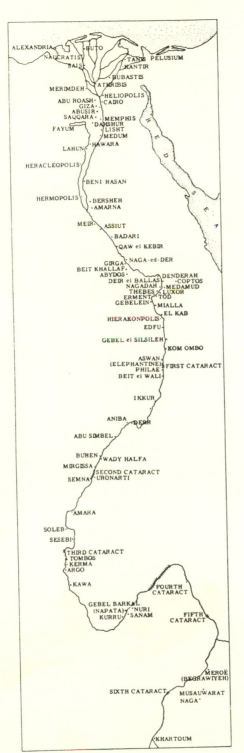

ALEXANDRIA
BUTO
NAUCRATIS
TANIS PELUSIUM
SAIS
KANTIR
BUBASTIS
MERIMDEH
ATHRIBIS
HELIOPOLIS
ABU ROASH
CAIRO
GIZA
ABUSIR
SAQQARA
MEMPHIS
DAHSHUR
FAYUM
LISHT
MEDUM
HAWARA
LAHUN

HERACLEOPOLIS

BENI HASAN

HERMOPOLIS
BERSHEH
AMARNA

MEIR
ASSIUT
BADARI
QAW el KEBIR
GIRGA
NAGA-ed-DER
BEIT KHALLAF
ABYDOS
DENDERAH
DEIR el BALLAS
COPTOS
NAGADAH
MEDAMUD
THEBES
LUXOR
ERMENT
TOD
GEBELEIN
MIALLA
EL KAB
HIERAKONPOLIS
EDFU
GEBEL el SILSILEH
KOM OMBO
ASWAN
(ELEPHANTINE)
FIRST CATARACT
PHILAE
BEIT el WALI

IKKUR

ANIBA
DERR
ABU SIMBEL

BUHEN
WADY HALFA
MIRGISSA
SECOND CATARACT
SEMNA
URONARTI

AMARA
SOLEB
SESEBI
THIRD CATARACT
TOMBOS
KERMA
ARGO

KAWA
FOURTH
CATARACT
GEBEL BARKAL
(NAPATA)
NURI
KURRU
SANAM
FIFTH
CATARACT

Map of Nile Valley

MEROË
(BEGRAWIYEH)
SIXTH CATARACT
MUSAUWARAT
NAGA

KHARTOUM

Map of the Nile Valley. Copied from W.S. Smith, *Ancient Egypt*, p. 192, with the permission of the Museum of Fine Arts, Boston.

*Ancient Egyptian
Science*

For Sue Once Again

Ancient Egyptian Science

A Source Book
by Marshall Clagett

Volume One

Knowledge and Order

Tome One

American Philosophical Society
Independence Square • Philadelphia
1989

Memoirs of the
AMERICAN PHILOSOPHICAL SOCIETY
Held at Philadelphia
for Promoting Useful Knowledge
Volume 184

Library of Congress Catalog card No: 89-84668
International Standard Book Number: 0-87169-184-1
US ISSN: 0065-9738
Jacket Illustration: <u>Front</u> Several depictions of Maat, from Lanzone, *Dizionario de mitologia egizia,*
            <u>Back</u> Re-Osiris, from the tomb of Nefertari, from Piankoff and Rambova, *The
            Tomb of Ramesses VI.*
End paper illustrations: <u>Front</u> The Shabaka Stone. Dynasty 24. From Breasted, ''The Philosophy
            of a Memphite Priest.''
            <u>Back</u> A vignette for Spell 110 of the *Book of the Dead,* from Naville, *Das
            ägyptische Todtenbuch,* vol. I.

Table of Contents

Volume One

Tome One

Tome Two

Preface

The work I have undertaken in this and the succeeding volumes grew from a more modest idea that came to me as I served on the committee for publishing Source Books in the History of the Sciences, namely to produce a Source Book in Ancient Egyptian Science consisting of enough extracts to illustrate some of the aspects of that science. However, when I considered the matter I realized that a few documentary extracts were insufficient to give a historian of science without any special knowledge of the Egyptian language and culture a well-rounded view of the growth and development of that science. Hence I decided to add substantial essays to introduce the documents. This resulted in a work independent of the Source Books series, a work whose first volume is published here.

It will be evident to the reader that the first section comprising Chapter One and Documents I.1-I.9 attempts to assay the importance for the development of Egyptian science--and its practitioners and institutions--of the invention and maturation of the art of writing in Egypt during the three thousand years or so after 3000 B.C. The first chapter supplies a general and connected account, and the documents present some detailed evidence to support that account. I have paid particular attention to the so-called Palermo Stone as my first document, since few if any efforts have been made to evaluate its content for the beginnings of Egyptian numerical, metrical, and calendaric techniques. Furthermore, no translator has included all the fragments together and at the same time rendered all of the many numbers that appear in the text. Previous authors have generally passed over the difficult numerical passages. My careful attention to numbers has yielded evidence of a previously undetected, rudimentary place-value system. The relevance of the rest of the documents to those points I have made in the introductory essay should be clear without further elaboration here.

The second section has the same general format as the first. Chapter Two attempts to show in a coherent way the fundamental religious context of Egyptian cosmogonic and cosmological ideas. The various schemes of the world and its creation are detailed and organized according to the temple centers in which they developed. Again, ample documentary material has been given as supplementary support for the general account. I have purposely left the more technical astronomical considerations for the next volume, in which I shall examine in detail calendars, astronomy, and mathematics. A third volume will treat Egyptian medicine and biology and will close with a detailed presentation of Egyptian techniques for representing nature.

A few remarks are in order concerning the English translations of the documents. For most of the documents I have had the help of translations into modern languages made by competent scholars and I have often followed them closely. However, in many cases I have rendered the texts in my own way, mainly to bring some consistency to translation. A case in point is my effort to translate ─𓏤𓏤𓇳 and 𓂋𓏤 almost always as "eternity" and "everlastingness", the first being the eternal past and the second the eternal future. Also,

I have at times had available to me a more complete Egyptian text than the earlier translators had. This is evident in the case of some of the translations of tomb inscriptions by Breasted. Revised texts by Sethe have allowed me to give a more complete interpretation. As I have already mentioned, my rendering of Document I.1, the so-called Palermo Stone, is more complete than any of the efforts in other modern languages, since it is based on all of the fragments and attempts to render all of the numbers. On the other hand, it will be clear to the reader familiar with the documents given in the second section, like the *Pyramid Texts* and the *Coffin Texts*, that these documents of mine are merely short excerpts from long originals, presented by me to illustrate sundry cosmogonical and cosmological concepts which I believe to be important. Certainly I make no pretense of giving definitive versions of even those passages that I have presented. More definitive versions would necessitate a careful rendering of the whole document to see if recent philological treatments of similar passages throughout the document throw further light on the passages in question. I am hoping that a student of the history of science coming to Egyptian culture for the first time will derive benefit from having these translations immediately available to him, incomplete though they might be.

A final word may be said about the title of this first volume: *Knowledge and Order.* It translates a pair of crucial Egyptian words: *rekh* ( ) and *maat* ( ). It will be noticed as we examine the documents of the first section that the scribal craft embraced an ideal of the knowledgeable man, who by his writing abilities was able to measure, count, and record. It is this ideal that is epitomized by *rekh*. Similarly, if we peruse the second section with its documents, it will be evident that the concept of cosmic rightness or order, one of the meanings of *maat*, lies at the heart of the ancient Egyptian efforts to describe the cosmos and its birth, together with the role of the gods and the king therein. By using these separate terms "knowledge" and "order" I do not mean to imply a more modern scientific method whereby systematic order in nature was intentionally and primarily sought by the careful gathering of knowledge. I merely mean that the concepts of "knowledge" and "order" arose as important aspects of the Egyptian intellectual achievement, and without their development Egyptian science, rudimentary as it was, would have taken some other form.

This volume and its successors are the result of many trips to Egypt and much reading, and I hope they will be of some use to budding historians of science, and perhaps even to those who have fully blossomed. I know that the study of Egyptian science has given me great pleasure, for I have turned aside from my many years of detailed Archimedean studies to an earlier cultural area of perennial fascination. Fortunately my colleague Otto Neugebauer not only gave me his entire collection of Egyptian reprints but has shared with me his learning at all stages of this work. This will perhaps be more clearly evident in the technical volumes that follow. I am as well indebted to Robert Bianchi for reading my manuscript with a careful eye and for the many pleasant and (to me) profitable hours we had together in Egypt and to Erik Hornung for his keen analytical and textual studies that have proved so useful to me in composing Section Two and for his cheerful letters. My research assistant Mark Darby read this work with his usual care and it has benefited from the close attention he has given it. Similarly my wife Sue, an editor by profession, has exercised her craft towards its improvement. Further, I owe much to her for photographing countless objects in the museums of Egypt, Europe, and America, and some of her many photographs have been included in the pages that follow. I must also thank my friend Dr. Alison Frantz for the skill and artistry with which she has copied and improved many older photographs that before her attention were scarcely readable.

The reader will notice that, for easy access, I have grouped all of the figures, i.e. the line drawings and photographs, at the end of the separately printed second tome, which also includes documents for the second section, a chronology, a bibliography and bibliographic abbreviations, and indexes. Permissions for and acknowledgments of the use of the illustrations are included in the legends accompanying them. Permission by the University of California Press to use the translations by Miriam Lichtheim of the Great Hymns to Osiris and Aten, the Bentresh Stela, and the Song from the Tomb of King Intef (i.e. The Song of the Harper) is gratefully acknowledged.

I initially composed this volume (on sundry different computers) with Nota Bene, a superior word-processing program, designing, by means of the font program Lettrix, some 500 hieroglyphs and a phonetic font needed to represent the glyphs. These fonts were designed for a dot matrix printer and are illustrated in my article "Computer-generated Hieroglyphs," *Proceedings of the American Philosophical Society*, Vol. 131 (June, 1987), pp. 197-223. Later I acquired a laser printer and converted both my manuscript and its glyphs for use with that printer, employing the font program Fontrix and its complementary printing program Printrix (mentioned and briefly described in the above-noted article). I also found it necessary to compose a font which includes the accented letters that appear so frequently in the quotations, notes, and bibliography of my work. This was necessary because the Fontrix fonts do not include the higher ASCII characters representing the accented letters. Though no ambiguity is present, I regret the manner in which some of my accented capital letters dangle below the normal base line. On the whole, Printrix did a yeomanly job with the often complex and highly formatted text and only failed on occasion to impose proper spacing and justification, in some cases leading to loose lines. Also notice that the dots inserted to connect quoted passages after an omission are sometimes preceded and sometimes followed by spaces added to aid justification. But, as usual, three dots indicate that no period marking the end of a sentence is present in the omission, while four signify the presence of one or more periods. I believe that these few infelicities of Printrix's laser printing are a small price to pay for the enormous saving in publication costs.

The computer knowledge of my son Michael was always at hand, and I made frequent use of it, particulary in solving the problems of converting Nota Bene text to Printrix text. Incidentally, in making that conversion I directly converted footnotes to endnotes. But, needless to say, an endnote must continue to be thought of as a continuation of the text at the point where the note number has been inserted, and accordingly any reference to "before" or "after" in a note relates to that point in the text where the note number occurs.

My secretary Ann Tobias has also participated in every step of preparing the initial manuscript and she it was who perfected many of the original glyphs. Needless to say, she has my warmest thanks, as does the staff of the Institute for Advanced Study and its library for supplying me with much of the equipment and books I needed. Indeed, the Institute has provided me with the ideal academic home for a quarter of a century. Finally, I must once again thank the American Philosophical Society for bringing another complex work of mine to light.

Marshall Clagett
Professor Emeritus
The Institute for Advanced Study

Section One

Knowledge

Section One

Chapter One

The Fruits of Scribal Activity
in Ancient Egypt

The fundamental role played by scribes in the development of the various professions in ancient Egypt was well recognized in a prayer addressed by a scribe to the god Thoth, the patron of his profession:[1]

> Come to me, O Thoth, august ibis, O god beloved of Khmun (i.e. Hermopolis), secretary of the Ennead (i.e. the nine gods),...come to me, to advise me; give me skill in thy craft which is better than all other crafts, for men have found that he who is skilled therein becomes a nobleman (or dignitary). I have seen many for whom thou didst act and [now] they are members of the Thirty (i.e. the traditional Grand Jury of Egypt), strong and wealthy because of what thou hast done.

That the craft of scribe excels all other crafts was a favorite theme of later authors, as is well illustrated by Documents I.7 and I.8 below. Not only was this a belief articulated by the scribes but it is borne out by an examination of the extraordinary careers in political and administrative professions as well as in the learned professions revealed in the biographies found in the tombs of nobles and officials throughout Egypt in all periods. The majority of these important officials held some scribal position in their careers. For example, consult the biography of Metjen in Document I.2 below, perhaps the earliest of the tomb biographies, his career spanning the end of the third and the beginning of the fourth dynasty (see the Appendix in Section III for a chronology of ancient Egypt). We learn from this biography that Metjen was the son of an honorary or pensioned scribe Anubisemankh and inherited from him the headship of the scribes of a provision bureau as that bureau's administrator, and along with that held many other important titles and posts. The high regard of officials for their scribal activities and training was also reflected in the fact that a great many of the prominent officials during the whole of Egyptian history had statues of themselves sculpted in the scribal position, with knees crossed and papyri on their laps (see Fig. I.1). Also they were occasionally represented as scribes on the reliefs in their tombs, as for example in the tomb of Hesyre, the well-known scribe, dentist, and physician of the third dynasty (see Fig. I.2).

To understand why the scribe was an important person in ancient Egyptian society, we have to realize how much the highly organized state and its culture depended on the invention and development of writing. Already in the days that preceded and introduced the dynastic period at the end of the fourth millennium B.C. a rudimentary written language is evident on palettes, mace-heads, tablets, sealings, stelas, and vases. The mace-head of the predynastic king Scorpion, who wears the tall white crown of Upper Egypt (see Fig. I.3), has before the head of the king a rosette (probably symbolizing the title of the king). It stands above the hieroglyph of a scorpion (apparently the king's name). Though we do not know the phonetic rendering of the name, that is, the syllables for which the hieroglyph stands, it is almost certain that the glyph did stand for his name rather than another kingly title as Baumgartel suggested,[2] for we notice that, on a vase found in Hieraconpolis (along with Scorpion's mace-head), in several places above the hieroglyph of the scorpion is the conventional Horus falcon, itself the hieroglyph indicative of one title of the king throughout dynastic history (see Fig. I.4). It is unlikely that the vase was to be identified by two titles rather than by a title and a name, as was usually the case. Such use of hieroglyphs to render proper names reflects the key step taken in the invention of writing: the use of pictorial signs not just to represent the things pictured but rather to represent names (and later abstract ideas) which have a similar sound. This is the rebus principle familiar to players of charades since time immemorial. A whole series of signs was devised to represent one, two or more consonants (see Figs. I.5-I.7). The signs for single consonants are sometimes called an alphabet, for in theory one could represent the consonants of all Egyptian words by using these signs alone. But note that vowels were not written down. Despite this development of phonetic representation of consonants, the pictorial element of hieroglyphics remained strong through the whole of dynastic history. Not only did a single sign often represent two or more consonants but in countless cases a single sign was used to express the whole word regardless of its length. Furthermore many such pictorial signs were used as determinatives following the already represented consonantal elements of the word. In this position the determinative sign was unpronounced and acted to distinguish the class to which the word written in consonants belonged. Such determinatives were needed because, without the writing of vowels, the consonants alone were not sufficient to distinguish words that shared the same consonants but had differing vowels and above all different meanings or to distinguish words that had the same vowels as well as consonants but still had different meanings. So, with the persistence of a large number of pictorial signs over and beyond those we can call alphabetic, the scribe was forced to learn a larger repertoire of signs--in all some 800 signs (which in the Ptolemaic and Roman periods multiplied tenfold), as well as the cursive forms of these signs (the so-called hieratic script) used to write on papyrus and bits of pottery and stone (and from the seventh century B.C. a still more cursive script named demotic).

More certain than the signs on the Scorpion mace-head as evidence of writing are the hieroglyphs and pictorial signs appearing on the famous palette celebrating the victory of King Narmer over the Delta people and thus the union of Upper and Lower Egypt at the beginning of or just before the first dynasty (Fig. I.8). Sir Alan Gardiner summarizes the significance of the recto of the palette for revealing an early form of Egyptian writing:[3]

> This is one of the oldest specimens of Egyptian writing known. The name of the king, written with the $n^c r$-fish and the mr-chisel, occupies the rectangle between the Hathor-heads. The other small hieroglyphs give the names or titles

of the persons over whose heads they are written; the captured chieftain may have been named Washi (harpoon *w^c*, pool *š*). The group at top on the right was probably intended as explanation of the picture in the centre; at this early date the gist of complete sentences could apparently be conveyed only by symbolical groups of which the elements suggested separate words. The conjectural meaning is: The falcon-god Horus (i.e. the king) leads captive the inhabitants of the papyrus-land *(T'-mḥw* 'the Delta').

The verso of this palette shows one figure with accompanying hieroglyphs that is of considerable interest for our account of scribal activity. In front of the king is a figure wearing a long wig who appears to have something that looks like scribal paraphernalia thrown over his shoulder. The figure is accompanied by the hieroglyphs standing phonetically for *tt*. There has been considerable discussion of the meaning of *tt*. Four different translations have been proposed. The first is "scribe"; this was supported by the appearance of the above-mentioned paraphernalia and by a very much later use of the term *tt* as the "staff" of the scribal-religious-medical organization commonly known as "The House of Life" (see below). The second translation assumes that *tt* is archaic writing for *wtt* and thus renders it as "the begotten one" or "son", and the third takes it for an old form for *t'ty* (i.e. "vizier"). All three of these translations are cogently rejected by

H. Kees, who believes that *ṯt* is archaic writing for *'tt* (i.e. tutor).[4] This same figure appears on the mace-head of Narmer (see Fig. I.9) along with the king's sandal bearer, who was also on the Narmer palette. He stands behind the king, who wears the crown of Lower Egypt and is seated on a throne in a pavilion at the top of some stairs. The whole scene may well represent the ceremony of Narmer's coronation as King of Lower Egypt after his victory over the North. Notice that in the top register the standards which are being carried (and presumably represent his allies and thus the worldly "followers of Horus") are the same as those on the verso of Narmer's palette: two of Horus, one of the wolf-god Wepwawet, and one with the royal placenta (or so this is usually identified). Finally notice that in the lowest register are recorded 400,000 oxen, 1,422,000 goats, and 120,000 prisoners, no doubt the fruits of Narmer's victory. This is clear evidence that the Egyptians had already invented the signs for larger powers of 10, namely 1,000, 10,000, 100,000, and 1,000,000 (see Fig. I.10). Incidentally the lesser powers (i.e. 1, 10, and 100) appear with signs for 1,000 and 10,000 on the bases of two statues of the second-dynasty king Khasekhem, found at Hieraconpolis in inscriptions which tell us that 47,209 or 48,205 enemies from the North have been slain (see Fig. I.11).

There is also evidence of the new writing on vases and leather bag sealings. On one of the latter we find two wavy lines (an old form for the sign meaning "water") preceded above by the sign for *m* (an owl), which acts as a phonetic complement. We can thus read the whole word as *mw* which means "water" (see Fig. I.12). The written language was also used early to express the names (royal and noble) found on countless stelas in or near the first- and-second-dynasty tombs at Abydos and Saqqara. The most perfect one artistically is certainly the celebrated stela of the first-dynasty Horus Djet (or better, Wadji) from Abydos, now in the Louvre (see Fig. I.13). There, in a serekh (the rectangular palace-facade design; see Document I.1, n. 24), surmounted by a falcon (=Horus), we see a serpent, which is the hieroglyph for $\underline{d}$ and apparently is an abbreviated writing for Djet or for Wadji. Another interesting one is the stela of the second-dynasty king Horus Reneb (or Nebre) from Saqqara and now in the Metropolitan Museum (see Fig. I.14a). In the serekh we see the sun sign ○ *(rᶜ)* signifying the sun-god Re above the basket sign ⏝ *(nb)* signifying "lord", giving the name the meaning "Re is the lord". See also the stela of Meryetneith, an early first-dynasty queen, in Fig. I.14b. It has the hoe sign for *mr* (standing for *mryt* "beloved") coupled with the sign of crossed arrows that is to be read as "Neith", and thus the whole may be translated as "Beloved of Neith".

Also of interest for the early stages of writing is the large number of labels or tablets that record events and thereby years of the reigns of the early dynastic kings. The lack of formal syntax in the "statements" on these tablets makes their exact translation difficult, and the archaic form of the hieroglyphs in which these statements are couched increases the difficulty of understanding them precisely. Nevertheless, let us look briefly at five such tablets. The first (see Fig. I.15) is a tablet from Naqada of the reign of Horus Aha, either the first or second king of the first dynasty. In the first register we have the name Horus Aha repeated twice (i.e., the falcon clutches the mace and shield which together mean "The Fighter"), then to their right a boat transporting the king in a shrine-like cabin (with a vulture or a falcon flying above), then the king's Horus name in a serekh, and finally a shrine (enclosed by three lines) which contains the signs for the Lady Cobra (of the North) and the Lady Vulture (of the Southland), signs which introduce the second, so-called *nebti* or "Two-Ladies" name of a king (for the king's titulary, see below Document I.1, n. 24). The name that follows seems to be *Men*, that is *Meni* or *Menes*, the traditional founding king of the united land. At first it was thought that this was to be read as the *nebti* name of Horus Aha written to the left of it and that this juxtaposition of the two names settled the question of which king (Narmer or Aha) was Menes. However, it seems equally plausible that since the *nebti* name *Men* is enclosed in lines that appear to form a shrine, the whole should rather be read as "the Shrine of *Nebti Men*" and we could accordingly translate the first register in the following manner: "Horus Aha proceeds by boat to the Shrine of *Nebti Men*", that is, to the shrine of his predecessor Menes,[5] who could then be identified with Narmer. Skipping the other two registers, which are more difficult to render with any precision, we pass to a second tablet, i.e. a wooden label, also from the reign of Aha (see Fig. I.16). It is replete with significant symbols. In the top register we see the Horus name of Aha; then the fox-skins sign for *ms* ("birth" or "making"); next a sign of a pelt on a rod later read as *'Imy-wt* ("He who is in the bandaging room"), which probably here designates Anubis (as it did from at least the third dynasty) and was produced in model form as a cult object of the god (see Document I.1, n. 19, below); farther to the right are two (?) boats, and below them the depiction of a sanctuary with the crossed-arrows symbol of the goddess Neith erected in the middle. Hence the whole register may be translated: "[Celebration of] the Birth (or Making) of the pelt (cult object of Anubis?) by the Horus Aha and his visit by two (?) boats to the Sanctuary of Neith [at Sais?] ". The second register appears to record further pilgrimages, translatable, from right to left: "And to the Sanctuary of the Heron of Buto (cf. Document I.1, n. 101), as well as to the Running of the [Apis?] Bull [at Memphis?] (cf. *ibid.* n. 46). The king makes an offering at Nekhen (i.e. Hieraconpolis)." This register then seems to be telling of pilgrimages to both the North and the South of Egypt.

Once more I skip the two lower registers and go on to the third tablet (Fig. I.17), an ebony tablet of the Horus Den (perhaps to be read Wedimu). On the left we see the crooked, stripped, and notched palm-branch sign ⌐ for *rnpt* ("year") and to its left the king seated in a shrine-like pavilion at the top of the stairs before a course indicated by three semicircles (course markers) at each end, a course which the king is shown to be running, all of this representing part of the Sed Festival of renewal of the king traditionally (but not invariably) held in the thirtieth year of rule (see Document I.1, n. 41). Then beyond a vertical bar we see the Horus name: Den or Wedimu, and to the left of that the name of an official: "Controller of the King of Lower Egypt, Hemaka". Thus this tablet has so far told us that it was made for Hemaka in the year of the Sed Festival of King Den. Again I pass over the rest of the tablet except to note that in the third register we see the hieroglyphs for *nsw-bit* (literally meaning "belonging to the sedge and the bee" but usually translated in the king's titulary as "King of Upper and Lower Egypt"; see Document I.1, n. 24). This introduces the so-called *nesu-bit* or *insibya* name of the Horus Den, that is Semti or Zemti, as the two sandy-hill-country signs are usually read. This tablet is of particular interest, for with its year sign distinguishing the king's activities of this year from the rest of the tablet it obviously directly reflects the practice by the royal scribes of keeping some record of the activities that gave to each year of the king's reign its name. Some such annals were probably composed for each reign, and together they provided the sources for Document I.1 below, the stone *Annals* composed in the fifth dynasty and usually called the Palermo Stone from its principal fragment. This latter document I have given in full as an example of one of the earliest systematic documents t̲ resulted from scribal activity and as one which showed the learned scribe in his early creativity. For in it he collected several kinds of data, not the least interesting of which, for our recounting of scientific activity, being the Nile heights for each year of the various reigns (at least from the time of Horus Djer onward). As we shall see, it also included the establishment and celebration of various festivals of the gods and the royal attendance at them, and it has further interest because it reflects old calendaric information and tells us something about the numerical systems used in Egypt at the earliest period of dynastic history.

The fourth tablet is an ivory label of Horus Den's reign (Fig. I.18, left) used to identify some sandals. It is dated to the "[Year of] the First Smiting of the East" (this can be read at the right edge of the tablet). It appears to refer to a year of Den's reign recorded in the *Annals* (see Document I.1, note 40). On the left we see the king smiting his enemies in a figure that is repeated throughout Egyptian history from the time of the Palette of Narmer to that of the temple pylons of the Greco-Roman period. Farther left is the name of the owner of the sandals marked by the tablet and it may be read something like *Akain*.

Finally let us look briefly at an ivory label from the reign of Semerkhet, the penultimate king of the first dynasty (Fig. I.18, right). At the far right we again see the stripped palm branch indicating the word "year" and with it the activity giving the year its name: "Year of the Following of Horus [in which took place at] the 'Mansion of the Great Ones' [the festivals of] the Great White One and Sokar" (for similar events recorded in the reigns of Djer and Den, see Document I.1, nn. 11, 18, and 33). Left of the vertical line we see the priest-like hieroglyph representing both the *insibya* and *nebti* names of Semerkhet, a name that some have read as Semenptah and others as Iryneter.[6] Though the rest of the tablet is by no means clear, it is evident from the hieroglyphs that it belonged to "the Royal Carpenter (or Maker of Axes) the Chief Count Henuka".

An equally if not more important source for early writing is the large number of seals and sealings of the first dynasties found in museums everywhere. I shall limit myself here to mentioning four (see Fig. I.19a). The top seal is of a priest of Neith named Shesh; the second one carries the name of Neithhotep, the wife of the Horus Aha; the third is a sealing from the time of "Seth Peribsen", of the second dynasty, and the last is one from the final king of that dynasty: "Horus-Seth Khasekhemuy in whom both gods are at rest", as can be read in the serekh. The last two sealings reflect the apparent contest (some would say civil war) between the followers of the God Horus and those of Seth.[7]

Another result of scribal activity that became a characteristic feature of Egyptian culture and funeral activity was the development of tomb biographies, in which are recorded the multiple activities of nobles and high officials, most of whom started as scribes. Needless to say, we shall not include here biographies that are largely confined to political activities but only a few of the many that reflect some kind of cultural and quasi-scientific activity. How did these tomb biographies arise? They have their roots in the stelas or marking stones of the protodynastic period that began, we have already seen, with the simple recording of a name (again see Figs. I.13 and I.14). But the biographies which interest us did not develop from the royal stelas but arose rather from private ones. No doubt the earliest of these stelas contained only the names of the courtiers as did the royal stelas the names of the kings. But very early the title or titles of the deceased began to be added along with the name. Of the 150 or so private stelas at Abydos (see Fig. I.20 for 43 of them) which date in great part from the first dynasty, we see that many of them also included titles.[8] In the context of this chapter I mention only two of them, the first being that represented in Fig. I.20, No. 43, where we read that the deceased was "Controller of Lower Egypt" and some kind of scribe (note that this is indicated by the sign for a scribe's outfit in the second register, consisting of a palette, a bag for the powdered pigments, and a reed holder).[9] On the whole these stelas are smaller than the royal ones. They are quite irregular in shape, though many of them have a curved top like the royal stelas. Presumably the earlier ones were erected separately in the ground around or near the kings' tombs and served largely as identification of the deceased's tomb and perhaps as a reminder of the name of the deceased, which had to be repeated in offering services. A good many of the stelas have the figure of the deceased in a sitting position, which no doubt also served as a hieroglyphic determinative for the name of the deceased. Some of the stelas had standing rather than seated figures. Indeed the most complex stela of these early ones (the second stela to be singled out) includes such a standing figure. This is the one of Sabef in the Cairo Museum (Fig. I.20, No. 48; Fig. I.21), probably dating from the reign of Ḳaᶜa, the last king of the first dynasty. Sabef stands at the bottom of the stela, holding a *kherep* scepter (signifying "to have control" or "to be at the head") in his right hand and a walking stick in his left hand. Behind him is his name, Sabef, in hieroglyphics, and above him are two registers of titles. They are by no means understood precisely. The first title may mean: "Controller of Festivals [at] the mansion called 'The protector is behind [us]'". Among the other titles are those that probably can be read as: "Companion in the Palace", "Controller of the Secrets of Decrees", and "Priest of Anubis".

In the North (Saqqara, Helwan, and Giza) quite a different development of stelas took place.[10] There the stelas were ordinarily rectangular, were almost all embedded in walls or ceilings, and had as their purpose the magical representation of the offering scene. Hence they all have the deceased seated before an offering table. In front of and around the table are representations of the offerings and in addition a list of cloth or linen materials that were to be provided for the deceased in the other world. In the upper register

or registers were the titles. There is some variation in
the location of the three major elements of the tomb
stelas of the north. I give here a few examples of
these stelas. The first is one from the end of the first
or the beginning of the second dynasty and was found
at Helwan (see Fig. I.22). The second is from Saqqara
and dates from the reign of Ka^{c}a at the end of the
dynasty. The deceased was the nobleman Merka (see
Fig. I.23). The third offering stela is that of a princess
of the second dynasty (Fig. I.24 left) and it may be
compared with another stela from the same dynasty
(Fig. I.24 right). The fourth is the stela of Tetenankh
(see Fig. I.25), from the third dynasty, and the fifth
that of Wepemnofret from the fourth dynasty (Fig.
I.26). It was not until the third dynasty that the
traditional elements of the offering scene were clearly
separated into titles, food-libation-purification offerings,
and linen offerings. I merely note here that in
Tetenankh's stela the name and titles are written in the
horizontal and vertical arms of the gnomon that
embraces the square including the deceased seated
before an offering table and surrounded by the various
items of offering (all properly identified by their
hieroglyphic signs). Beyond the vertical arm of the
gnomon is a column, which at the top includes the
traditional list of linen materials to be offered to the
deceased and below that more offerings. The
formulistic request for 1000 of each offering item is
evident under the offerings, where we see the lotus
signs that mean "1000" (Gardiner, *Egyptian Grammar*,
1957, p. 480, sign M 12). The name and titles are of
interest to us in the context of this chapter: (vertical
column) "Controller of scribes, Scribe of petitions in the
House of the Nome, Tetenankh" and in the horizontal

column "Scribe of petitions, Familiar of the King, Tetenankh". By the third and fourth dynasties these offering scenes and particularly the title lists had expanded greatly into the various rooms of the tombs. We see them expand (1) into the offering niches of the third-dynasty tombs like the panels in Hesyre's tomb (see Fig. I.2), which were found in six niches of the western wall of the tomb, and like the reliefs in the offering niche of the tomb of Khabawsokar (Fig. I.27), and (2) into the false doors which dominate tombs for the remainder of ancient Egyptian history (Fig. I.28). These were "doors" above the burial chambers that allowed the deceased to come forth and return to his tomb ("false doors" because the doors in fact were mere recesses in the walls in which they were constructed). Around these doors titles and family information began to be included, while the offering scene itself became fixed above the door. We cannot study these developments in detail, but we can look briefly at the two panels from Hesyre's tomb given in Fig. I.2. The left one reports his titles, among which we particularly note "Head of Royal Scribes" and "Magnate of the Ten of Upper Egypt".[11] The right panel has a list of titles above the offering scene. The first title is the one of most interest to us: "Chief of Dentists and Physicians" (wr ibḥ swnw). The list also includes the already mentioned titles of "Head of Royal Scribes" and "Magnate of the Ten of Upper Egypt".

It will be obvious that in describing the development of the title lists, I have throughout this chapter (both in regard to the cases illustrated here and in the documents I have included) emphasized those officials who were scribes. Before listing some of the various kinds of scribes, I ought to mention an interesting list of scribal names which dates from the time of King Djoser in the third dynasty (see Fig. I.29). Each column includes two scribes, first giving the title "Scribe" and then the name. We can report the names as follows, starting from the left and reading the names at the tops of the columns first: (top) ---, ---, Tjenet-ty, Senedjemib, Kanefer, ---(Wepwawetsaes ?), Amkhent; (bottom) Mesa, Samery, Inkhemu, Ikau, Wedjwer, Serefka, Shepseska. What the purpose of this list was, I do not know, but it is interesting that such a group should be singled out in some way, perhaps not surprising in a reign that saw the building of the great stone funerary complex of King Djoser at Saqqara.

It is not enough to say that a great many occupants of the tombs were at one time or another scribes, for the title lists report a truly extraordinary variety of scribes:[12]

> Scribe of the Royal Documents, Overseer of Scribes of the Pyramid of Khufu, Overseer of Scribes of the Crews, Scribe of a Phyle, Judge and Overseer of Scribes, Tutor of the King's Sons, Inspector of Scribes of the Granary, Scribe of Divine Book(s), Judge and Boundary Official, Judge and Overseer of Scribes of the Great Court, Director of Scribes and Members of the Great Jury, Scribe of the Royal Documents in the Presence, Inspector of Bookkeepers, Overseer of the Scribes of the Lands, Overseer of the Scribes of the Royal Sealed Documents, Scribe of the Royal Linen, Scribe of the

Expedition, Director of Scribes of the Great Broad Hall, Overseer of Scribes of the King's Repast, Scribe of the Treasury of the Estate 'Mansion of Menkaure', Bookkeeper of the Royal Documents, Overseer of the Scribes of the Land in the Two Houses of Upper and Lower Egypt, Director of the Scribes of Petitions, Director of Scribes of the House of the Master of the Largesse, Scribe of the King's Expedition in Wenet, Serer, Tep and Ida, Scribe of the Archives, Judge and Overseer of Scribes of the Herds, Scribe of the Troops of the Lord of the Two Lands, Scribe of the Altar of the Temple of Ptah, Scribe of the Lord of the Two Lands, Scribe of the Treasury of the Pyramid of Merykare, Scribe of the Two Granaries and of the Pyramid-town, Overseer of Royal Scribes of the Army of Upper and Lower Egypt, Scribe of the Treasury of the Estate of Amun, Scribe and Counter of the Grain in the Granary of Divine Offerings of Amun, Scribe of Divine Writings in the estate of Amun, Counter of Cattle of the God's Wife of Amun, Scribe of Recruits of the Ramesseum in the Estate of Amun, Scribe of the Divine Offerings of the Gods of Thebes, Scribe of the Royal Documents of the Granary, Scribe of the Altar of the Royal Apartments, Scribe of Divine Offerings of the Temple of Ptah, Scribe of the Documents of the Chief Steward, Scribe of the Counting of Cattle of the House of the Overseer of the Seal, Great Scribe of the Counting of Amun, Keeper of the Writing Material of the King, Scribe of the Silver and Gold of Ptah, Royal Scribe of Accounts of Everything in the Temple of Imhotep, Son of Ptah, Scribe of the Two Granaries of the Temple of the Aten in Memphis, Scribe of the Doors of the Temple of Neith, Mistress of Sais, Scribe of the Great Prison, Overseer of Writing in the Palace, Overseer of Writing in the House of Life, Overseer of Scribes of the Fields, Temple Scribe and Chief Accountant of the Divine Adoratrice Nitocris, and many, many others.[13]

In addition to their scribal activities, a great many of the occupants of the tombs had titles which indicated some attention to "quasi-learned" professions, particularly to those we shall encounter in the remaining chapters of this work. The most common of such professions was that of physician *(swnw)*. The title of physician may go back to the first dynasty.[14] At any rate, we recall that by the third dynasty the above-mentioned Hesyre built a tomb at Saqqara with celebrated wooden reliefs on which he is entitled: "Chief of Dentists and Physicians" (see Fig. I.2). Among the

98 physicians listed by Jonckheere 42 were from the Old Kingdom, 16 from the Middle Kingdom, 29 from the New Kingdom, and 11 from the Late Period, a list corrected and elaborated by Ghalioungui to include 52 names of persons from the Old Kingdom, 20 from the Middle Kingdom, 40 from the New Kingdom, and 15 from the Late Period.[15] Jonckheere, Ghalioungui, and von Känel report the following titles: Physician, w^cb-Priest of Sekhmet (a kind of physician; see below, n. 24), Overseer of w^cb-Priests of Sekhmet, Conjurers and Protective Magicians of Selket (physicians specializing in stings and bites; *ibid.*), Chief Physician and/or Chief of Physicians, Overseer of Physicians, Chief of Physicians of Lower Egypt, Chief of Physicians of Upper and Lower Egypt (or of Lower and Upper Egypt), Chief of the Physicians of the Lord of the Two Lands (i.e. of the Pharaoh), Chief of Physicians of the King, Physician or Chief of the Physicians of the Great House (i.e. the Royal Palace), Physician of the House (i.e. Temple) of Amun, Inspector of Physicians (and Inspector of Physicians of the Great House or of the King), Dean of Physicians and Dean of the Physicians of the Great House, Chief of the Physicians of the Mansion of Life (Hwt ^cnh instead of Pr ^cnh translated as "House of Life"), Physician of the Company (or Troop), Overseer of the Two Teams of Physicians of the Great House (*lit.* Overseer of the Two Sides of the Barge of Physicians of the Great House),[16] Physician of the Queen's House and Chief of the Physicians of the Queen's House, Directress of Female Physicians (a title given to one Peseshet in the Old Kingdom, the only known female physician),[17] Physician of the Eyes (i.e. oculist), Physician of the Eyes in the Great House and Chief of the Physicians of the Eyes in

ANCIENT EGYPTIAN SCIENCE

the Great House, Controller of the Physicians of the
Eyes in the Great House, Physician of the Stomach and
the Eyes, Physician of the Stomach, Physician of the
Stomach in the Great House, Dentist, Chief of Dentists
and Chief of Dentists of the Great House, Interpreter of
the Secret Art (liberally translated by Junker as
"Interpreter of the Internal Organs of the Body"),[18]
Interpreter of Liquids (urine?; *lit.* "water") inside the
ntnt.t (bladder?), Guardian (or Shepherd) of the Anus
(i.e. Proctologist). I should observe that often
physicians had more than one of these titles, and in one
case the physician Irenakhty II (end of the Old Kingdom
or First Intermediary Period) had the following titles on
his stela: Physician of the Great House, Inspector of the
Physicians of the Great House, Physician of the Eyes in
the Great House, Physician of the Stomach in the Great
House, Dean of Physicians of the Great House,
Shepherd of the Anus, and Interpreter of Water inside
the *ntnt.t*.[19] A short biography of one successful
physician of the fifth dynasty is given as Document I.3
wherein is recounted the reward for his career: two
false doors for his tomb provided by the king.

No doubt allied with the physician were those
simply called "savants" (*rḥw* or *rḥw-ḥt*), and sometimes
they were surely the same person. Such would appear
to be the case of the savants appealed to in the
late-period story of the curing of the princess Bentresh,
the daughter of the prince of Bakhtan:[20]

It happened in year 23, second
month of summer, day 22, while his
majesty was in Thebes-the-
Victorious, the mistress of cities,
performing the rites for his father
Amen-Re, lord of Thrones-of-the-

Two-Lands, at his beautiful feast of Southern Ipet, his favorite place since the beginning, that one came to say to his majesty: "A messenger of the prince of Bakhtan has come with many gifts for the queen" (i.e. *Nefrure*, his daughter). He was brought before his majesty with his gifts and said, saluting his majesty: "Hail to you, Sun of the Nine Bows! Truly, we live through you!" And kissing the ground before his majesty, he spoke again before his majesty, saying: "I have come to you, O King, my lord, on account of Bentresh, the younger sister of Queen *Nefrure*. A malady has seized her body. May your majesty send a learned man *(rḫw-ḫt)* to see her!"

His majesty said: "Bring me the personnel of the House of Life and the council of the residence." They were ushered in to him immediately. His majesty said: "You have been summoned in order to hear the matter; bring me one wise of heart with fingers skilled in writing from among you." Then the royal scribe Thothemheb came before his majesty, and his majesty ordered him to proceed to Bakhtan with the messenger.

The learned man reached Bakhtan. He found Bentresh to be

possessed by a spirit: he found him to be an enemy whom one could fight.[21]   Then the prince of Bakhtan sent again to his majesty, saying "O King, my lord, may your majesty command to send a god [to fight against this spirit.   The message reached] his majesty in year 26, first month of summer, during the feast of Amun while his majesty was in Thebes.   His majesty reported to Khons-in-Thebes-Neferhotep, saying: "My good lord, I report to you about the daughter of the prince of Bakhtan."   Then Khons-in-Thebes-Neferhotep proceeded to Khons the Provider, the great god who expels disease demons.   His majesty spoke to Khons-in-Thebes-Neferhotep: "My good lord, if you turn your face to Khons-the-Provider, the great god who expels disease demons, he shall be dispatched to Bakhtan."   Strong approval twice.   His majesty said: "Give your magical protection to him, and I shall dispatch his majesty to Bakhtan to save the daughter of the prince of Bakhtan."   Very strong approval by Khons-in-Thebes-Neferhotep.   He made magical protection for Khons-the-Provider-in-Thebes four times.   His majesty commanded to let Khons-the-Provider-in-Thebes proceed to the great bark with five boats and a chariot, and many horses from east to west.

This god arrived in Bakhtan at the end of one year and five months. The prince of Bakhtan came with his soldiers and officials before Khons-the-Provider. He placed himself on his belly, saying: "You have come to us to be gracious to us, as commanded by the King of Upper and Lower Egypt, *Usrmare-sotpenre*!" Then the god proceeded to the place where Bentresh was. He made magical protection for the daughter of the prince of Bakhtan, and she became well instantly.

As is apparent from this quotation and from the evidence in Chapter Two below and in Volume Three, Chapter Four, magic played an important part in the fabric of religious, cosmological, and medical thought. This is illustrated in a literary context by the magical tales recounted in the Westcar Papyrus (see Document I.6) where it was the lector-priest (*ḥr.ḥb* or *ḥry.ḥbt*; lit. "he who carries the ritual roll") who was cast as a magician, no doubt because he was the priest charged with the production and knowledge of the sacred books of ritual and theology which had as their major objective the protection of the king from evil, and the preservation of the right order of the world (*mꜣꜥt*). Furthermore, leaving the imaginary world of story, we note that it was the lector-priest who was summoned, along with the physician, when in the fifth dynasty the king's vizier, chief judge, and architect Washptah fell ill and died during a visit by the king to a building being erected by the architect (see Document I.4). We find that some physicians themselves also bore the title of Lector-priest.[22] Other professionals involved in the use of magic had the titles of Magician (*ḥkʾ* or *ḥkʾy*), Overseer of Magicians (*imy-r ḥkʾw*), Prophet of the God Heka (or the Goddess Hekat), Conjurer (or authoritative one) of the Goddess Selket (*ḥrp Srḳt*), and Protective Magician (*sʾw*) or Protective Magician of Selket (*sʾw Srḳt*).[23] We know of physicians (*swnw*) who also bore these various titles of magicians, the most important being the last mentioned Conjurers and Magicians of Selket, both of whom pale in medical importance before the *wᶜb*-Priest of Sekhmet, who was widely mentioned in medical contexts and strictly speaking is a physician.[24] Thus in the Edwin Smith Surgical Papyrus (Document V.1, Case 1, Gloss A) we read: "Now if the priest of Sekhmet or any physician puts his hands (or) his fingers [upon the head, or upon the back of the] head, upon the two hands, upon the pulse, upon the two feet, [he] measures (*ḥʾy*) the heart...." Furthermore in the Ebers Papyrus (Document V.2, Sect. XCIX) the same passage concerning the pulse as the measurer of the heart is repeated, except that to the priest of Sekhmet and physician in the Smith Papyrus has been added the magician designated as *sʾw* (-*Srḳt?*) in the Ebers Papyrus. Among the other professionals of ancient Egypt who interest us is the hour-watcher or astronomer (*imy-wnwt* or simply *wnwty*),[25] whose activities will concern us in Volume Two, Chapter Three. And finally we should mention the reckoner or calculator (*ḥsb*), or scribe of counting or reckoning (*sš ḥsb* or *sš nt ḥsb*, or *nisw*), responsible not only for accounting and the recording of all kinds of things but also no doubt for the mathematical papyri we shall examine in Volume Two, Chapter Four.

References to institutions in which these scribes and derivative professionals were active go back at least to the Old Kingdom. On the stela of Wepemnofret, King Khufu's son (see Fig. I.26), we see him described as a "Priest of Seshat presiding over the House of Book(s) *(ḥm nṯr Sš¹t ḫntt pr mḏ¹t)*. This same institution is mentioned in connection with a scribe represented in the tomb of Kanenesut in the early fifth dynasty,[26] and is also found in the tomb of Tetu, where we find the name and title of his son given as "Nefereshemka, Inspector of the Scribes of the House of Book(s)".[27] Presumably this is the organization called the "House of Sacred Book(s)" mentioned in the tomb of Chief Lector-priest Medunefer, where he is entitled as "Scribe of the House of Sacred Book(s) *(sš pr mḏ¹t nṯr)*. It may be that it is also the same as the "Place of Records" *(st-ᶜ)* which King Djedkare (Dynasty V) visited (see Document I.5). I should not be surprised if the "chest of writings" that King Neferirkare had brought to him when Washptah fell ill and died was kept in just such a house of books (see Document I.4). I also suspect that it was this place that in the late Old Kingdom came to be called a House of Life and appeared in a number of locations in the course of Egyptian history. At any rate, we should examine this institution at some length.[28]

The "House of Life" is no doubt to be distinguished from the Old Kingdom "Mansion of Life" (Gardiner, *JEA* 24, p. 83). Still the expression "House of Life" is found in some sources of the Old Kingdom, though whether it was applied to one or more organizations at this early time is not known. The god

ANCIENT EGYPTIAN SCIENCE

Khnum is called "Lord of the House of Life" already in the fifth dynasty, and we find references in two decrees of Pepi II (*ibid.*, p. 160) to "the apparatus of the House of Life," presumably including "papyrus, reed-pens, ink, medical instruments, perhaps even the whole pharmacopoeia". Among Middle Kingdom references to the House of Life we note a stela (from Abydos) which calls the prince Mentuhotep (time of Sesostris I) "Master of the Secrets of the House of Life," and we see (Gardiner, p. 160; Ward, p. 45) the deceased Iha speaking of himself as "one who sees to the propitiation of the gods, [who is] overseer of writings in the House of Life, to whom all private matters are revealed". On a Middle-Kingdom scarab appears the title "Instructor of the House of Life" (Ward, p. 149), though references to teaching in the House of Life are scarce and it is doubtful that any regular courses were taught in the houses of life. Also in the Middle Kingdom we find the earliest use of the title "Scribe of the House of Life" for one Keku (Gardiner, p. 160; Ward, p. 160, No. 1380). Proceeding to the eighteenth dynasty, we can mention a brick that came from an actual House of Life in Amarna, a discovery of Pendlebury's reported by Gardiner (p. 160):

> The 'House of Life' consists of two buildings, Q.42.19 and Q.42.20, which lie 400 metres to the south of the great temple and 100 metres east of the small temple and royal estate that are themselves to the east of the Palace. The 'House of Life' abuts upon the so-called Records Office....'The place of correspondence of Pharaoh',...as befits the similarity

of these activities....The only object
of any importance found [here] was a
fragmentary funerary papyrus...now
in the Ashmolean Museum.

Particularly interesting as illustrative of the
variety of activity in the House of Life is a reference
in Tomb 111 at Thebes (Dynasty XIX) belonging to
Amenwahsu, who is called "scribe of the sacred book(s)
in the house of Amun, w^{cb}-priest of Sekhmet in the
house of Amun...scribe who wrote the annals of the
gods and the goddesses in the House of Life" (Gardiner,
p. 161; von Känel, pp. 45-46). In the same tomb we find
the statement that "this inscription has been written in
this tomb by the scribe of the House of Life
Amenwahsu in his own hand" (von Känel, p. 46) and
indeed elsewhere Amenwahsu is entitled as "engraver
($s\check{s}$ $t^{j}y$ $m\underline{d}^{j}t$) in the House of Life". Before leaving
Amenwahsu, we should note that a royal scribe with
the name Khaemope, whom Gardiner identified as
Amenwahsu's son of the same name (Gardiner, p. 161), a
claim disputed by von Känel (p. 48), engaged in an
activity similar to that of Amenwahsu when he (i.e.
Khaemope) "wrote the annals of all the gods in the
House of Life". In view of these statements, it is
tempting to imagine that the annals that appear as
Document I.1 were composed in a House of Life since,
of course, the King himself was the "Good God" and a
great many of the events by which the years are
designated in the annals are festivals celebrating the
"births" of the various gods (see below, Document I.1, n.
6).

The great Ramesses II did research on Thebes as
the original land of creation in the writings of the
House of Life (see Chap. 2 below, n. 3). In the reign of

Ramesses IV a stela reports the king as investigating "[the annals?] of Thoth who is in the House of Life; I have not left unseen any of them at all, in order to search out both great and small among the gods and goddesses, and I have found...the entire Ennead,[29] and all of thy [Osiris's] forms are more mysterious than theirs" (Gardiner, p. 162). Ramesses' love of such recondite learning produced in the House of Life is also extolled in inscriptions in the Wadi Hammamat. The king is said to be "excellent of understanding like Thoth, and he hath penetrated into the annals like the maker thereof, having examined the writings of the House of Life" (*ibid.*). Among other documents of this period we find that Amenope, the author of the Onomasticon given below as Document I.9 (a great list of names arranged under the various categories in which the author or general Egyptian tradition saw the world), has the title "scribe of the sacred book(s) in the House of Life." His Onomasticon gives a hint of the variety of the activity of the members of the House of Life. A pursuit similar to that of Amenope seems to be implied in the title given to the specialized god Horus in *Snwt,* "Who is known to have magical powers...[and] be a master of words [and] of exalted rank in the House of Life, a creator in the library" (Gardiner, p. 164). These titles ascribed to the god reflect, I suppose, what the scribes of the House of Life were doing.

The magical activity of the House of Life is also clear from a magical papyrus wherein we read: "The first spell of all water-enchantments--now the head ones [i.e. the lector-priests] have said with regard to it, Open the heart to no strangers concerning it--a true secret of the House of Life" (*ibid.*). Furthermore, one scene in a painted coffin of a scribe Ankhefenamun links Isis (well

known for her magical powers) with the House of Life
(*ibid.*, p. 165).

In the Saite period (Dynasty XXVI) Peftuauneith,
the Chief Physician of King Apries, had recorded on his
statue (Louvre A 92) an inscription that mentions his
rebuilding of the temple of Osiris at Abydos, apparently
during the reign of Apries' successor Amasis. Following
this account the inscription further tells us:

> I restored the House of Life after
> (its) ruin. I renewed the sustenance
> of Osiris, and put all of his (or its?)
> ordinances in their proper place
> (Gardiner, p. 165).

Similarly under the king Darius I the Chief Physician
Udjahorresne was sent from Persia back to Egypt

> in order to restore the department(s)
> [or establishment] of the House(s) of
> Life...[30] after they (it?) had
> decayed....I did as His Majesty had
> commanded me; I furnished them
> with all their staffs consisting of
> persons of rank, not a poor man's son
> among them. I placed them in the
> charge of every learned man [in
> order to teach them?] all their crafts.
> His Majesty had commanded [me] to
> give them every good thing that
> they might carry out all their crafts.
> I supplied them with everything
> useful to them, with all their
> equipment that was on record, as
> they had been before. His Majesty
> did this because he knew the worth
> of this guild in making well those

that are sick, in making endure
forever the names of all the gods,
their temples, their offerings, and the
conduct of their festivals.[31]

From this statement we can perhaps deduce that
not only were magic and medicine important subjects at
the House of Life, but perhaps also (1) astronomy in
connection with the determination of festivals, (2) the
preparation and preservation of offering rituals, and (3)
the development and recording of the detailed aspects
of the gods and their temples.

It was the ideal House of Life at Abydos which
was described in a mysterious work of the Late Period
or the Ptolemaic Period contained in Papyrus Brit. Mus.
10051 (Salt 825): [32]

The House of Life. It shall be
in Abydos and composed of four
[side] bodies and an interior body
[made] of covered reeds. *The four
[bodies called] Houses and [the
central body called] the Living One.*
The Living One is Osiris, while the
four Houses are Isis, Nephthys, Geb,
and Nut (! Horus and Thoth?). Isis is
on one side and Nephthys is on the
other. Horus is on the third side and
Thoth on the last one. These are the
four corners [as shown in Fig. I.30].
Geb is the ground floor of it (the
House of Life) and Nut its ceiling.
The hidden one who rests within is
the Great God. The four outer
bodies are of stone which is from the
Two Houses (?). The ground floor is

of sand. The exterior is pierced in all by four doors (two times): one to the south, another to the north, a third to the west, and a fourth to the east.

It shall be very, very, secret, not known and not seen. It is only the solar disk which looks upon its mystery.

The people who enter into it are the staff of Re: and they are the scribes of the House of Life. The people who are inside are (1) the "Shaven-headed Priest" *(fkty)*, who is Shu; (2) the "Slaughterer" *(ḥnty)*, who is Horus, who slays those who rebel against his father Osiris; (3) the "Scribe of the Sacred Book(s)," who is Thoth, who recites [the ritual of] glorification every day, without being seen or heard. [Properly] silent of mouth, their mouths and bodies covered, they are far removed from any repulsive violence.

No Asiatic [i.e. foreigner] will be allowed to enter there; he shall not see it and you will be far removed from it.

The books which are inside [the House of Life] are the "Emanations of Re," wherewith to keep alive the god and to overthrow his enemies. The staff of the House of Life, who are in it, are the

> "Followers of Re" who protect his
> son every day....They (the gods or
> their priestly representatives at the
> House of Life) are personally
> occupied in protecting the god, in
> defending the king in his palace, and
> in overturning those who rebel
> against him.

The editor of this papyrus submits this passage
and indeed the whole text to a profound and subtle
analysis. The detailed rituals described therein show
that the major objective of the House of Life is the
defense of the gods, the king, and the right order by
which society and the world run smoothly, that is
maat.[33] He paraphrases the ideal-physical description
of the House of Life at Abydos as follows (see Fig.
I.30):[34]

> The House of Life ought to be found
> at Abydos. It ought to be built of
> four bodies plus an interior body
> made of covered reeds (like a
> pavilion)....The four exterior bodies
> are of stone and form an enclosure.
> The ground floor of the House of
> Life is made of sand and the exterior
> is pierced by four doors....It ought to
> be impenetrable to profane gaze. It
> cannot be known and cannot be seen.
> Only the solar disk ought to gaze on
> its secret.

Surrounded by these walls or bodies (each assigned to a
god), the House of Life is apparently open to the sky
except for the reed-covered pavilion in the center
occupied by a statuette of "Osiris, First of the

Westerners", i.e. the dead. The scribes of the House of Life, that is the "Staff of Re" or "Followers of Re", produce and guard the books, called "Emanations (i.e. *Bas*) of Re", which contain the details of the rites necessary to its purpose, namely to revivify the king and Osiris, and the magical charms and spells made use of in those rites. According to Derchain's belief, the House of Life also contained:[35]

> treatises of medicine [presumably like those of Volume Three, Chapter 5 below], of astronomy [cf. Vol. Two, Chap. 3], of mathematics [cf. Chap. 4], of mythological narratives [cf. Chap. 2] (like the annals of gods and goddesses), catalogues of divinities, manuals of the decoration of temples, rituals for embalming, exemplar manuscripts of the Book of the Dead from which copies could be made, without counting the more diverse manuals among which are those of dream interpretation, and various commentaries, all of the works constituting the information for which a ritualist might have need. Doubtless one ought to find there other works as well, e.g. geographical notes describing the nomes of Egypt....Finally, as the care of preparing royal tombs fell upon the personnel of the House of Life, it ought also to have contained manuscripts of cosmogonic compositions which we know to be

> sculpted on the walls of the rock-cut
> tombs in the Valley of the Kings [cf.
> Chap. 2]....Finally it is also there [at
> the House of Life] that the
> descriptions of Egypt which we call
> Onomastica were compiled [cf. Doc.
> I.9]. In a word, one ought to find
> there the complete totality of all the
> philosophic and scientific knowledge
> of the Egyptians.

I should add that the evidence assuring us that the various works listed by Derchain were in fact prepared and/or contained in the House of Life is scarce but not wholly missing (e.g. see particularly the quotation given above from the biographical statement concerning Udjahorresne). Even before the study made by Derchain, the wide variety of subjects considered at the House of Life was described by Volten.[36] Since his main objective was the study of Dream Interpretation,[37] he stressed the connection of this subject with the House of Life. Volten particularly emphasized the importance of magic and medicine[38] at the House of Life, but he also thought that astronomy and mathematics were important in connection with preparation and determination of the great religious festivals. After listing the various subjects pursued at the House of Life, Volten concludes (and this Gardiner had specifically denied) that the House of Life was a kind of university. Though this may be doubtful, that it functioned as a scriptorium for the production of many kinds of works like those that we shall study is scarcely to be gainsaid, just as we cannot deny its great importance in the determination of ritual.

But probably the House of Life was not the only

institution to serve as a scriptorium. We have already mentioned the Record Hall at Amarna that was located in the vicinity of the House of Life. Furthermore we note references to a "hall of writing" and an "office of writing" in a letter from the scribe Hori (of about the time of the reign of Ramesses II) to the scribe Amenemope, where he describes himself as:[39]

> The scribe of noble parts, patient in discussion, at whose utterances men rejoice when they are heard, skilled in hieroglyphics; there is nothing he does not know. He is a champion in valour and in the art of Seshyt [i.e. Seshat, the goddess of writing]; servant of the lord of Khmun [i.e. Thoth, lord of Hermopolis] in the hall *(is)* of writing; assistant-teacher (*or, in a variant reading*, teacher of subordinates) in the office (*ḥ*ꜣ) of writing.[40] First of his companions, foremost of his fellows, prince of his contemporaries, without his peer. His merit is proved in every stripling [i.e., he is a good teacher]....Swift to inscribe empty rolls....Unraveling the obscurities of the annals like him who made them.

In connection with the production and preserving of books, we should mention finally the temple libraries. It appears that normally each temple had a House of Books *(pr mdꜣt)*. The only ones now extant are in the temples at Philae and Edfu.[41] These consisted of a single niche (Philae) or a small room (Edfu). In both cases there was very little space and hence it is a safe conclusion that these "libraries" contained only books that were needed for the festivals at the temple. They thus contrast with the libraries at the House of Life, which were more like research libraries. But in terms of its purpose, the library at Edfu can be clearly tied in with a House of Life (one presumably at Edfu). Its reliefs show that it had some of the same objectives as those of a House of Life like that already described at Abydos: the annihilation of the king's enemies and the protection of the life of the king. For example, a rite is described which is entitled "Overthrowing the enemies of his father Osiris each day".[42] It is executed on behalf of "Osiris, the First of the Westerners, the Great God, Lord of Abydos, who made resplendent the House of Life by means of his ka".[43] Established in the library is the god Horus *imy Snwt* elsewhere mentioned as "the lord of books...the master of discourse, the Old One in the House of Life, who is installed in the House of Books...the redoubtable lord of the House of Books".[44] Furthermore Seshat, the goddess of writing, appears in the friezes on the four walls of the library at Edfu and also lower on the east wall of that library (see Fig. I.31b), and she on occasion has the titles of "Lady of the House of Books" and "Lady of the House of Life".[45] In conclusion note that a catalogue of more than thirty books of the library is given on the south wall.[46]

To this point I have briefly sketched the invention of writing and scribal activities. Using the fruits of that invention for recording and describing, certain people became specialized in the nascent scientific activities mentioned here but reserved for detailed treatment later. Now we may proceed to the first set of documents.

Notes to Chapter One

1.   A. H. Gardiner, *Late-Egyptian Miscellanies* (Brussels, 1937), p. 60; R. A. Caminos, *Late-Egyptian Miscellanies* (London, 1954), p. 232; and P. Montet, *Everyday Life in Egypt in the Days of Ramesses the Great* (Philadelphia, 1981), p. 275.

2.   E. J. Baumgartel, *The Cultures of Prehistoric Egypt*, Vol. 2 (London/New York/Toronto, 1960), p. 103, and "Scorpion and Rosette and the Fragment of the Large Hierakonpolis Mace Head," *Zeitschrift für ägyptische Sprache und Altertumskunde*, Vol. 93 (1966), pp. 9-13. For the possible identification of the rosette as a designation of the king, see W. Helck, *Untersuchungen zu den Beamtentiteln des ägyptischen Alten Reiches* (Glückstadt/Hamburg/New York, 1954), p. 24.

3.   A. H. Gardiner, *Egyptian Grammar,* 3rd ed. (London, 1957), p. 7.

4.   H. Kees, "Archaisches [tt=ỉtt] 'Erzieher'?" *Zeitschrift für ägyptische Sprache und Altertumskunde,* Vol. 82 (1957), pp. 58-62.

5.   A. H. Gardiner, *Egypt of the Pharaohs* (Oxford, 1961), pp. 405-07.   For a review of the literature on the meaning of the ivory tablet from Naqada, see J. Vandier, *Manuel d'archéologie égyptienne,* Vol. 1 (Paris, 1952), pp. 827-31.

6.   W. B. Emery, *Archaic Egypt* (Harmondsworth, England, 1961), p. 84, adopts Semenptah as his *nebti* and *nesu-bit* names. Grdseloff reads the name as Iryneter (see Vandier, *Manuel,* Vol. 1, p. 856).

7.   Evidence of writing in these seals and sealings, and indeed in all of the tablets, vases, and the

like which we have briefly examined to this point, serve only to illustrate the early period of scribal activity. The reader who wants fuller evidence may consult the invaluable collection of inscriptions from the early period presented and discussed by P. Kaplony, *Die Inschriften der ägyptischen Frühzeit*, Vols. 1-3 (Wiesbaden, 1963), *Supplementband* (Wiesbaden, 1964), together with his *Kleine Beiträge zu den ägyptischen Frühzeit* (Wiesbaden, 1966). See also Fig. I.19b for some inscriptions in early cylinders.

8. Vandier, *Manuel*, Vol. 1, pp. 731-32. We are of course primarily dependent on W. M. F. Petrie, *The Royal Tombs of the First Dynasty*, Part I (London, 1900), plates XXXI-XXXVI, and *The Royal Tombs of the Earliest Dynasties*, Part II (London, 1901), plates XXVI-XXXA.

9. See signs Y 3 and Y 4 in Gardiner, *Egyptian Grammar*, p. 534. It appears to be sign Y 4 that occurs on this stela, with the reed holder now missing because of the deteriorated state of the stela.

10. Vandier, *Manuel*, Vol. 1, pp. 733-74, gives a very valuable, detailed description of the development of these stelas.

11. For remarks on the Magnates of the Ten of Upper Egypt, presumably an administrative and judicial council, see J. H. Breasted, *A History of Egypt*, 2nd ed. (New York, 1912), pp. 79-80. I have followed the conventional rendering of this title (cf. Helck, *Untersuchungen zu den Beamtentiteln des Alten Reiches*, pp. 18-19). But see H. Goedicke, "Die Laufbahn des Mtn," *Mitteilungen des Deutschen Archäologischen Instituts, Abteilung Kairo*, Vol. 21 (1966), pp. 57-62, who reviews this title (and the literature on it) in detail and comes to the translation "Grosser des Katasters von

Oberägypten" (Great One of the Cadastre of Upper Egypt). Perhaps it was already a title of a rank rather than of a specific administrative office. See K. B. Gödecken, *Eine Betrachtung der Inschriften des Meten im Rahmen der sozialen und rechtlichen Stellung von Privatleuten im ägyptischen Alten Reich* (Wiesbaden, 1976), p. 80, who believes that the shift from office-title to rank-title had taken place by the early fourth dynasty.

12.   In listing the various scribal titles, I have primarily used three standard works: B. Porter and R. L. B. Moss, *Topographical Bibliography of Ancient Egyptian Hieroglyphic Texts, Reliefs, and Paintings*, Vols. 1-3, 2nd ed. (Oxford, 1960-78); M. A. Murray, *Index of Names and Titles of the Old Kingdom* (London, 1908); and W. A. Ward, *Index of Egyptian Administrative and Religious Titles of the Middle Kingdom* (Beirut, 1982). H. Goedicke, "Diplomatic Studies in the Old Kingdom," *Journal of the American Research Center in Egypt*, Vol. 3 (1964), pp. 31-41 (whole article), has (p. 31) some wise statements concerning the rise of the office of king's scribe: "In the III Dynasty the position of scribe for the king develops into an established office, and the appearance of a 'leader of the king's scribes' suggests the formation of a royal chancery. The early holders of this position, to judge from their burials, were persons of highest social status. From this early title subsequently develops a more specific $z\check{s}$ ^{c}-nswt, 'scribe of the King's documents,' a title of which various compounds are attested." The authority for these remarks is Helck, *Untersuchungen zu den Beamtentiteln des Alten Reiches*, pp. 71 ff., and, in addition, the above noted work of Kaplony, *Die Inschriften der ägyptischen*

Frühzeit, Vol. 1, p. 583; for a list of titles involving scribes, see Vol. 2, p. 1215 (under *zš*, given alone and in compound).

13. See the long list of additional titles in Ward, *Index*, pp. 156-68, which I make no attempt to reproduce here; see also Porter and Moss, *Topographical Bibliography*, Vol. 3, 2nd ed., pp. 928, 934, and the long list of titles given in the index (under *sš*) of F. von Känel, *Les prêtres-ouâb de Sekhmet et les conjurateurs de Serket* (Paris, 1984), pp. 324-25.

14. Petrie, *Royal Tombs*, Part I, p. 38.

15. F. Jonckheere, *Les médecins de l'Égypte pharaonique. Essai de prosopographie* (Bruxelles, 1958) and P. Ghalioungui, *The Physicians of Pharaonic Egypt* (Cairo, 1983). See L. Habachi and P. Ghalioungui, "Notes on Nine Physicians of Pharaonic Egypt," *Bulletin de l'Institut d'Égypt*, Vol. 51 (1969), pp. 15-24. See also Porter and Moss, *Topographical Bibliography*, Vol. 3, 2nd ed., p. 932, and von Känel, *Les prêtres-ouâb de Sekhmet*, p. 324 (*swnw*). Incidentally, I have followed Gardiner, Faulkner, and Ghalioungui in transcribing the hieroglyphs used for "physician" as *swnw* rather than as *sinw* used by Jonckheere throughout, though a case can be made for *zinw* in the Old Kingdom (see Gardiner, *Egyptian Grammar*, p. 512, sign T 11).

16. Jonckheere, *Les médecins*, pp. 116-17. Note that von Känel, *Les prêtres-ouâb de Sekhmet*, p. 227, substitutes for Jonckheere's title "Physician of the Troop" the reading "Physician and Magician of Selket (*s'w Srḳt)*.

17. Peseshet's stela is reproduced in Jonckheere, *Les médecins*, Fig. 9. He incorrectly translates it "Directrice des médecins" as if the reading were *imyt-r swnw* when in fact it is *imyt-r swnwt* and hence it is

obvious that her title should be translated "Directress of Female Physicians". Cf. Ghalioungui, *The Physicians of Pharaonic Egypt*, p. 18.

18. Jonckheere, *Les médecins*, p. 67, n. 1.

19. *Ibid.*, p. 25, and Fig. 2 for the stela, cf. von Känel, *Les prêtres-ouâb de Sekhmet*, pp. 167-68.

20. M. Lichtheim, *Ancient Egyptian Literature*, Vol. 3 (Berkeley/Los Angeles/London, 1980), pp. 91-92. For printing purposes I have removed, both in the text and the next footnote, the hyphens in the gods' names as given in Miss Lichtheim's translation, but I have restored them by hand.

21. This conclusion reflects ordinary medical procedure, whereby the physician after diagnosing the case comes to the conclusion "an ailment to be treated" or "an ailment not to be treated". In the case of Princess Bentresh, the learned man saw that as a case of possession her ailment could be treated by a specialist (who it turned out was the cult image of the god called Khons–the–Provider–in–Thebes). Miss Lichtheim's note on the god is of interest: "The Theban god Khons was worshipped under several distinct manifestations, with Khons–in–Thebes–Neferhotep occupying the leading position, while the outstanding trait of Khons...[the-Provider-in–Thebes] was that of healer."

22. Jonckheere, *Les médecins*, pp. 126-27.

23. A. H. Gardiner, "Some Personifications. I. ḤĪKE, The God of Magic," *Proceedings of the Society of Biblical Archaeology*, Vol. 37 (1915), pp. 253-62; "Professional Magicians in Ancient Egypt," *ibid.*, Vol. 39 (1917), pp. 31-44, 138-40, and the work of von Känel cited in note 13.

24. Gardiner, "Some Personifications," pp. 261-62;

Jonckheere, *Les médecins*, pp. 127-28. For a recent and detailed study of w^{cb}-priests of Sekhmet and the Charmers of Serket as medical personnel, see von Känel, *Les prêtres-ouâb de Sekhmet.*

25. Ward, *Index*, pp. 9, 58, 86; O. Neugebauer and R. A. Parker, *Egyptian Astronomical Texts*, Vol. 3 (Providence, Rhode Island, and London), 1969, p. 213; A. H. Gardiner, *Ancient Egyptian Onomastica*, Vol. 1 (Oxford, 1947), pp. 61*-62*.

26. G. A. Reisner, *A History of the Giza Necropolis*, Vol. 1 (Cambridge, Mass., and London, 1942), p. 341.

27. *Ibid.*, p. 502. For the succeeding reference to Medunefer, see p. 491.

28. Many of the initial references to the House of Life have been taken from A. H. Gardiner, "The House of Life," *Journal of Egyptian Archaeology*, Vol. 24 (1938), pp. 157-79 (abbreviated in the next paragraphs simply as "Gardiner"). The first reference (abbreviated as "Gardiner, *JEA* 24") is to another article in the same volume of the journal: "The Mansion of Life and the Master of the King's Largess," *ibid.*, pp. 83-91. I have also in the passages occasionally cited Ward's *Index* merely as "Ward" and von Känel's *Les prêtres-ouâb de Sekhmet* as "von Känel."

29. The name Ennead is one that embraced the nine gods at Heliopolis: Atum, Shu, Tefnut, Geb, Nut, Osiris, Seth, Isis, and Nephthys. For the variations in composition and number of the Ennead, see E. Hornung, *Conceptions of God in Ancient Egypt: The One and the Many* (Ithaca, 1982), pp. 221-23, where the pertinent literature is cited. See also below, Chap. 2, n. 29.

30. I have generally followed Lichtheim, *Ancient Egyptian Literature*, Vol. 3, pp. 39-40, but occasionally

have preferred the reading of Gardiner, pp. 157-58. The translation here of "departments" instead of "establishment" is a case in point. Gardiner goes on to say that the missing part may have completed the phrase as follows: "the department(s) of the House(s) of Life dealing with medicine". Miss Lichtheim objects: "But medicine was only one of several crafts practiced by the members of the House of Life."

31. It is this last sentence that gives us concrete evidence of the wide variety of subjects pursued at the House of Life, at least at this late date.

32. P. Derchain, *Le Papyrus Salt 825 (B.M. 10051), rituel pour la conservation de la vie en Égypte, Académie Royale de Belgique, Classe des Lettres, Mémoires*, Vol. 58 (Brussels, 1965), pp. 139-40; Part III, pp. 7*-10*. For the possible (but doubtful) location of Abydos' House of Life in the Second Osiris Hall of the Temple of Sethos I, see R. David, *A Guide to Religious Ritual at Abydos* (Warminster, Wilts., England, 1981), pp. 147-48.

33. Derchain, *op. cit.*, Part I, *pass.*

34. *Ibid.*, p. 49.

35. *Ibid.*, pp. 56-57.

36. A. Volten, *Demotische Traumdeutung (Pap. Carlsberg XIII und XIV verso), Analecta aegyptiaca*, Vol. 3 (Copenhagen, 1942), pp. 17-44.

37. *Ibid.*, p. 40.

38. *Ibid.*, p. 30. Note that L. Habachi and P. Ghalioungui discovered Priests of Sekhmet and physicians apparently connected with a House of Life at Bubastis: "The 'House of Life' of Bubastis," *Chronique d'Égypte*, Vol. 46 (1971), pp. 59-71. See also P. Ghalioungui, *The House of Life: Per Ankh. Magic and Medical Science in Ancient Egypt* (Amsterdam, 1973),

pp. 66-67.

39. A. H. Gardiner, *Egyptian Hieratic Texts: Series I. Literary Texts of the New Kingdom. Part I. The Papyrus Anastasi and the Papyrus Koller* (Leipzig, 1911), p. 6*. I have omitted Gardiner's notes except for the note I have numbered as 40.

40. *Ibid.*, n. 6: "*O.P.* [Petrie Ostracon] continues differently thus: '[skilled in (?)] his profession; knowing the secrets of heaven and earth....; there is none who repels(?) ....in writing. First of his fellows in the midst of his neighbors; chief of his contemporaries, they are not equal [to him]; teacher of subordinates in the office of writing; his merit is proved in every stripling. Lamp....' (end)."

41. Derchain, *op. cit.* in n. 32, p. 58. Both libraries are discussed at some length by Derchain, pp. 58-61.

42. E. Chassinat, *Le temple d'Edfou*, Vol. 3 (Cairo, 1928), p. 345, E'o. 1 d., lin. 1.

43. *Ibid.*, p. 346.

44. Derchain, *op. cit.*, p. 60.

45. *Ibid.* See Chassinat, *Le temple d'Edfou*, Vol. 3, p. 350, E'e. 2 g. I, lin. 2, and Gardiner, p. 164 (23). See also Document I.1, n. 44.

46. Chassinat, *Le temple d'Edfou*, Vol. 3, pp. 347(E's. 2 d., lin. 2)-348(E's. 2 d., lin. 6) and 351(E's. 2 g., lin. 3-6). See H. Brugsch, "Bau und Maasse des Tempels von Edfu," *Zeitschrift für ägyptische Sprache und Alterthumskunde*, Vol. 9 (1871), pp. 43-45 (full article pp. 32-45), and M. Weber, *Beiträge zur Kenntnis des Schrift- und Buchwesens der alten Ägypter* (Cologne, 1969), pp. 131-34. Most of the titles in the catalogue are unknown elsewhere, many are in the form of abbreviated titles, and many are difficult to translate

precisely. The first set of works (E's. 2 d., lin. 2-6) includes the following: "Many Chests Containing Books Together with a considerable [Number of] Rolls of Leather: (1) The Overthrowing of Seth; (2) Repelling of Crocodiles; (3) Protection of the Hours; (4) Guarding of the Sacred Bark; (5) Opening of the *Nam.t*-Bark; (6) Book of Making the King Rise (i.e. his coronation?); (7) Guides to Ritual; (8) Great Glorifications of Him Who is on the Deathbed; (9) The Protection of a City; (10) The Protection of a House; (11) The Protection of the White Crown; (12) The Protection of Thrones; (13) The Protection of the Year; (14) The Protection of Graves (or Beds); (15) The Appeasement of Sekhmet; (16) The Guardians (*not listed by Weber*); (17) The Totality of Books (or the Book of the Totality?) Concerning the Hunting of a Lion, the Repelling of Crocodiles, the Guarding of ____(?), and the Repelling of Snakes; (18) The Craft of all Priests of the Temple-Kitchen (or Knowledge of All Secrets of the Laboratory [for the production of unguents and the like]); (19) The Knowledge of Your Offerings to the Gods in All Their Images and to Your Families on Your (Birth?)days and Every Inventory of Your Secret Godly Forms and the Forms of Your Ennead." The second set of titles (E's. 2 g., lin. 3-5) is: "(20) The Book of What is in the Temple; (21) The Book of *Rth* (Dread?); (22) Book of All Writings Concerning Arms (or Battles or Tools?); (23) Book of the Management (or Plan) of a Temple; (24) The Book of Guards (or Officials) Who Belong to the Temples; (25) Rules for Painting the Wall and the Observation (or Protection) of Body Forms; (26) Book of the Protection of the King in his Palace; (27) Spells for the Repelling of the Evil Eye; (28) Knowledge of the Periodic Returns of the Two Celestial Spirits: the

Sun and the Moon; (29) The Governing of the Periodic Returns of the Stars; (30) The Numbering of All the Sepulchers and the Knowledge of Those Who are in Them; (31) All Consultation-books of the Summoning of Your Majesty to Your Temple in Your Festivals." It is obvious that items (17), (22), and (31) seem to refer to more than one book. Weber in the above-cited work (pp. 113-31) gives other lists of titles, and S. Sauneron, *Les prêtres de l'ancienne Égypte* (Paris, 1957), p. 136, translates some of the titles in the Edfu catalogues somewhat differently. Sauneron also mentions the remains of a similar catalogue at Tod (southeast of Luxor), and he tells us (p. 137) that the works themselves from one of these temple libraries have been discovered in the small village of Tebtunis (in the Fayyum).

Document I.1: Introduction

The Early Egyptian *Annals* on Stone, Generally called the Palermo Stone

Our first document is, as I have stated in my general remarks above, the earliest historiographical document extant from ancient Egypt's long history. It is one of the most important by-products of the Egyptian development of a written language. It consisted of a rectangular block of black diorite, on both sides of which were inscribed the principal events of the reigns of the kings of the first four dynasties and a part of the fifth. It was composed in the fifth dynasty, perhaps from now lost annals of early kings, or if not from formal annals at least from many tablets and labels giving the year names in terms of events.[1] From this one (or less likely more than one)[2] stone seven fragments have been found (Figs. I.32-I.43): one now in Palermo, five in Cairo, and one in London. Valiant efforts have been made to reconstruct the size and even the content (at least in terms of the number of years in each reign) of the whole stone on the basis of these fragments and various extant lists of kings (see the literature listed below and Fig. I.44). But it is fair to say that none of these constructions is entirely convincing, for they are all based in some significant degree on unproved and implausible assumptions.[3] Still, the most useful are the reconstructions of Kaiser, Helck, and Giustolisi (see Figs. I.42 and I.43 for the latter two). The size of the stone has been variously estimated: the length ranging from six to ten feet and the height agreed upon as somewhat more than two feet.[4]

Details of the document have been discussed in the notes that accompany it, but we can briefly summarize here its most important aspects.

(1) The stone represents the first partially extant, extensive set of annals in Egyptian history, which covered in all likelihood about 600 years of pharaonic rule (from ca. 3000 B.C. to ca. 2400 B.C.). As I have said above, its author of the fifth dynasty probably had access to annals prepared in the earlier dynasties.

(2) The annals of the first three dynasties consist almost exclusively of events that give the years their names. Thus for those dynasties the document is largely a list of year names rather than true annals of the most important royal events in the reign of each king. In these early years two events were generally sufficient to identify the year. The first event was often a repeated event such as the "Following of Horus", which was either a festival celebrating the conquest of Egypt by Horus and his allies or a biennial tour of Egypt by the king and his officials, perhaps for tax purposes (see Document I.1 below, note 11). Since this event was repeated every other year, a second event was needed to identify the year more completely. The second event was frequently (though not exclusively) the celebration of a religious festival, often entitled the "Birth of Such-and-Such God" (see Document I.1, n. 6). Occasionally an event that happened only once (or that the original annalist thought would happen only once) was chosen by itself as the name of the year. For example, the third year of Horus Djer's reign in the

first dynasty was named exclusively as "The Year of [the Festival of] the Birth of the Two Children of the King of Lower Egypt" (see *ibid.*, n. 16). An alternative to taking a single unusual event as the name of the year was the practice of taking a more common event and using an ordinal number to precede it. So, Year 9 of Djer's reign was named "The Year of the First Occurrence of the Feast of Djet (Uto *or* Wadjet)" (*ibid.*, n. 22). As I have said, sometimes the unusual single event by which a year was named had no religious significance but was a secular event. Thus the Year X + 2 of the Horus Den in the first dynasty was named "The Year of the Smiting of the Asiatics" (*ibid.*, n. 34). Similarly the Year Y + 2 of the same king was called "The Year of the Smiting of the Troglodytes [i.e. Easterners]" (*ibid.*, n. 40). Needless to say, even when the event was secular it concerned an action of the king, for these are royal annals. We should note that the first year of a king's reign is characterized by the celebrations accompanying his assumption of the throne, namely, ceremonies of "the Union of the Two Lands and of the Circuit of the Wall" (*ibid.*, end of n. 13).

(3) While the principal purpose of the *Annals* reflected in the first three dynasties was the recording of events which gave the names of the years, an important supplementary datum was included for each year, the Nile height at full flood, whose measurement or at least recording apparently started by the time of the Horus Djer (*ibid.*, n. 14). This is important as illustrating Egyptian concern from a very early date with regular measurements, and it illustrates the early use of the linear units of cubit, span, palm, and finger and their fractions. In fact, the flooding of the Nile was of such importance that Year Y + 4 of the reign of

Horus Den apparently received its name from an unusually high flooding: "Year of the Filling [i.e. Flooding] of all the Lakes [or Nomes] of the Rekhyt-Folk in the West and the East of Lower Egypt [i.e. in the Delta]" (*ibid.*, n. 42).

Another important "measuring" event that is reflected in the early years of the *Annals* is that connected with laying out the ground plan or "stretching the cord" as the first step in the construction of temples or mansions. Year Y + 7 of Den's reign was called "The Year of Stretching the Cord at the Great Door of the Castle [called] 'Seats of the Gods' by the Priest of Seshat" (*ibid.*, n. 44). Similarly the Year X + 2 of Horus Ninetjer in the second dynasty was named "The Appearance of [the king as] the King of Upper Egypt [at] the Stretching of the Cord for the Mansion [called] 'Hor-ren'" (*ibid.*, n. 57). In the next dynasty, Year 4 of King Djoser's reign, the king appears at the "Stretching of the Cord for the Mansion [called] 'The Refreshment of the Gods'".

(4) By the second dynasty the biennial survey called the "Following of Horus" attracts to itself the supplementary characterization of the "counting" of the wealth of the land. The significant point is that along with the specification of the "counting" an ordinal number began to be used. For example, the Year X + 3 (=8?) of Ninetjer is called "The Year of the Following of Horus [in which took place] the Fourth Occurrence of the Counting" (*ibid.*, n. 58). Two years later it was the "fifth" occurrence of the counting, two years after that the "sixth", and successively every two years, the "seventh", "eighth", and "ninth" occurrences of the counting. The general "counting" without specification of what is being counted which originated in the second

dynasty seems to have spawned specific countings in the third. For example, in Year X + 1 (=3?) of Horus Zanakht's reign we read of the "First Occurrence of the Counting of Gold" (*ibid.*, n. 66). This was followed in the next year by the "Second Occurrence of the Counting", which probably was confined to the counting of the cattle and the cultivated land. By the Year Y + 3 (=14?) of this reign the counting of the gold and that of the fields were merged and the year was called "The Year of the Following of Horus [in which took place] the Seventh Occurrence of the Counting of the Gold and the Fields" (*ibid.*, n. 70). Compare also Year Y + 5 (=16?). Though these biennial countings were not specifically mentioned in the next reign, that of the great King Djoser who was responsible for building the step pyramid at Saqqara, no doubt the "countings" were subsumed by the biennial "Followings of Horus". Mention of the biennial occurrences of the countings was restored in the records of the fourth dynasty, in the first reign, that of Sneferu (see *ibid.*, n. 86). The references to the countings in Sneferu's reign appear for the most part to have been general references, but note that in the year X + 1 (=4?) the annalist speaks of the "Second Occurrence of the Counting of Silver and Lapis lazuli" (*ibid.*, n. 81).

There is one peculiarity concerning the system of "countings" in the reign of Sneferu. In all previous references to the countings, at least to the nonspecific countings, the countings are always recorded for alternate years, that is, the system was clearly a biennial one. But notice that in the reign of Sneferu the eighth counting follows in the next year after the seventh counting (*ibid.*, n. 90). This seems to have been an aberration only, for the biennial system was still in place later in the fourth and also in the fifth and sixth dynasties. One further point is worth noting in connection with Sneferu's reign. In Year W + 1 the designation of the counting includes "small cattle", and presumably also oxen (see below C-4 r, line 2, Nr. 1).

      The next most important step in freeing the system from identifying regnal years by names and instead substituting a completely numerical system can be noted in the *Annals* of the fifth dynasty when the Year X + 1 (=3?) of Weserkaf's reign is designated as "The Year *after* the First Counting of the Oxen" (*ibid.*, n. 97).[5] By adding *after*, which I have italicized, the chronographers have achieved a system which ties every regnal year (except the first) to an ordinal numerical count, so that from the second year the years of a reign would be successively numbered: Year of first occurrence of the counting, Year after the first occurrence, Year of second occurrence, Year after the second occurrence, and so on. I have said "except the first" because it is generally believed that the Year of the first occurrence of the counting was the second year of a reign. Hence we would have these equations: Year of the assumption of the throne = Year 1, Year of the first occurrence of the counting = Year 2, Year after the first occurrence = Year 3, and so on. It is not known exactly when the practice of numbering the even and odd years in the manner just described became a system in which every year was simply given its own number.[6] This was achieved either by shifting to an annual counting or by simply dropping the use of the system of cattle counting as the basis of numbering the years. What is known is that the designation of an odd-numbered year as the "The Year *after* the *n*th occurrence of the counting" was dropped (it appears that the word *khet* or *m-khet*, meaning "after", disappeared in Pepi II's reign at the end of the sixth dynasty). Furthermore it seems clear that at some time after Dynasty VI the expression "The Year of the *n*th occurrence of the counting" in its abbreviated form "Year of the *n*th occurrence" came simply to mean "Regnal year *n*". [7]

(5) Though the system of numerical regnal years took many centuries to develop, it is evident from these *Annals* that the divisions of "months" and "days" as the basic units of the year were in effect from at least the first dynasty. From the listing of the number of months and days of the last calendar year which Aha served before his death, followed by the number of months and days of the first calendar year of Djer's reign, it is obvious that some kind of calendar year was in use (*ibid.*, n. 13). We cannot know from the data the length of this year. It could well be that it was the civil year of 12 months of 30 days plus five epagomenal days that was demonstratively in effect in the Old Kingdom and was evident in these *Annals* in the fourth dynasty at the end of Menkaure's reign and the beginning of that of Shepseskaf (*ibid.*). I shall return to calendaric questions later in Volume Two, Chapter Three, at which time I shall discuss the problem of the time of the installation of the civil calendar.

(6) Beginning with the fourth dynasty, the *Annals* now begin to resemble chronicles of which the *raison d'être* is to recount a multiplicity of memorable events in each year of a reign. This change is not unconnected with the rise of a quasi-numerical system of designating the regnal years, so that the text itself is freed from the purpose of simply giving an event by which the year can be named and can be devoted to

several important events of the year. For example, the Year Z + 2 of Sneferu in the *Annals* records the following events: "The Building with *meru*-wood of a 100-cubit Dewatowe ship and 60 sixteen-[oared?] barges, The Smiting of Nubia and taking of prisoners numbering 4,000 men and 3,000 women, together with 200,000 large and small cattle, the Building of the Wall of the Southland and the Northland [called] 'The Houses of Sneferu', The Transporting of 40 ships filled with *ash*-wood (so-called 'cedar')" (*ibid.*, nn. 87 and 88). Not only are the variety and extent of the information notable but also the fact that all of these events are secular activities. The same is true for the following year of Sneferu's reign, though the fragments of other years of his reign contain a mixture of secular and religious events. This was also true even of the fifth dynasty, in which religious donations predominated, for in the Year Z + 1 (=15?) of the reign of Sahure we find reported the importation of copper from the Malachite Country and myrrh and metals from Punt.

(7) The flurry of secular events reported in the previous paragraph should not blind us to the dominance of the reporting of festivals and other religious activities throughout the *Annals*, as the reader will see if he peruses the text at random. Note the following references to gods or their heralds (the citations in parentheses are either to the document's notes or to its marginal numbers).

First dynasty: Anubis (nn. 6, 9, 21, 25; C-1 r, lin. 3, Nr. 4), Sokar (nn. 18, 28, 37, 43), Yamet (n. 19; or probably the cult-object later called *Imy-wt*, "He who is in the bandaging room", i.e. Anubis--n. 21), Min (n. 20), Wadjet (n. 22; Pr, lin. 3, Nr. 5), Sed (n. 27; Pr, lin. 3, Nr. 11), Ha (n. 29), Neith (? n. 30), The Great White One

(? n. 33), Saw or Ptah (n. 39), Seshat (nn. 44, 47), Harsaphes (Pr, lin. 3, Nr. 9), the Apis Bull (n. 46), Mafdet (n. 47); *second dynasty*: the Apis Bull (n. 59; Pr, line 4, Nr. 10), Sokar (Pr, lin. 4, Nr. 6; Nr. 12), Horus of Heaven (Pr, lin. 4, Nr. 8), Wadjet (n. 61), Nekhbet (n. 61); *third dynasty*: Min (Pr, lin. 5, Nr. 10); *fourth dynasty*: the Apis Bull (? C-4 r, lin. 2, Nr. 2), Sed (n. 92), the Horus Bull (C-2, lin. 2, Nr. 1), Bastet (n. 94), Seshed (Pv, lin. 1, Nr. 2), the Two Wepwawets (*ibid.*); *fifth dynasty*: the Souls of Heliopolis (C-1 v, lin. 2, Nr. 2; Pv, lin. 2, Nr. 2; Pv, lin. 4, Nr. 2; Pv, lin. 5, Nr. 2), Re (C-1 v, lin. 2, Nr. 1; Pv, lin. 2, Nr. 2; Nr. 3; lin. 3, Nr. 1; lin. 4, Nr. 1; Nr. 2; lin. 5, Nr. 1; Nr. 2), Hathor (same as for Re, except for the third citation and the last two), the Gods of the Sun-Temple called "Sep-Re" (Pv, lin. 2, Nr. 2), Gods of the Heron of Djebakherut (?*ibid.*), Sepa (*ibid.*), Nekhbet (*ibid.*, lin. 2, Nr. 2; lin. 3, Nr. 1), Wadjet (*ibid.*, lin. 2, Nr. 2; lin. 3, Nr. 1; lin. 5, Nr. 2), Gods of the Shrine of the South (Pv, lin. 2, Nr. 2), Min (*ibid.*, Nr. 3), Mesenkhet (*ibid.*, lin. 3, Nr. 1), Semkhet (*ibid.*), Khenti-yawatef (*ibid.*), the White Bull (*ibid.*), Divine Ennead (*ibid.*, Nr. 2; lin. 4, Nr. 2), Seshat (*ibid.*, lin. 4, Nr. 1), the Gods of Kheraha (*ibid.*, Nr. 2), Re-senef (*ibid.*), and Ptah (*ibid.*, lin. 5, Nr. 2).

There are also numerous festivals and ceremonies which are general or ambiguous, or where the gods to whom they are dedicated are not known. For example, mention is made of a Festival of Desher (nn. 15, 31), of the "Censing the Decapitated Folk" (n. 17), of the "Birth of the Two Children of the King of Lower Egypt" (dedicated to the gods Shu and Tefnut[?]; see nn. 16, 85).

We should also single out the reference to the building out of stone of a temple called "The Goddess abides" (n. 69), for if the reign in which this took place is correctly identified as Nebka's, then we have here the earliest reference to a stone building in ancient Egypt (though stone was used for flooring, stairs, gates, and portcullis blocking in the first dynasty). I should note that there are references to pyramids (n. 96; C-1 v, lin. 2, Nr. 1; Nr. 2) and to Sun-Temples (Pv, lin. 2, Nr. 2; lin. 3, Nr. 1; lin. 5, Nrs. 1-2). There is also reference to the deeply religious Sed-festival, the festival at which the king's rule was renewed (n. 41).

(8) While I forbear citing detailed references to other temples and shrines in the *Annals*, I must stress the historical importance of the *Annals* for its plethora of information concerning the granting of regular offerings and of arable land to a host of temples and shrines in the fifth dynasty, and above all I single out the gifts to Re (see the references given to Re in the preceding paragraph), reflecting as they do Re's primacy in that dynasty.

(9) The gifts of land mentioned in the *Annals* also yield precious information to the historian of Egyptian numeration and measurement. The measures of land in these grants involve $ḥ^{ꜣ}$ (a 10-aroura measure), $st^{ꜣ}t$ (unit-aroura measure), *rmn* (1/2 aroura), *ḥsb* (1/4 aroura), $s^{ꜣ}$ (1/8 aroura), *mḥ* (a cubit-area, i.e. 1/100 aroura). If we start with a cubit-area (i.e. an area 1 cubit wide and 100 cubits long), then 1/8 aroura = 12 1/2 cubit-areas, 1/4 aroura = 25 cubit-areas, 1/2 aroura = 50 cubit-areas, 1 aroura = 100 cubit-areas, and 10 arouras = 1000 cubit-areas (which reveals why the lotus sign [Gardiner sign M 12] read as $ḥ^{ꜣ}$, meaning 1000, was used for the 10-aroura measure; see Fig. I.50). In expressing the various areas of the land grants, the annalist has sometimes made use of a primitive place-value system, a

fact which I have not seen mentioned before (see Document I.1, nn. 99, 107). In this system we find numbers where the 10-aroura measures are numbered first in units without an expected preceding 10-aroura sign, then followed by a unit-aroura sign which is itself followed by the counting of those unit-arouras in units. We also find numbers where 100-aroura measures are counted in units without any preceding 100-unit sign, then followed by the 10-aroura sign which is itself followed by the counting of 10-aroura measures in units. But the annalist was not always consistent in the use of the place-value technique (*ibid.*, nn. 99, 103) and in fact the use of this technique in later times was rare.

Texts and Studies of the Fragments

I. *The Palermo Fragment.* Abbreviated as Pr and Pv for the recto and verso.
    Text:
        H. Schäfer, "Ein Bruchstück altägyptischer Annalen," *Abhandlungen der Königlichen Preussischen Akademie der Wissenschaften, 1902, Phil.-hist. Abh.* (Berlin, 1902), pp. 3-41, with plates of Pr and Pv (see Figs. I.32, I.34) and a German translation.
        K. Sethe, *Urkunden des Alten Reichs*, Vol. 1, 2nd ed. (Leipzig, 1933) (= *Urkunden* I), pp. 235-49, a revised text of the parts containing Dynasties IV and V; this includes additions from fragments C-1 through C-4.
    Studies and Translations:
        A. Pellegrini, "Nota sopra un'iscrizione egizia del Museo di Palermo," *Archivio storico*

siciliano, n. s., Anno xx (1895), pp. 297-316, with reproductions of Pr and Pv (see Figs I.33, I.35).

E. Naville, "La Pierre de Palerme," *Recueil de travaux relatifs à la philologie et à l'archéologie égyptiennes et assyriennes*, 25me année (1903), pp. 64-81, with a French translation of Pr and a discussion of Pv.

K. Sethe, *Untersuchungen zur Geschichte und Altertumskunde Ägyptens*, Vol. 3: *Beiträge zur ältesten Geschichte Ägyptens* (Leipzig, 1905).

L. Borchardt, *Die Annalen und die zeitliche Festlegung des Alten Reiches der ägyptischen Geschichte* (Berlin, 1917).

E. Meyer, *Ägyptische Chronologie* (Berlin, 1904).

J. H. Breasted, *Ancient Records of Egypt*, Vol. 1 (Chicago, 1906), pp. 51-72, a translation based on Schäfer's text and thus of the Palermo fragment alone.

II. *The Cairo Fragments.* Abbreviated as C-1, C-2, C-3, C-4, and C-5.

H. Gauthier, "Quatre nouveaux fragments de la Pierre de Palerme," *Le Musée Égyptien*, Vol. 3 (1915), pp. 29-53, with photographs, partial transcriptions, and some translations of fragments C-1 to C-4 (see Figs. I.36-I.39).

G. Daressy, "La Pierre de Palerme et la chronologie de l'Ancien Empire," *Bulletin de l'Institut Français d'Archéologie Orientale*, Vol. 12 (1916), pp. 161-214, with further transcriptions, corrections, and suggestions regarding fragments C-1 to C-4.

F. W. Read, "Nouvelles remarques sur la

Pierre de Palerme," *ibid.*, pp. 215-22.

J. H. Breasted, "The Predynastic Union of Egypt," *ibid.*, Vol. 30 (1931), pp. 709-24; he established that line 1 in C-1 r contains the names of predynastic kings of a united Upper and Lower Egypt.

See also K. Sethe, *Urkunden*, Vol. 1, as above, who makes use of C-1 to C-4 for his text of the parts of the *Annals* concerning the fourth and the fifth dynasties.

J. L. de Cenival, "Un nouveau fragment de la Pierre de Palerme," *Bulletin de la Société Française d'Égyptologie*, Vol. 44 (1965), pp. 13-17, reporting C-5 (see Fig. I.40).

III. *The London Fragment.* Abbreviated as L (see Figs. I.41a-b).

W. M. F. Petrie, "New Portions of the Annals," *Ancient Egypt*, 1916, pp. 114-20, including a reproduction of Lr.

C. N. Reeves, "A Fragment of Fifth Dynasty Annals at University College London," *Göttinger Miszellen. Beiträge zur ägyptologischen Diskussion*, Heft 32 (1979), pp. 47-50, with photographs and a transcription of Lv (see Fig. I.41c).

H. M. Stewart, *Egyptian Stelae, Reliefs and Paintings from the Petrie Collection. Part Two: Archaic Period to Second Intermediate Period* (Warminster, England, 1979), p. 6.

IV. *Other studies of all or several fragments.*

A. Weigall, *A History of the Pharaohs*, Vol. 1 (New York, 1925), includes a dogmatic interpretation of the *Annals* which is now usually rejected.

G. Godron, "Quel est le lieu de provenance de la 'Pierre de Palerme'?" *Chronique d'Égypte*, Vol. 27 (1952), pp. 17-22; his tentative conclusion: Memphis.

W. Helck, *Untersuchungen zu Manetho und den ägyptischen Königslisten* (Berlin, 1956), especially pp. 9-10, 12, 77-81.

W. Kaiser, "Einige Bemerkungen zur ägyptischen Frühzeit. II. Zur Frage einer über Menes hinausreichenden ägyptischen Geschichtsüberlieferung," *ZÄS*, Vol. 86 (1961), pp. 39-61.

V. Giustolisi, "La 'Pietra di Palermo' e la cronologia dell'Antico Regno," *Sicilia archeologica*, Anno I, Nr. 4, Dec. 1968, pp. 5-14; Nr. 5, March, 1969, pp. 38-55; Anno II, Nr. 6, June, 1969, pp. 21-38, being a good overall summary of all the fragments, with an Italian translation of the *Annals* (except for the difficult sections of the fifth dynasty including the donations to shrines and temples) (see my Fig. I.43).

W. Helck, "Bemerkungen zum Annalenstein," *MDAIK*, Vol. 30 (1974), pp. 31-35 (see my Fig. I.42).

P. F. O'Mara, *The Palermo Stone and the Archaic Kings of Egypt* (La Canada, Calif., 1979) and *The Chronology of the Palermo and Turin Canons* (La Canada, Calif., 1980), studies which I believe to be entirely unsatisfactory since the basic point of departure is that the stone commences with the reign of Horus Den, which is easily refutable.

W. Barta, "Die Chronologie der 1. bis 5. Dynastie nach den Angaben des rekonstruierten Annalenstein," *ZÄS*, Vol. 108 (1981), pp. 11-23.

A. Roccati, *La Littérature historique sous l'ancien empire égyptien* (Paris, 1982), "Annales des IVe et Ve dynasties," pp. 36-58, with a number of translations that differ from mine. Note that Roccati interprets the month and day designations as specific dates rather than as the number of months and days in the first or last regnal year, as I have done following Borchardt.

D. B. Redford, *Pharaonic King-Lists, Annals and Day-Books: A Contribution to the Study of the Egyptian Sense of History* (Mississauga, Ontario, Canada, 1986). Has no translation or detailed analysis of the Palermo Stone, but sets it in an illuminating study and analysis of the ancient Egyptian approach to history. See particularly pp. 86-90, 134-35. Attributes the *Annals* to "a heightened consciousness of the past and a desire to edit it...evidenced from the reign of Neferirkare".

The English Translation

In my translation I have kept my eye on the previous efforts of Breasted, Schäfer, Gauthier, Daressy, Cenival, Giustolisi, and others. It is, I believe, the most complete translation of all the fragments yet made in any language; it attempts to translate all of the numerical details of the donations mentioned in the course of the fifth dynasty. I have added brackets both for doubtful but probable readings and for additional phrases that make the account less syncopated than the original text without (I trust) altering the intent of the original annalists.

The various fragments are noted in the left margins of the translation by using the abbreviations mentioned in the description of sources given above (P, C-1, C-2, C-3, C-4, C-5, and L, supplemented by r or v for recto or verso where appropriate). The additional citations of Nr. 1, Nr. 2, etc. represent the numbers of the boxes for the successive years of the reigns, starting from the right. This will be clear to the reader if he examines Figs. I.32-I.43 where the fragments are depicted.

The detailed notes following the document indicate some of the difficulties involved in translating accurately the early forms of glyphs found in the *Annals*. They also give general information about early dynastic culture that might be helpful to the non-specialist.

Notes to the Introduction of Document I.1

1. W. M. F. Petrie, *The Making of Egypt* (London and New York, 1939), p. 98, suggested a successive composition of the *Annals*: "The primary text was issued under Sneferu at the close of the IIIrd (!beginning of the IVth) dynasty; and it continued to receive additions until nearly halfway through the Vth dynasty." Earlier in his *History of Egypt*, Vol. 1 (XIth ed. rev., London, 1924), p. 9, Petrie had declared that the *Annals* were composed in the reign of Userkaf (Weserkaf). "After that Sahura and Neferkare (!Neferirkare) scratched their annals slightly upon the stone." Cf. Redford, *Pharaonic King-lists*, pp. 134-35.

2. Helck, "Bemerkungen," p. 33 (see literature below), has presented a convincing argument that all of the fragments are from the same stone, answering all of the arguments presented by Kaiser, who believed that Fragment C-4 alone was from a different stone. Earlier Gauthier, "Quatre nouveaux fragments," p. 30, believed that Fragments P, C-1, C-2, and C-3 were from the same stone. But Borchardt, *Die Annalen*, pp. 22-23, argued that P and C-1 were from different stones. In opposition to this, Breasted, after presenting new measurements of P and C-1 and answering Borchardt's arguments one by one, concludes ("The Predynastic Union of Egypt," p. 719): "A fair consideration of the measurements, however, both horizontal and vertical, makes it very probable that the two fragments [i.e. C-1 and P]...formed parts of the same monument. In any case the identical divisions and disposition of the surface of the stone in laying out the first five rows

make it perfectly certain that the records on the two fragments are parts of the same document, and that they may be employed to supplement each other in our endeavors to reconstruct the complete record once inscribed on the front of the slab." Kaiser, "Einige Bemerkungen," p. 44, n. 2, essentially supporting Gauthier, concludes: "Allein Fragment K 4 [= C-4] stammt sowohl nach der Stärke der Platte wie der Art der Feldereinteilung mit Sicherheit von einem anderen Annalenstein und gibt so den wertvollen Hinweis, dass mehrere, und zwar unterschiedlich gestaltete Annalenplatten existiert haben." Helck opposes the arguments supporting this conclusion in the article mentioned above.

3. The devastating review which T. E. Peet made of Borchardt's *Die Annalen* in the *Journal of Egyptian Archaeology*, Vol. 6 (1920), pp. 149-54, can be extended to the assumptions of others who have attempted to reconstruct the stone with precision from the fragments. I must admit that, after attempting somewhat similar constructions of my own, I have complete sympathy with the remarks of W. F. Edgerton, "Critical Note," *The American Journal of Semitic Languages and Literature*, Vol. 53, (1937), pp. 187-97, and especially p. 197, n. 23: "In my opinion the charge of inaccuracy in the underlying measurements [which Borchardt later made against his own earlier reconstruction], while certainly true, was of minor importance. What makes the reconstruction completely worthless is the fact that it rested on assumptions which are at best unprovable, not to say improbable. This was pointed out in detail by Peet....On its face Peet's criticism eliminates not merely the reconstruction of the Old Kingdom Annals which Borchardt published

in 1917 but every similar reconstruction which may be published in the future, no matter how accurate the underlying measurements may be."

4. Breasted, *Ancient Records of Egypt*, Vol. 1, p. 52: "some seven feet long and over two feet high." Daressy, "La Pierre de Palerme," p. 180: "La longueur du tableau...serait ainsi de 2m. 65cent." (=8.69 feet). The complicated calculations of Borchardt which have been criticized so severely by Peet in the review mentioned in the previous note need not be reported in detail here. But we can say that his calculation of the length of the Palermo Stone (which he distinguished from the stone from which Fragment C-1 came) was a little over eight feet (ca. 8.05 feet), while the Cairo stone he computed to be somewhat longer (ca. 8.50 feet) (see Borchardt, *Die Annalen*, pp. 13-30 and plates 1 and 2).

5. A. H. Gardiner, "Regnal Years and Civil Calendar in Pharaonic Egypt," *Journal of Egyptian Archaeology*, Vol. 31 (1945), pp. 14-15, quotes a somewhat earlier use of the expression of the year after a counting: "*the 17th day of the second month of Winter in the year after the first occasion*, i.e. year 3" taken from the tomb of Meresankh III, the wife of King Chephren (misidentified by Gardiner as the niece of Chephren's wife).

6. K. Sethe, *Untersuchungen*, Vol. 3, p. 88, gives several examples from the Middle Kingdom where there is no mention of the "counting" but only the regnal year. See also below, Document I.5, n. 3, where a year is simply designated by a number without any reference to an "occurrence" (of a counting).

7. *Ibid.*, pp. 69-100, for the classic history of regnal dating in ancient Egypt. See the subsequent contributions of E. Edel, "Zur Lesung von 𓏤

'Regierungsjahr'," *Journal of Near Eastern Studies*, Vol. 8
(1949), pp. 35-39, J. von Beckerath, "Die Lesung von 𓏏𓏏
'Regierungsjahr': Ein neuer Vorschlag," in *ZÄS*, Vol. 95
(1969), pp. 88-91, and W. Barta, "Das Jahr in
Datumsangaben und seine Bezeichnungen," *Festschrift
Elmar Edel: 12. März 1979* (Bamberg, 1979), pp. 35-41,
tracing the readings for the expression "regnal year".
"Regnal year" was used in both the eighth and eleventh
dynasties (see Barta, p. 39).

Document I.1

Early Egyptian Stone Annals:
A Translation of the Fragments of
Palermo, Cairo, and London

[The Gods as Rulers][1]
(*no part on fragments*)

[Kings of Upper Egypt][2]
(*no part on fragments*)

Pr, line 1

Kings of Lower Egypt:[3] ___pu, Seka, Khayu, Teyew, Tjesh, Ni-heb, Wadjenedj, Mekh, _a,_____

C-1 r, line 1

[Some Predynastic] Kings of Upper and Lower Egypt.[4]

[First Dynasty]

[Horus Narmer]
(*no part on fragments; may be predynastic*)

[Horus Aha?][5]

C-5, line 1, Nr. 1

[Year X + 1] [The Year of....in which took place the Festival of] the Birth of Anubis.[6]

[Nile height:] *not recorded.*[7]
Nr. 2
[Year X + 2] [The Year of....in which took place ....] Bull.[8]
    [Nile height:] *not recorded.*
Nr. 3
[Year X + 3] [The Year of....in which took place the Festival of] the Birth of....[9]
    [Nile height:] *not recorded.*
[After four years or so, the Palermo Fragment continues the same reign as follows.][10]
Pr, line 2, Nr. 1
[Year X + 7 (?) + 1] The Year of the Following of Horus [in which took place the Festival of] the Birth of Anubis.[11]
    [Nile height:] *not recorded.*
Nr. 2
[Year X + 7 (?) + 2] [The last civil year of the reign of the King, of which he reigned the first] six months and seven days.
    [Nile height:] *not recorded.*

[Horus Djer?][12]

Nr. 3
[Year 1] [The first civil year of the reign of the king in which he reigned the last] four months and thirteen days [after his enthronement and in which took place the ceremonies of] the Union of the Two Lands and of the Circuit of the Wall.[13]
    [Nile height:] 6 cubits.[14]
Nr. 4
[Year 2] The Year of the Following of Horus [in which took place] the Festival of Desher.[15]

[Nile height:].....
Nr. 5
[Year 3] The Year of [the Festival of] the Birth of the Two Children of the King of Lower Egypt.[16]

[Nile height:] 4 cubits, 1 palm.
Nr. 6
[Year 4] The Year of the Following of Horus [in which took place the Festival of] the Censing of the Decapitated Folk.[17]

[Nile height:] 5 cubits, 5 palms, 1 finger.
Nr. 7
[Year 5] The Year of [the First Occurrence of] the Festival of Sokar [celebrated] behind [or at] the Castle [called] "Companion of the Gods".[18]

[Nile height:] 5 cubits, 5 palms, 1 finger.
Nr. 8
[Year 6] The Year of the Following of Horus [in which took place the Festival of] the Birth of the Goddess Yamet (*or* the cult-symbol for Anubis).[19]

[Nile height:] 5 cubits, 1 palm.
Nr. 9
[Year 7] The Year of the Appearance of the [king as] King of Upper Egypt [at the Festival of] the Birth of Min.[20]

[Nile height:] 5 cubits.
Nr. 10
[Year 8] The Year of the Following of Horus [in which took place the First Occurrence of the Festival of] the Birth of Anubis.[21]

[Nile height:] 6 cubits, 1 palm.
Nr. 11
[Year 9] The Year of the First Occurrence of the Festival of Djet (Uto *or* Wadjet).[22]

[Nile height:] 4 cubits, 1 span.

Nr. 12

[Year 10]....(*destroyed*).[23]

C-1r, above line 2

Horus Djer, King and [Horus] of Gold Itet, whose mother was Khened (priestess of?) Hap.[24]

C-1r, line 2, Nr. 1

[Year X + 1 (=20?)] The Year of the Following of Horus [in which took place the Second Occurrence of the Festival of] the Birth of Anubis.[25]

[Nile height:]....

Nr. 2

[Year X + 2 (=21?)] The Year of the Festival of Traversing the Two Lakes (?).[26]

[Nile height:]....

Nr. 3

[Year X + 3 (=22?)] The Year of the Following of Horus [in which took place the Festival of] the Birth of the God Sed (?).[27]

[Nile height]....

Nr. 4

[Year X + 4 (=23?)] The Year of [the Second Occurrence of] the Festival of Sokar [celebrated] behind (*or* at) the Castle [called] "Companion of the Gods".[28]

[Nile height:]....

Nr. 5

[Year X + 5 (=24?)] The Year of the Following of Horus [in which took place the Festival of]...

[Nile height:]....

Nr. 6

[Year X + 6 (=25?)] The Year of the Appearance of [the king as] the King of Upper Egypt [at the

Festival of] the Birth of [the desert God] Ha.[29]
      [Nile height:]....
Nr. 7
[Year X + 7 (=26?)]   The Year of the Following
of Horus [in which took place the Festival of] the
Birth of Neith(?).[30]
      [Nile height:]....
Nr. 8
[Year X + 8 (=27?)]   The Year of the Festival of
Desher [held] behind (*or* at) the castle [called]
"Companion of the Gods".[31]
      [Nile height:]....
Nr. 9
[Year X + 9 (=28?)]   The Year of the Following
of Horus [in which took place the Festival of] the
Birth of....[32]
      [Nile height:]....

            [Horus Wadji]
         (*no part on fragments*)

C-5, Pr, above line 2
                  Horus Den (Wedimu),
            [King Zemti whose] mother
            [was Me]ryet[-Neith].

C-5, line 2 (=Pr line 3), Nr. 1
      [Year X + 1 (=18?)]   The Year of ....The Great
White One (?)[33]
      [Nile height:]....
Nr. 2
[Year X + 2 (=19?)]   The Year of the Smiting of
the Asiatics.[34]
      [Nile height:] 5 cubits

Nr. 3

[Year X + 3 (=20?)] The Year of the [Festival of the] Birth of the pelt [of Anubis (?) later called Imy-wt] at the *Senuty*-Sanctuary (i.e. the Double Shrines).[35]

[Nile height:]....cubits.

Nr. 4

[Year X + 4 (=21?)] The Year of the Smiting of the Wolf (?) People.[36]

[Nile height:] 6 cubits, 1 palm, 2 fingers.

Nr. 5

[Year X + 5 (=22?)] The Year of the Festival of Sokar [celebrated] behind (*or* at) the Castle [called] "Companion of the Gods".[37]

[Nile height:]....cubits....

[*After five years or so, the Palermo Fragment continues the same reign.*][38]

Pr, line 3, Nr. 1

[Year Y + 1 (=28?)] The Year of the [King's?] Sojourn (*or* Station) in the Temple of Saw (*or* Ptah?) in the City of Heka....[39]

[Nile height:] 3 cubits, 1 palm, 2 fingers

Nr. 2

[Year Y + 2 (=29?)] The Year of the Smiting of the Troglodytes (*Intyw*).[40]

[Nile height:] 4 cubits, 1 span.

Nr. 3

[Year Y + 3 (=30?)] The Year of the Appearance of [the king] as King of Upper Egypt and [his] Appearance as King of Lower Egyp[t] [at] the [Royal] Sed Festival.[41]

[Nile height:] 8 cubits, 3 fingers.

Nr. 4

[Year Y + 4 (=31?)] The Year of the Filling [i.e.

Flooding] of all the Lakes [or Nomes] of the Rekhyt-Folk in the West and the East of Lower Egypt [i.e. in the Delta].[42]

[Nile height:] 3 cubits, 1 span.

Nr. 5

[Year Y + 5 (=32?)] The Year of the Second Occurrence of the Festival of Djet (Uto or Wadjet).

[Nile height:] 5 cubits, 2 palms.

Nr. 6

[Year Y + 6 (=33?)] The Year of the Festival of Sokar [celebrated] behind (or at) the Castle [called] "Seats of the Gods".[43]

[Nile height:] 5 cubits, 1 palm, 2 fingers.

Nr. 7

[Year Y + 7 (=34?)] The Year of Stretching the Cord at the Great Door of the Castle [called] "Seats of the Gods" by the Priest of Seshat.[44]

[Nile height:] 4 cubits, 2 palms.

Nr. 8

[Year Y + 8 (=35?)] The Year of the Opening of the Lake of the Castle [called] "Seats of the Gods" and of Shooting the Hippopotamus.[45]

[Nile height:] 2 cubits.

Nr. 9

[Year Y + 9 (=36?)] The Year of the [King's?] Sojourn (or Station) on the Lake of the Temple of Harsaphes in Heracleopolis.

[Nile height:] 5 cubits.

Nr. 10

[Year Y + 10 (=37?)] The Year of the Journey to Sahseteni and of the Smiting of Wer-ka.

[Nile height:] 4 cubits, 1 span.

Nr. 11

[Year Y + 11 (=38?)] The Year of [the Festival of]
the Birth of the God Sed.
[Nile height:] 6 cubits, 1 palm, 2 fingers.
Nr. 12
[Year Y + 12 (=39?)] The Year of the Appearance
of [the king as] the King of Lower Egypt [at] the
First Occurrence of the Running of the Apis
Bull.[46]
[Nile height:] 2 cubits, 1 span.
Nr. 13
[Year Y + 13 (=40?)] The Year of the [Festival of
the] Birth of Seshat and [that of the Birth of]
Mafdet.[47]
[Nile height:] 3 cubits, 5 palms, 2 fingers.
Nr. 14
[Year Y + 14 (=41?)] The Year [of the Appearance
of the king as] the King of Upper Egypt [at the
Festival of] the Birth of....
[Nile height:]....

[Horus Andiyeb or Adjib (Enezib),
King of Upper and Lower Egypt,
Merpibia?][48]

C-1 r, line 3, Nr. 1
[Year X + 1]....[49]
[Nile height:]....

C-1 r above line 3
Horus Semerkhet (?), King of
Upper and Lower Egypt and
Favorite of the Two Ladies
Semenptah(?), whose mother is
Baterits(n?)[50]

C-1 r, line 3, Nr. 2

[Year 1] The Year of the Appearance of [the king as] the King of Upper Egypt and [his] Appearance [as] the King of Lower Egypt [at the Ceremony] the Union of the Two Lands.[51]

[Nile height:] 4 cubits, 4 palms.

Nr. 3

[Year 2] The Year of the Following of Horus [in which took place]....

[Nile height:] 4 cubits, ...4 (?) palms.

Nr. 4

[Year 3] The Year of the Appearance of [the king as] the King of Upper Egypt [at the Festival of] the Birth of Anubis.

[Nile height:] 4 cubits,....palms.

Nr. 5

[Year 4] The Year of the Following of Horus [in which took place]....

[Nile height:] 4 cubits,....palms.

Nr. 6

[Year 5] The Year of....[and of the Festival of] the Birth of....

[Nile height:]....

Nr. 7

[Year 6] The Year of the Following of Horus [in which took place the Festival of] the Birth of ....

[Nile height:] 4 cubits, 4 palms.

Nr. 8

[Year 7] The Year of the Appearance of [the king as] the King of Upper Egypt and [his] Appearance [as] the King of Lower Egypt [at]....

[Nile height:] 4 cubits,....palms.

Nr. 9

[Year 8] The Year of the Following of Horus [in which took place]....
      [Nile height:] 4 cubits,....palms.
Nr. 10
[Year 9] The Year of the Appearance of [the king as] King of Upper Egypt and [his] Appearance [as] King of Lower Egypt [at the Festival of] the Birth of....[52]
      [Nile height:]....
               [Horus Ḳaᶜa?][53]
Nr. 11
[Year 1] The Year of....[54]
      [Nile height:]....

[The Second Dynasty]

[Horus Hetepsekhemuy]
(*no part on fragments*)

[Horus Nebre]
(*no part on fragments*)

Pr, above line 4

Horus Ninetjer,
Son of Nub-[Nufer]....[55]
line 4, Nr. 1

[Year X + 1 (=6?)] The Year of the Following of Horus [in which took place the Third Occurrence of the Counting].[56]
      [Nile height:]....
Nr. 2
[Year X + 2 (=7?)] The Appearance of [the king as] the King of Upper Egypt [at] the Stretching of

the Cord for the Mansion [called] "Hor-ren".[57]

      [Nile height:] 3 cubits, 4 palms, 2 fingers.

Nr. 3

[Year X + 3 (=8?)] The Year of the Following of Horus [in which took place] the Fourth Occurrence of the Counting.[58]

      [Nile height:] 4 cubits, 2 fingers.

Nr. 4

[Year X + 4 (=9?)] The Year of the Appearance of [the king as] the King of Upper Egypt and [his] Appearance [as] King of Lower Egypt [at] the Running of the Apis Bull.[59]

      [Nile height:] 4 cubits, 1 palm, 2 fingers.

Nr. 5

[Year X + 5 (=10?)] The Year of the Following of Horus [in which took place] the Fifth Occurrence of the Counting.

      [Nile height:] 4 cubits, 4 palms.

Nr. 6

[Year X + 6 (=11?)] The Year of the Appearance of [the king as] the King of Upper Egypt [at] the Second Occurrence of the Festival of Sokar.

      [Nile height:] 3 cubits, 4 palms, 2 fingers.

Nr. 7

[Year X + 7 (=12?)] The Year of the Following of Horus [in which took place] the Sixth Occurrence of the Counting.

      [Nile height:] 4 cubits, 3 fingers.

Nr. 8

[Year X + 8 (=13?)] The Year of the First Occurrence of the Festival of the Worship of Horus of Heaven [in which also took place] the Destruction of the Mansion of Shem-Re and of the Mansion of the North.[60]

[Nile height:] 4 cubits, 3 fingers.

Nr. 9

[Year X + 9 (=14?)] The Year of the Following of Horus [in which took place] the Seventh Occurrence of the Counting.

[Nile height:] 1 cubit.

Nr. 10

[Year X + 10 (=15?)] The Year of the Appearance of [the king as] the King of Lower Egypt [at] the Second Occurrence of the Running of the Apis Bull.

[Nile height:] 3 cubits, 4 palms, 3 fingers.

Nr. 11

[Year X + 11 (=16?)] The Year of the Following of Horus [in which took place] the Eighth Occurrence of the Counting.

[Nile height:] 3 cubits, 5 palms, 2 fingers.

Nr. 12

[Year X + 12 (=17?)] The Year of the Appearance of [the king as] the King of Lower Egypt [at] the Third Occurrence of the Festival of Sokar.

[Nile height:] 2 cubits, 2 fingers.

Nr. 13

[Year X + 13 (=18?)] The Year of the Following of Horus [in which took place] the Ninth Occurrence of the Counting.

[Nile height:] 2 cubits, 2 fingers.

Nr. 14

[Year X + 14 (=19?)] The Year of the Appearance of [the king as] the King of Lower Egypt [at] the ...(?) Festivals of Djet (Uto or Wadjet) and Nekhbet.[61]

[Nile height:] 3 cubits.

Nr. 15

[Year X + 15 (=20?)] The Year of the Following of Horus [in which took place] the Tenth Occurrence of the Counting.
[Nile height:]....
Nr. 16
[Year X + 16 (=21?)]....
[Nile height:]....

[Horus Sekhemib and Seth Peribsen][62]
(*partly on C-1, but not readable*)[63]

[The last kings of the IInd Dynasty: Sened, Neferka, Neferkaseker, Khasekhem, and Khasekhemuy][64] (*no part on fragments*)

[Third Dynasty]

[Horus Zanakht, King Nebka?][65]

Lr, line 1, Nr. 1
[Year X + 1 (=3?)] The Year of......[in which took place] the First Occurrence of the Counting of the Gold.[66]
[Nile height:]....
Nr. 2
[Year X + 2 (=4?)] The Year of the Following of Horus [in which took place] the Second Occurrence of the Counting.
[Nile height:] 3 cubits, 6 palms, 2 fingers.
Nr. 3
[Year X + 3 (=5?)] The Year of....the Rekhyt-Folk.[67]
[Nile height:] 3 cubits, 1 palm.
Nr. 4

[Year X + 4 (=6?)] The Year of [the Following of Horus in which took place the] Third [Occurrence of the Counting].[68]

[Nile height:]....[2+]1 cubits....

Pr, line 5, Nr. 1

[Year Y + 1 (=12?)] The Year of the Following of Horus [in which took place] the Sixth Occurrence of the Counting.

[Nile height:] 2 cubits, 4 palms, 1 1/2 fingers.

Nr. 2

[Year Y + 2 (=13?)] The Year of the Appearance of [the king as] King of Upper Egypt and [his] Appearance as King of Lower Egypt [at] the Building out of Stone of [the Temple called] "The Goddess abides".[69]

[Nile height:] 2 cubits, 3 palms, 1 finger.

Nr. 3

[Year Y + 3 (=14?)] The Year of the Following of Horus [in which took place] the Seventh Occurrence of the Counting of the Gold and the Fields.[70]

[Nile height:] 3 2/3 cubits.

Nr. 4

[Year Y + 4 (=15?)] The Year of the Making of a Copper [statue called] "Exalted is King Khasekhemuy".[71]

[Nile height:] 2 cubits, 6 palms, 2 1/2 fingers.

Nr. 5

[Year Y + 5 (=16?)] The Year of the Following of Horus [in which took place] the Eighth Occurrence of the Counting of Gold and Fields.

[Nile height:] 4 cubits, 2 palms, 2 2/3

fingers.
Nr. 6
[Year Y + 6 (=17?)] The Year of the Fourth Occurrence of Bringing the Wall (?) of Dewadjefa and
of Shipbuilding.[72]
        [Nile height:] 4 cubits, 2 palms.
Nr. 7
[Year Y + 7 (=18?)] The [last] year [of King Nebka
(?) in which he reigned only] two months and 23
days [of the whole civil year].[73]

[Horus Netjeri-khet, King Djoser][74]

Nr. 8
[Year 1] The Appearance of [the king as] the
King of Upper Egypt and [his] Appearance [as]
King of Lower Egypt [at the Ceremonies of] the
Union of the Two Lands and of the Circuit of the
Wall.
        [Nile height:] 4 cubits, 2 palms, 2 2/3
fingers.
Nr. 9
[Year 2] The Appearance of [the king as] the
King of Upper Egypt and [his] Appearance [as]
King of Lower Egypt [at] the Double Shrines.[75]
        [Nile height:] 4 cubits, 1 2/3 palms.
Nr. 10
[Year 3] The Year of the Following of Horus [in
which took place the Festival of] the Birth of
Min.
        [Nile height:] 2 cubits, 3 palms, 2 3/4
fingers.
Nr. 11
[Year 4] The Year of the Appearance of [the

king as] the King of Upper Egypt and [his]
Appearance as King of Lower Egypt [at] the
Stretching of the Cord for the Mansion [called]
"The Refreshment of the Gods".

[Nile height:] 3 cubits, 3 palms, 2 fingers.
Nr. 12
[Year 5] The Year of the Following of Horus [in
which took place]....[76]

[Nile height:]....

[Horus Sekhemkhet, King Djoser-tety]

(apparently all six years are on Fragment C-1 r,
line 4, but are quite unreadable)[77]

[Horus Khaba(?), King --ka]

(apparently the first two or so years of the
six-year reign of this king, whose complete king's
name is not known and whose Horus name is
merely guessed at, are also on Fragment C-1 r,
line 4, but are unreadable)[78]

[King Huny]
(no part of this reign is on any fragment)[79]

[Fourth Dynasty]

[Horus Nebmaat, King Sneferu,
the son of Merlisankh.[80]

C-4 r, line 1, Nr. 1
[Year X + 1 (=4?)]   The Year of....Sneferu....[in
which took place] the Second Occurrence of the

Counting of Silver and Lapis lazuli.[81]

[Nile height:] 3 cubits

Nr. 2

[Year X + 2 (=5?)] [The Year of the following events: the Appearance of the king as the King of Upper Egypt at] the Shrine Per-wer [and his Appearance as King of Lower Egypt at] the Shrine Per-nu,[82] and of fashioning in copper of a statue of the Horus Nebmaat (i.e. King Sneferu),[83] and of....

[Nile height:] 3 cubits, 5 palms.

L, line 2, Nr. 1

[Year Y + 1 (=10?)] The Year of....[84]

[Nile height:]....

Pr, line 6, Nr. 1

[Year Z + 1 (=12?)] [The Year of....and of the Ceremony of the Birth of] the Two Children of the King of Lower Egypt.[85] [The Sixth Occurrence of the Counting.][86]

[Nile height:]....

Nr. 2

[Year Z + 2 (=13?)] The Year of [the following events:] The Building with *meru*-wood of a 100-cubit Dewatowe ship[87] and 60 sixteen-[oared?] barges. The Smiting of Nubia and the taking of prisoners numbering 4,000 men and 3,000 women, together with 200,000 large and small cattle. Building of the Wall of the Southland and the Northland [called] "The Houses of Sneferu". The Transporting of 40 ships filled with *ash*-wood (so-called "cedar").[88]

[Nile height:] 2 cubits, 2 fingers (*or perhaps* 1 1/2).

Nr. 3

[Year Z + 3 (=14?)] [The Year of the following events:] The Erection of 35 Houses, and also enclosures (?) for 122 oxen. The Building of one 100-cubit Dewatowe ship of "cedar" and two 100-cubit ships of *meru*-wood. The Seventh Occurrence of the Counting.

[Nile height:] 5 cubits, 1 palm, 1 finger.

Nr. 4

[Year Z + 4 (=15?)] [The Year of the following events:] The Erection of "Exalted is the White Crown of Sneferu" upon the Southern Gate and of "Exalted is the Red Crown of Sneferu" upon the Northern Gate.[89] The making of "cedar" gates for the Royal Palace. The Eighth Occurrence of the Counting.[90]

[Nile height:] 2 cubits, 2 palms, 2 3/4 fingers.

Nr. 5

[Year Z + 5 (=16?)]....

[Nile height:]....

C-4 r, line 2, Nr. 1

[Year W + 1] The Year of....[and of the....Counting of Oxen] and small Cattle.

[Nile height:]....cubits, 2 palms.

Nr. 2

[Year W + 2] The Year of [the following events:] The Appearance of [the king as] the King of Upper Egypt [at] the Fourth Occurrence of the Running of the Oxen (*or* Apis Bull?). The Fashioning of A Gold Statue of the Horus Nebmaat for honoring the Gods. Bringing from Libya 1,100 prisoners and 13,100 large and small cattle. Going forth to the Building of the Fortress, *T-t* (?)....

[Nile height:]....

Pr, line 7

[Horus Medjed,
King of Upper and Lower Egypt
Khufu (=Cheops) whose] mother
[was Hetepheres].[91]

C-2, line 1
[Year W + 1] The Year [of the following events:]
....14 statues....Khufu....100 cubits....
[Nile height:] 3 cubits, 6 palms, 3 1/2
fingers.

C-1 r, line 7
[Year X + 1] The Year of Fashioning a Statue of
the Horus....
[Year X + 2] The Year of....Sneferu....
[Year X + 3] The Year of....[there is none] beside
him....
[Nile heights for these years unobtainable]

C-4, line 3
[Year Y + 1] The Year of [the following events
of] the King of Upper and Lower Egypt
Khufu....He made [it] as his monument for....made
of Lapis lazuli....and as his monument for....
[Nile height:]....

C-2, line 2, Nr. 1
[Year Z + 1] The Year of [the following events:]
The King of Upper and Lower Egypt
[Khufu]....Building....The Establishing of
Sed[92]....Birth of the Horus Bull....Opening the
mouth of all (?) the Gods[93]....
[Nile height:]....

Nr. 2

[Year Z + 2] The Year of [the following events:] The Appearance of [the king as] King of Lower Egypt [at] ....The Following....Names....
[Nile height:]....

[King Djedefre]

C-3, line 2, Nr. 1
[Year X + 1] The Year of [the following events:] [Building] 20+ (?) barks....Engraving of the Double Shrine....[A block] 14 cubits, 2 fingers, in length. Granite from [the quarries of] Hatnub.
[Nile height:]....
Nr. 2
[Year X + 2 (or is it a part of X + 1?)] The Year of [the following events of] the King of Upper and Lower Egypt Djedefre. He made [it] as his monument for his (?) mother(?) Bastet....in....(? Bubastis?).[94]
[Nile height:]....

[King Menkaure (Mycerinus)]

C-1 v
[Year X + 1]....
[Nile height:]....3/4.[95]
Pv, line 1, Nr. 1
[Year Y + 1] The [last civil] year [of which Menkaure reigned] [4] months and 24 days.

[King Shepseskaf]

Nr. 2
[Year 1] [After the king's enthronement there

remained of the civil year] [3] + 4 months and 11
days [and the following events took place:] The
Appearance of [the king as] the King of Upper
Egypt and [his] Appearance [as] the King of
Lower Egypt [at the Ceremonies of] the Union of
the Two Lands and the Circuit of the Wall. The
Festival of Seshed. The [Festival of the] Birth of
the two Wepwawets. The Year of the King's
Following of the Gods who United the Two
Lands. The Establishing of the Estate of the
Garden Lake and the Selection of the Place for
the Pyramid [called] "Shepseskaf is
Purified".[96]....20 [portions] every day for the
Double Shrines of the South and the North....
1,624.... 600 (300 + 300?) ....

[Nile height:] 4 cubits, 3 palms, 2 1/2
fingers.

[Fifth Dynasty]

[King Weserkaf]

L-1 v,line 2, Nr. 1

[Year X + 1 (=3?)] The Year [of the following
events of the King of Upper and Lower Egypt
Weserkaf:] .... Coming from the first journey (or
way) .... gifts which they brought to the Pyramid
of Weserkaf [called] "Purest of Places" as well as
70   women of foreign countries. The Year after
the First Counting of the Oxen.[97]
[Nile height:]....
Nr. 2
[Year X + 2 (=4?)] The Year of [the following
events of] the King of Upper and Lower Egypt

Weserkaf. He made [it] as his monument for (I) the Souls of Heliopolis:[98] the establishing for them of the following divine invocation-offerings: 242 (?) offerings of bread and beer, 43 oxen, 4 (?) oryx, 132 fowl, 12 pintail ducks, on the First Occurrence of the Festival of *It* and on every annual return of that festival, with abundance of offerings forever; for (II) Re: [a gift of] arable land in the following quantity of arouras (Egyptian: *st'wt*): 44·10 + 8 + 1/4 + 1/8 [*total in modern terms*: 448 3/8];[99] for (III) Hathor: arable land in the following quantity of arouras: 23·10 + 5 + 1/2 [*total in modern terms*: 235 1/2]; building [of a shrine] for Hathor in the estate of the Pyramid of Weserkaf [called] "Purest of Places" and building [of a shrine] for Hathor in the estate [called] "The Lake of Weserkaf is Purified".

[Nile height:] 3 cubits, 2 palms, 2 1/2 fingers.

Pv, line 2, Nr. 1

[Year Y + 1 (=5?)] The Year of.... the Third Occurrence of the Inventory of the House of Horus-Seth.[100] The Year after the Second Occurrence of the Counting.

[Nile height:]....

Nr. 2

[Year Y + 2 (=6?)] The Year [of the following events of] the King of Upper and Lower Egypt Weserkaf. He made [it] as a monument for (I) the Souls of Heliopolis: 20 invocation-offerings of bread and beer at every festival of the Sixth Day (?), 20 invocation-offerings of bread and beer at every Festival of *It* and arable land in the following quantity of arouras: 35·10 + 3 + 1/2 +

1/4 + 1/8 [*total in modern terms*: 353 7/8] in the Domain of Weserkaf; for (II) the Gods of the Sun-Temple [called] "Sep-Re": arable land in the quantity of 24 arouras in the Domain of Weserkaf, and 2 oxen and 2 pintail ducks everyday; for (III) Re: arable land in the quantity of 44 arouras in the nomes of the Northland; for (IV) Hathor: arable land in the quantity of 44 arouras in the nomes of the Northland; for (V) the Gods of the House of the Heron of Djebakherut(?):[101] arable land in the quantity of 54 arouras [for] the erection of a chapel of his [i.e. the Heron's] temple at Buto in the Nome of Xois; for (VI) Sepa:[102] arable land in the quantity of 2 arouras [for] the building of his shrine; for (VII) Nekhbet in the Shrine of the South: 10 invocation-offerings of bread and beer every day; for (VIII) Wadjet in the Shrine of Per-nu [in Buto]: 10 invocation-offerings every day; for (IX) the Gods of the Shrine of the South: 48 invocation-offerings of bread and beer every day. The Year of the Third Occurrence of the Counting of the Oxen.

[Nile height:] 4 cubits, 2 1/2 fingers.
Nr. 3
[Year Y + 3 (=7?)] The Year of [the following events of] the King of Upper and Lower Egypt Weserkaf. He made [it] as his monument for Re: arable land in the quantity of 1,804 (?) + 1/2 + 1/4 arouras and 13 [area] cubits (?) [*in modern terms with cubits converted to arouras*: 1,804 22/25 arouras][103] in the Northland; for Min: arable land in the quantity of....arouras....in the Northland....(*and the rest of the year is lost*).

[King Sahure]

C-1 v, line 3, Nr. 1

[Year X + 1 (=1?)] [The Year of the following events of] the King of Upper and Lower Egypt Sahure. He made [it] as a monument for....The Festival of the Opening of the Mouth in the House of Gold (ḥwt-nb) (i.e. the sculptor's or goldsmith's workshop) of statues of....and that of the Opening of the Mouth in the House of Gold of six statues of Sahure. The First Occurrence of Going to the South and Inventorying the House of Horus-Seth.[104]   The Year of the First Occurrence of the Circuiting.

[Nile height:]....

Nr. 2

[Year X + 2 (=2?)]....(*nothing decipherable from this year*)

[Nile height:]....

Pv, line 3, Nr. 1

[Year Y + 1 (=5?)] The Year of [the following events of] the King of Upper and Lower Egypt Sahure. He made [it] as his monument for (I)....in Heliopolis....[the Shrine of ?] the Divine Bark [upon its four supports?][105]....Son of Re....[the Shrine of?] the Divine Bark [upon its four supports?], 200 w^{c}b-priests of [the Shrine of?] the Divine Bark [upon its four supports?]; for (II) Nekhbet, Mistress of Per-wer: 800 daily portions of invocation-offerings of bread and beer; for (III) Wadjet, Mistress of Per-nezu (!Per-nu): 4,800 daily portions of invocation-offerings of bread and beer; for (IV) Re in the Double Shrines:

138 daily portions of invocation-offerings of bread and beer; for (V) Re in the Shrine of the South: 40 daily portions of invocation-offerings of bread and beer; for (VI) Re in Tep-hut: 74 daily portions of invocation-offerings of bread and beer; for (VII) Hathor in the Sun-Temple [called] "Sekhet-Re": 4 daily portions of invocation-offerings of bread and beer; for (VIII) Re in the Sun-Temple [called] "Sekhet-Re": arable land in the quantity of 24 arouras in the Nome of Xois; for (IX) Mesenkhet:[106] arable land in the quantity of 2 arouras in the Nome of Busiris; for (X) Semkhet: arable land in the quantity of 2 arouras in the Nome of Busiris: for (XI) Khenti-yawatef: arable land in the Nome of Memphis in the following quantity of arouras: $2 \cdot 100 + 2 \cdot 10 + 8 + 1/4 + 1/8$ [total in modern terms: 228 3/8];[107] for (XII) Hathor in the Ro-she of Sahure: arable land in the Nome of the East in the following quantity of arouras and cubits: $2 \cdot 100 + 2 \cdot 10 + 6 + 1/4$ arouras and 4 cubits [the total in modern terms, with cubits converted to arouras: 226 29/100 arouras]; for (XIII) Hathor in the pyramid [called] "The Soul of Sahure Appears": arable land of $2 \cdot 100 + 2 \cdot 10 + 1/4$ arouras in the Libyan Nome (No. 7); for (XIV) the White Bull: arable land in the Near Eastern Nome (Nr. 14) in the following quantity of arouras and cubits: $23 \cdot 100 + 2 \cdot 10 + 1/4$ arouras and 10 cubits [total in modern terms, with cubits converted to arouras: 2,320 7/20]. The Third Ocurrence of the Inventorying of the House of Horus-Seth. The Year after the Second Occurrence of the Counting.

[Nile height:] 2 cubits, 2 1/4 fingers.
Nr. 2
[Year Y + 2 (=6?)] The Year of [the following events of] the King of Upper and Lower Egypt Sahure. He made [it] as his monument to the Divine Ennead in the House of God....the House of...., and for the Double Shrines and the Tep-Hut: arable land in the Nome of the West (Nr. 3) in the quantity of .... arouras.... (*the rest of the year and its Nile height are lost*).

Pv, line 4, Nr. 1

[Year Z + 1 (=15?)] The Year of [the following events of] the King of Upper and Lower Egypt Sahure. He made [it] as his monument.... (*about 7 columns under this superscription are missing*): for Re, Hathor, and the House of Seshat, in the North and the South, arable land in the quantity of....arouras for Re, [2·10?] + 8 arouras for Hathor, and 2·10 + 4 arouras for Seshat; .....everybody. There was brought from the Malachite Country 6,000 [units] of copper, from Pewenet (i.e. Punt) 80,000 measures of myrrh, 6,000 [units] of $\underline{d}^{c}m$-gold (i.e. electrum),[108] 2,900 [units] of *sn*-gold,[109] and 23,020 [measures] of..... The Year after the Occurrence of the Seventh Counting.[110] [The reign of King Sahure terminated after] nine months and 28 days [of this civil year].[111] [Nile height:]....

[King Neferirkare]

Pv, line 4, superscription
Horus Weserkhau, King of Upper and Lower Egypt, Favorite of the Two Goddesses

Khaemsekhemu (?), [Horus ?] of Gold....
Nr. 2
[Year 1] [The first civil year of which the king reigned the last] two months and seven days, [the year in which took place the ceremonies of] the Birth of the Gods,[112] the Union of the Two Lands, and the Circuit of the Wall, [and in which] the King of Upper and Lower Egypt Neferirkare made [it] as his monument for (1) the Divine Ennead in the Divine Double Shrines in the city [called] "Neferirkare Beloved of the Ennead": arable land in the quantity of 3·100 + 30 +....arouras in the Nome of Memphis, under [the charge of] the House of Neferirkare beloved of his son (?); and for (2) the Souls of Heliopolis: in the Eastern Nome in the city [called] "Neferirkare Beloved of the Souls of Heliopolis" arable land in the quantity of 110·100 + 10 arouras;[113] for (3) the Souls of Heliopolis and (4) the Gods of Kheraha[114]: in the Near Eastern Nome (Nr. 14) arable land in the following quantity of arouras: 352·100 + 20 + 1 + 1/2 + 1/4 [*total in modern terms*: 35,221 3/4 arouras], the one parcel under the charge of the Two Great Seers of his temple[115] and the other under the charge of the Officials and Priests of his temple and both parcels as divine offerings being exempt from taxes like the domain of the God (i.e. the King); for (5) Re-senef and (6) Hathor: an altar for each in the establishment [called] "Hutty" [provided] every day with 210 portions of invocation-offerings of bread and beer for the one and 204 for the other, with appropriate magazines and serfs established for each altar; for

(7) the Festival of the Opening of the Mouth of a statue of Ihy [i.e. Son of Hathor] made of electrum and the procession [with it to the Temple of] Hathor [Mistress of] the Sycamore, in Meret-Sneferu; for (8) Re [in the shrine of] Tep-hut, making for him these....the House of the Thirty[116] and likewise ....the Way.... (*the rest of the year is lost*).

Lv

[Year 2(?)] [The year of the following events of the King of Upper and Lower Egypt Neferirkare. He made it as his monument for]... 2 (*or* 10).... 5 (*or* 13).... 31 (*or* 41).... arable land in the quantity of y·10 + z arouras....[117]

[Nile height:] 3 cubits....

Pv, line 5, Nr. 1

[Year Y + 1 (=10?)] [The Year of the following events of the King of Upper and Lower Egypt Neferirkare. He made it as his monument for....] the Festival of the Opening of the Mouth in the House of Gold [of the statue of].... and the Festival of the Opening of the Mouth in the House of Gold [of the statue of].... the levying of taxes (?).... Neferirkare.....; for Re in the Sun-Temple [called] "Favorite Seat of Re".... making for him a Circuit of the Wall.... and making for him the Estate (?) ....; for King Huny:[118] arable land in the quantity of.... arouras. The Year of the Fifth Occurrence of the Counting.

[Nile height:]....

Nr. 2

[Year Y + 2 (11?)] The Year of [the following events:] The Appearance of [the king as] the King of Upper Egypt and [his] Appearance as King of Lower Egypt [at].... The Erection of the Wall of the Sun Bark at the Southern Corner [of the Sun-Temple called "Favorite Seat of Re"].   The King of Upper and Lower Egypt Neferirkare made [them] as his monument for (1) Re in the Sun-Temple [called] "Favorite Seat of Re": [models of] the Evening Sun Bark and the Morning Sun Bark, each of copper and each eight cubits long; for (2) the Souls of Heliopolis:.... made of electrum....; for (3) the Shrine of Ptah-South-of-his-Wall: (?) arouras of land.....; for (4) Wadjet in the Southern City: ....made of electrum ....

[Nile height:]....

The rest of the text is lost.

{For the notes to this document, see page 97.}

Notes to Document I.1

1. Though there is no evidence for or against it, it seems possible that the original stone contained in its first line the names of the gods who were sometimes considered to be forerunners of the human kings of Egypt, as is evident in the list of kings called the Turin Canon (composed in the reign of Ramesses II, ca. 1290-1224 B. C.) and in Manetho's *History of Egypt* (3rd cent. B. C.). In the Turin Canon the dynastic kings (starting with Meni) are preceded by gods and "spirits *(ʾḫw)*, [i.e.] the Followers of Horus *(šmsw Ḥrʾ)* (see A. H. Gardiner, *The Royal Canon of Turin* [Oxford, 1959], plate I, Col. II, lines 1-9). The "Akhu, Followers of Horus", no doubt equivalent to Manetho's "Spirits of the Dead and Demigods" (see W. G. Wadell, *Manetho with an English Translation* [London and Cambridge, Mass., 1940, repr. 1980], p. 5), may well have included divinized predynastic kings like those named here in the Palermo Stone (see L. V. Žabkar, *A Study of the Ba Concept in Ancient Egyptian Texts* [Chicago, 1968], p. 35).

2. It is a likely supposition that, since the stone contained the names of predynastic kings of Lower Egypt as well as those of predynastic kings of a united Upper and Lower Egypt (as we shall see), the stone also contained names of kings of Upper Egypt. Since the stone was composed in the fifth dynasty, and thus in the tradition of the dynastic unifiers from the south, it would make sense that names of Upper Egypt would precede those of Lower Egypt.

3. I have used this rubric without brackets because each of the names of kings here listed in the

first line of the Palermo Stone has as its hieroglyphic
determinative a figure of a king wearing the red crown
of Lower Egypt (see Fig. I.32, line 1). Schäfer, "Ein
Bruchstück," p. 14, having only the Palermo fragment
with the kings of Lower Egypt, suggested that if the
stone was produced in a temple of Lower Egypt perhaps
it did not include names of kings of Upper Egypt. But
in view of the fact noted in the preceding footnote that
the stone contained kings of a predynastic kingdom of
Upper and Lower Egypt, it seems much more likely that
the stone also included the names of kings of Upper
Egypt before those of Lower Egypt, as I propose.

    4. When the Cairo fragment (C-1) was first
studied both Gauthier ("Quatre nouveaux fragments," p.
31) and Daressy ("La Pierre de Palerme," p. 162)
identified the predynastic kings in the first line (Fig.
I.36b) as kings of Upper Egypt, i.e., the determinatives
were figures wearing the white crown of Upper Egypt
[though Daressy believed that the third figure perhaps
wore the crown of Lower Egypt; but he thought this to
be either an error or the result of wearing]. Breasted
later ("The Predynastic Union," pp. 710-12) made an
exhaustive examination of the Cairo fragment and
showed that the kings on the top row were wearing not
merely the crown of Upper Egypt but rather the double
crown of Upper and Lower Egypt; or, to put it more
precisely, there are ten royal figures in the top band "of
which the last three heads (at the left) have been
broken off. The remaining seven (Nos. 1-7 in Fig. I.36c)
all show sufficient traces of the crowns to make it
quite certain that each figure is wearing the double
crown". This was an interesting discovery, for it
seemed to show that there was a tradition of a
predynastic union of Upper and Lower Egypt, as

Newberry and Sethe had thought (*ibid.*, pp. 720-21). Incidentally, Breasted also suggested that the top band included a long list of kings of Upper Egypt preceding those of Lower Egypt.

5. Most students have concluded that the first king given in the second line of the stone is Aha. If this is so, then Narmer (whose palette we mentioned above) would perhaps have been given as the last of the predynastic kings in the preceding line. However, since we have no reliable figures for the lengths of Narmer's and Aha's reigns (the numbers given in the vestiges of Manetho's account being generally unreliable), it could well be that both reigns appeared on the second line of the Stone to the right of the Palermo Fragment. The Palermo fragment contains on its right side the last two years of what appears to be Aha's reign, and further to the right the fifth fragment of Cairo seems to contain evidence of three earlier years of the reign of Aha.

6. The word *mst* is here translated "Birth". It was also used in the sense of "making" or "fashioning" statues (see K. Sethe, *Dramatische Texte zu altägyptischen Mysterienspielen* [Leipzig, 1928], p. 49). Hence it is possible that at the various ceremonies celebrating the "birth" of some god or other, it was in fact the fashioning of his statue that was being celebrated. See Gardiner, "Regnal Years," p. 13, n. 2: "I see no reason why the 'Birth of Anubis' and the 'Birth of Min' should not be interpreted as the creation of statues of those deities; the fact that these occurrences are mentioned twice each [in Djer's reign] is hardly an objection, since more than one statue, or different types of statues, may have been made. The only case in the Palermo Stone which is at all likely to have had a different sense is

ANCIENT EGYPTIAN SCIENCE

'Birth of the Gods' in Vs, 4, 3, apparently a reference to the epagomenal days......If my theory is correct we have here fresh evidence of the vast importance which was attached, in the early dynasties, to such artistic creations; this was the age in which the traditional attitudes and attributes received their stereotyped forms. However, it must be remembered that from the Egyptian point of view such events will have been regarded less as artistic achievements than as acts of piety." Later Gardiner in his *Egypt of the Pharaohs* (Oxford, 1961), p. 414, while even yet interpreting "the birth of gods" as the fashioning of cult-images, suggests that the word "birth" used in the naming of these ceremonies is "the consequence of the belief that the statues became really alive after the ceremony of 'Opening the Mouth' had been performed over them". The ceremony of Opening the Mouth performed on cult-images was the same as that performed on mummified corpses to revivify them. It is described by E.A.W. Budge, *The Mummy*, Collier Books ed. (New York, 1972), p. 172: "When everything has been brought in this chamber, and the tables of offerings have been arranged, a [Sem] priest, wearing a panther skin, and accompanied by another who burns incense in a bronze censer, approaches the mummy, and performs the ceremony of 'opening the mouth'.....*un-re* [*wn-r* or *wpt-r*], while a [lector] priest in white robes reads from a roll of papyrus or leather. The act of embalming [not to say, the fact of dying] has taken away from the dead man all control over his limbs and the various portions of his body, and before these can be of any use to him in the nether-world, a mouth must be given to him, and it must be opened so that...[he] may be able to speak [and eat]. The twenty-first and twenty-second chapters of the 'Book of the Dead' refer to the giving a mouth to the deceased....In the vignette to the twenty-third chapter a priest is seen performing the operation of opening of the mouth ... *arit apt re* [*irt wpt-r*], with the [small adze-shaped] instrument...and the deceased says in the text, 'Ptah has opened my mouth with that instrument of steel (*!*) with which he opened the mouth of the gods.'" Cf. A. J. Spencer, *Death in Ancient Egypt* (Harmondsworth, England, 1982), pp. 52-54, and especially A. H. Gardiner and N. de G. Davies, *The Tomb of Amenemhet* (London, 1915), pp. 57-61. A. Erman, *A Handbook of Egyptian Religion* (London, 1907), p. 134, emphasizes that after the ceremony the deceased is able to partake of the food offerings presented to him. For a recent discussion of the ceremony and its literature, see J. G. Griffiths, *The Origins of Osiris and His Cult* (Leiden, 1980), pp. 69-74. Particularly pertinent is his remark on pp. 71-72: "In its earliest form it is a ceremony concerned with the statue, and it aims at the preparation and animation of the statue in the *ht-nb* ('House of Gold') before its transport into the shrine." See also S. Morenz, *Egyptian Religion* (Ithaca, 1973), p. 155: "But we must add that from early times onward Egyptians were not satisfied with just fashioning an image, i.e. with the creation of a work of art. On the contrary, a ritual was performed on the statues while they were still in the sculptor's workshop (the 'gold house'), as a result of which the work of human hands was thought to come alive. This ceremony of 'opening the mouth' had the purpose of making all the organs serviceable and so vitalizing the image....The surviving sources which mention the ritual performed on statues go on to mention acts and texts relevant to embalmment, sacrificial ritual and certain temple rituals." Incidentally the variety of statues and cult-images produced in the sculptor's workshop (the House of Gold) is interestingly presented on a stela of the eighteenth or nineteenth dynasty (Leyden V 1; see A. H. Gardiner, *Ancient Egyptian Onomastica*, Vol. 1 [Oxford, 1947], pp. 52-53): "He (the King) appointed me to take charge of operations when I was but a weanling, he found me estimable in his heart, and I was introduced into the House of Gold in order to fashion the forms and images of all the gods, and none of them was hidden from me. I was a master of secrets seeing Re (R^c) in his changing appearance and Atum in his true shape. Then there was Osiris, lord of Abydos, in front of the Lords of the Sacred Land, and there was Thoth, lord of Khmun .....I saw Shepsy in his mysterious secrecy, and Unwet in her changing appearances. There was Min cleaving to his beauty, and Horus dwelling in Hasroet ..... [followed by many more gods] .....It was I who caused them to rest in their eternal shrines, carrying them in the conduct of the king's festival with which I was charged (?)." The most complete treatment of the ceremony of opening the mouth is that of E. Otto, *Das ägyptische Mundöffnungsritual*, 2 vols. (Wiesbaden, 1960).

Still other explanations for "birth" in the names of individual festivals have been advanced. For example, the "Birth of Min" has been interpreted in terms of the changing status of Min in the course of a festival like that recorded on the north wall of the second court of the Temple of Ramesses III at Medinet Habu, where Min is first associated with Osiris and is thus interpreted as a remote, perhaps dead deity like Osiris and then later in the ceremony after cutting a stalk of emmer he becomes a living god identified with

Horus, the transition from the one to the other being interpreted as a "birth" (see W. J. Murnane, *United with Eternity* [Chicago and Cairo, 1980], p. 37).

Needless to say, the simplest explanation of "birth" is that a day was established as an anniversary of the god's birth, for as we shall see in Chapter Two, gods were capable of birth and death.

For specific mention of the fashioning of statues in the Palermo Stone, see Pr, line 5, Nr. 4, which describes a statue of King Khasekhemuy, and Pv, line 4, Nr. 2, a statue of the god Ihy. V. Giustolisi, "La 'Pietra di Palermo'," 3ª puntata, pp. 28-29, believes that this year and the second after it are years of the Following of Horus, which he persists in calling the *Festa di Horo* (see note 11 below), because, in the later years recorded on the Palermo fragment, this Horus event is listed for one of its two years. This is reasonable, but his suggestion that the second year after this also saw the Festival of the Birth of Anubis as well as the *Festa di Horo* is unlikely because then there would be nothing to distinguish the two years X + 1 and X + 3, and the second event in each Horus year was clearly selected to distinguish the years.

7. It will be seen that from the next reign onward, the maximum height of the Nile in flood is recorded below each year. It will be evident from the years remaining here from C-5 line 1 and Pr line 2 of Aha's reign that the fifth-dynasty author of the *Annals* did not have access to the Nile heights for this reign. Perhaps no record of them was kept in the reign of Aha and before.

8. It is not clear as to what ceremony is being referred to here. The last sign is that of a bull. J. L. de Cenival, "Un nouveau fragment," p. 15, thinks it is

probably a reference to an Apis Bull. Compare the references to the Apis Bull in Pr, line 3, Nr. 12, and Pr, line 4, Nos. 4 and 10. See Fig. I.16 (second register) for the representation of a running bull (possibly Apis), and perhaps this is in celebration of the same event as here appears on the Cairo fragment.

9. Not enough of this year is visible for any more specific translation than that given here. The only thing that seems clear to me is the bottom part of the sign for *mst*. Giustolisi suggests the festival was that of the Birth of Anubis, which I believe is wrong; see note 6.

10. I suggest here that about four years separate fragment C-5 from the Palermo fragment. I have done this on the basis of the distance between the fragments in line 3 and the ratio between the sizes of the year segments in lines 2 and 3.

11. "Following of Horus" is a literal rendering of *šmsy-Ḥrw*. There has been considerable discussion of this phrase and its analogous forms. For Schäfer and Breasted it meant some ceremony of the worship of Horus. But it is now often interpreted as a biennial tour of the realm undertaken by the king and his officials, perhaps with the objective of ascertaining the wealth of the land for the purpose of tax assessment or collection. See J. v. Beckerath, "*šmsj-Ḥrw* in der ägyptischen Vor- und Frühzeit," *Mitteilungen des Deutschen Archäologischen Instituts, Abteilung Kairo*, Vol. 14 (1956), pp. 5-6 (whole article, pp. 1-10). See also Gardiner, "Regnal Years," p. 13, where he describes these tours as "royal progresses by river". The emphasis on travel by river arises from the fact that *šmsy-Ḥrw* is determined on the stone by a ship with a falcon on the foredeck and the sign for "following" on the afterdeck.

It may be that these biennial tours were the forerunners of the biennial "countings" of the wealth of the land which we shall mention below.

12. Most scholars believe that the second line of the stone began with the reign of Aha, as I noted above, and continued through the first two years recorded on the right side of the Palermo Stone. If that is so, then the third year on the Palermo Stone should begin the reign of the Horus Djer. This argument appears to be confirmed by evidence drawn from the first Cairo fragment. For, if the various estimates of the distance (in years) between the left end of the Palermo Stone and the right end of the Cairo fragment (estimates that range from 9 to 14 years) are even gross approximations of the true distance, then that distance would not be great enough to contain the end of a reign prior to that included on the Cairo fragment. Hence the years given on the two fragments are parts of the same reign, namely that of Djer, since the superscribed name of the king above line 2 of the Cairo fragment is almost certainly that of Djer (see note 24 below). A brief word should be added to explain my conclusion that the lacuna between the fragments would not have been large enough to have included the end of a preceding reign begun in the Palermo Stone. Studying the various superscribed royal names in the two fragments (those names above lines 2 and 3 of the Cairo fragment and the partial one above line 4 of the Palermo Stone), we can deduce that the superscribed name ordinarily occupied a space of at least seven years. Furthermore, it is evident from the name over line 3 of the Cairo fragment that such superscribed names are so placed that just as many years precede the beginning of the superscription as follow the end (i.e.,

that the name is placed as nearly as possible over the middle years of the reign). But there are nine years of the reign beginning in line 2 of the Palermo Stone and there is no trace of a superscribed name above those nine years. Hence if that reign is said to have ended in the lacuna between the two fragments, the lacuna will have had at least sixteen years recorded in it, that is, the seven years under the name plus nine years to balance at the left end the nine years given at the beginning and recorded on the Palermo Stone. But that 16 years (which is only an estimated minimum) exceeds even the largest estimate of the distance between the fragments. In fact, the lacuna probably would have had to include far more than just 16 years, for we know that Djer's reign must have been a fairly long one. This judgment is based not merely on the untrustworthy figures of 31 or 39 years found in the remains of Manetho's account but rather on the quite extensive archeological remains around the tomb of Djer at Abydos (see W. M. F. Petrie, *A History of Egypt*, Vol. 1 [11th ed. London, 1924], p. 15). Hence the lacuna would have had to have had not only at least 16 years for the end of the reign that began in the Palermo Stone but an additional minimum of at least 11 years for the beginning of the reign of Djer. Hence we seem to have confirmed that the reign of Djer began in the Palermo Stone and continued in both the lacuna between the fragments and in the Cairo fragment.

13. The figure of "four months and thirteen days" was interpreted by Schäfer and Breasted as a date, namely as the thirteenth day of the fourth month. It was Borchardt (*Die Annalen*, pp. 2-5) who correctly saw these and the similar numbers on the Palermo Stone as being time periods which are fractions of civil

(or, as he called them, calendar) years. But notice in this first example that, if we add to the four months and thirteen days of Djer's first year the six months and seven days of the last year served by his predecessor, the total is ten months and 20 days, instead of the full civil year of twelve months and five days (as was the case in the year of transition from the reign of Sahure to that of Neferirkare, where the nine months and 28 days of the end of Sahure's reign may be added to the two months and 7 days of the beginning of Neferirkare's reign to equal 12 months and 5 days [see the Palermo Stone, verso, line 4, Nos. 1 and 2], and apparently also in the year of the change to the reign of Shepseskaf where a plausibly-read [4] months and 24 days may be added to [3+] 4 months and 11 days to equal 12 months and 5 days [ibid., line 1, Nos. 1 and 2]). Now we do not know whether the calendar year of twelve months and five days which existed in the Old Kingdom prevailed in the first dynasty. All we know from the recital of months and days given at the end of Aha's reign and that given at the beginning of Djer's reign is that some kind of calendar with divisions of months and days was in use (assuming that the compositor of the fifth dynasty was using a first-dynasty source). If the 365-day calendar was already being used, then here in the case of the transition to Djer's reign we lack 1 month and 15 days of a full civil year. Hence between the reigns there must have been 1 month and 15 days or that period plus one or more years. It might be argued that, since there was no Nile height recorded for the end of the preceding reign, while we have such a height designated for the first year of Djer's reign, the two time spans are fractions of a single year and thus the two reigns were separated by only one month and fifteen days. This argument is considerably weakened by the previous observation that no Nile height is recorded for *any* of the extant years of the reign of Aha, and so it is not significant that no such height was recorded in his last year. But an even stronger argument against there being an interval of only one month and fifteen days is the fact that the author not only has a straight line that extends vertically to the bottom of the line above to indicate the end of the reign but he also includes to the left of that vertical line the top of the palm branch that constitutes the hieroglyphic sign for "year", thus giving us the impression that not only do we have a new reign to the left of the vertical line but also a new civil year. However, in Palermo Stone, recto, line 5, seventh year (see Fig. I.32) there is a clear case where the civil year is divided up between the two reigns, for to the left of the vertical line ending the one reign there is no whole palm branch indicating a new year, but rather there immediately follow the signs indicating the initial ceremonies of the beginning of a new reign. One clear conclusion emerges, namely that the years being recorded in the annals are calendar years and not regnal years, as the last case cited shows. No doubt the cases where the fractions add up to twelve months and five days also show this to be so, for it is unreasonable to suppose that the new king after the lapse of one or more full years would start his reign on the exact day which would allow his fraction of the year when added to the fraction of the preceding king's last year to equal exactly twelve months and five days. Incidentally in those cases where the fractions add up to twelve months and five days the tops of the reign-ending lines are absent either because the fragment was broken (Palermo Stone, verso, line 1) or because the line was worn away (*ibid.*, line 4). Presumably if the vertical lines were still intact we would find that there were no palm branches indicating new years to the left of the lines ending the reigns.

The Ceremonies of the Union of the Two Lands and the Circuit of the Wall were traditional ceremonies of the coronation of the King. The "Wall" was presumably the "White Wall" of Memphis, perhaps built by the first of the dynastic kings (Menes?) at the founding of Memphis. The procedures of Succession and Coronation as persisting into the New Kingdom are described in lively fashion in H. Frankfort, *Kingship and the Gods* (Chicago, 1948), pp. 101-09.

14. Quite clearly one of the main services of the early annals was the inclusion of the maximum height of the Nile for each year, which no doubt served as a measure of the produce due. It is supposed that the measurements recorded here were taken in the neighborhood of Memphis or of Old Cairo, on a standard Nilometer from some agreed zero point. The numbers were most often in terms of cubits, palms, and fingers with an occasional use of spans. The royal cubit equaled 523 mm. or 20.6 inches = 7 palms = 28 fingers. There is another shorter cubit of 6 palms and two different spans, one of 3 1/2 palms and the other of 3 palms. See F. Ll. Griffith, "Notes on Egyptian Weights and Measures," *Proceedings of the Society of Biblical Archaeology*, Vol. 14 (1891-92), pp. 403-04 (whole article, pp. 403-50). In regard to the Nile height we may conveniently quote the brief account of H. Kees, *Ancient Egypt* (Chicago and London, 1961; Phoenix edition, 1977), pp. 50-52, based on the research of Borchardt and others: "In the annals from the Thinite

Period up to Dynasty V, between about 2950 B.C. and 2500 B.C., the rise of the Nile, probably measured in the neighborhood of Old Cairo, was on an average about 4 cubits (approximately 7 feet); therefore a recorded High Nile of 8 cubits and 3 fingers caused in the following year [according to Sethe's interpretation of Palermo Stone, recto, line 3, No. 4 given below] 'flooding of all the western and eastern nomes' in the Delta. Lists compiled in the reign of Sesostris I, about 1950 B.C., give the following, far higher, figures for the desirable height of the flood-waters at various points on the Nile: Elephantine, 21 cubits, 3 1/3 palms (approximately 39 feet); 'the House of the Inundation' near Old Cairo, 12 cubits, 3 palms and 3 fingers (about 21 1/2 feet); for Diospolis or Tell Balamun, the most northerly town of the Delta, 6 cubits, 3 palms, 3 fingers (about 11 feet). The many measurements recorded up to Roman times reveal a further rise of about 20-30 per cent with the result that the figure for Elephantine reaches 24 cubits, 4 palms (about 42 feet) and, as an idealized figure, 28 cubits (i.e. equal to 4 x 7); for the 'House of the Inundation' at Old Cairo the figure becomes 14-16 cubits, while for the Northern Delta it remains unchanged at 6-7 cubits. This increase can only partly be explained by the rise in the bed of the river which, according to Lyons, amounts to about 4 inches a century; in the course of the centuries separating the reign of Sesostris I from 150 B.C. the rise of the bed would amount to about 6 feet or 3 cubits, 3 palms. The fact that ancient writers made use of theoretical and idealized figures is proved by a completely reliable statement by Strabo (Book XVII, 788) that when Petronius was Prefect 12 cubits, that is about 21 feet, of flood-water assured an abundant harvest. He adds that with only 8 cubits there was still no shortage whereas before his time apparently 14 cubits had to be attained before bountiful crops were assured. This measurement of 12 cubits corresponds almost exactly with the Memphite standard under Sesostris I about 2,000 years earlier. As a check on these figures it should be mentioned that in the Third Century B.C. for the purpose of constructing dykes at Memphis the figure of 12 cubits was taken as the high-water mark whereas the actually recorded heights attained by the flood-waters in the years 259 B.C. and 258 B.C. were respectively 10 cubits, 3 palms, 1 1/6 fingers and 10 cubits, 6 palms, 2 2/3 fingers. An inundation that reached the height of 14 cubits at Memphis must therefore have overflowed the dykes.

"The heights recorded in these figures were not apparently measured from low water, for its level on the monument of Sesostris II is taken to be almost the same throughout the whole length of the Nile with 4 cubits, 2 palms, 3 1/3 fingers for Upper Egypt and 4 cubits, 3 fingers for Lower Egypt. According to Borchardt, however, all the Nilometers in the country measured from a fixed zero at Roda with a theoretically assumed fall from Elephantine to Memphis. The big rise in the measured numbers, especially for Elephantine, cannot be accounted for by the fact that because of the narrowing of the river through the cataract the highwater mark at Elephantine is higher above the low water than is the case at Memphis (Lyons estimates about 23 feet for the former and about 16 feet 6 inches for the latter), or in the Delta where the river broadens to an incomparable extent. The explanation must be sought in the predetermined zero on the gauge."

ANCIENT EGYPTIAN SCIENCE

The classic account of Nilometers is that of L. Borchardt, "Nilmesser und Nilstandsmarken," *Abhandlungen der Königlichen Preussischen Akademie der Wissenschaften*, 1906 (*Abhandlungen nicht zur Akademie gehöriger Gelehrter, Phil.-hist. Abh.* I, pp. 1-55). See also W. Helck, "Nilhöhe und Jubiläumsfest," *Zeitschrift für ägyptische Sprache und Altertumskunde*, Vol. 93 (1966), pp. 74-79; K. W. Butzer, "Die Naturlandschaft Ägyptens während der Vorgeschichte und den dynastischen Zeitalter," *Akademie der Wissenschaften und der Literatur, Mainz, Math.-Naturwiss. Kl., Abhandlung* No. 2 (1959); and B. Bell, "The Oldest Records of the Nile Floods," *The Geographical Journal*, Vol. 136 (1970), pp. 569-73. Bell concludes concerning the Nile heights recorded on the Palermo Stone: "Under either of these assumptions about the zero-point of the scale [i.e. either that the zero-point of the scale rose with the alluvium or that the zero-point was fixed by the nilometer's being built into a quay or wall]...it is clear that the height of the inundation, and thus the amount of the summer monsoon rainfall over East Africa, averaged less from Dynasty II onward than in Dynasty I. The difference between the average flood-height for Dynasty I and for Dynasties II-V is 0.7 metres, under the assumption of a zero-point that rose at a uniform rate with the alluvium. Under the assumption of a fixed zero for the nilometer, the decline in flood height is greater, and is also progressive with time. If the alluvium actually rose more rapidly than the rate I have assumed..., an even larger decline in the flood volume would be indicated."

The connection of the measure of the Nile height with taxes was noted by Seneca in his description of the Nilometer at Aswan (quoted by K. Baedeker, *Egypt and the Sûdân* [Leipzig, 1929] p. 383): "The Nilometer is a well built of regular hewn stones, on the bank of the Nile, in which is recorded the rise of the stream, not only the maximum but also the minimum and average rise, for the water in the well rises and falls with the stream. On the side of the well are marks, measuring the height sufficient for the irrigation and the other water levels. These are observed and published for general information.... This is of importance to the peasants for the management of the water, the embankments, the canals, etc., and to the officials on account of the taxes. For the higher the rise of water, the higher are the taxes." See *ibid.*, p. 113, for an account of the Nilometer on the Isle of Roda.

15. Note that *Desher* has as its hieroglyphic determinative a ship. Compare with this the determinative of the Festival of *Djet* in No. 11 below. Presumably in these festivals movement by ship was involved, so much so that the ship becomes a customary determinative for various festivals. The literal meaning of *desher* is "red" and so we have here a "Festival of the Red". Incidentally the word in the feminine means "the desert land" or "the Red Crown". But here it is given in the masculine.

16. It is unlikely that this is a reference to the birth of twins of the Horus Djer, since it is repeated later (Pr, line 6, Nr. 1). According to Sethe, *Untersuchungen*, Vol. 3, p. 63, the reference is probably to the Birth of Shu and Tefenet, the children of the sun-god. As a ceremony it would symbolize the pouring of life into Shu and Tefenet by Atum (see Frankfort, *Kingship and the Gods*, pp. 134-35) and have significance for the earthly king as well.

17. The event being celebrated here is mysterious but appears to represent the early defeat and subjection of the *Rekhyt*-Folk of the Delta. One thinks of the pile of decapitated people on the Palette of Narmer (see Fig. I.8 right) and similarly of the lap-wings *(rhyt)* hanging from standards on the mace-head of the Scorpion king (see Fig. I.3). Consult the thorough (but rather speculative) account of the hieroglyphs that describe this event in P. Kaplony, *Kleine Beiträge zu den Inschriften der ägyptischen Frühzeit* (Wiesbaden, 1966), pp. 65-71. The interpretation of the *Rekhyt*-Folk as inhabitants of the Delta is questioned in a long and thoughful account in A. H. Gardiner, *Ancient Egyptian Onomastica*, pp. 98*-108*.

18. Schäfer translates this as follows: "Planen (?) des Hauses *Ḥsf-nṯrw*. Fest des Sokaris (?)." Breasted changes it slightly: "Design (?) of the House (called): 'Mighty of the Gods' *(shm-nṯrw)*. Feast of Sokar." My translation differs in two respects. I reject utterly the translation of *ḫ'* by either *Planen* or *Design*, preferring rather the translation "behind" or "at". It could hardly be the planning or design of the castle that is involved, since the same event is repeated a few years later in the same reign (see C-1 r, line 2, Nr. 4), and surely "behind" is the normal rendering of it. Furthermore I read *smr-nṯrw* instead of either Schäfer's or Breasted's readings. Hence I have translated the name of the castle as "Companion of the Gods". Note that Kaplony, *Kleine Beiträge*, p. 69, has read *smr(?)-nṯrw* within a castle outline appearing on the second register of an ivory label bearing Djer's name (which, incidentally, Kaplony always writes as *Shtj*). See also his "Gottespalast und Götterfestungen in der ägyptischen Frühzeit," *Zeitschrift für ägyptische Sprache und*

Altertumskunde, Vol. 88 (1962), p. 12, n. 5 (full article pp. 5-16). A conclusive bit of evidence that this was a castle of Djer's is found on a stone vessel in the Berlin Museum (Borchardt, *Annalen*, p. 31 and my Fig. I.45). Kaplony in the article just quoted mentions six castles or fortifications that have *ntrw* as a part of the name and all are in the first three dynasties. These *Götterfestungen* are distinguished from the *Gottespalast*.

Incidentally I add here "[the First Occurrence of]" so that this year can be adequately distinguished from the later entry in C-1 r, line 2, Nr. 4, where I add "[the Second Occurrence of]".

19. Schäfer remarked that the goddess Yamet was named in the later Pyramid texts. With Giustolisi, I think that it is probable that the sign read by Schäfer as *Yamet* is actually the sign later named *Imy-wt* (at least from the sixth dynasty), the well-known symbol of a pelt hanging from a rod, which (probably from the first dynasty and certainly from the third) symbolized the god Anubis. The name *Imy-wt* may be translated: "He who is in the bandaging room". Such a symbol from the Middle Kingdom was found in a wooden shrine during the Metropolitan Museum's excavations at Lisht in 1914 (see A. M. Lythgoe, "Excavations at the South Pyramid at Lisht in 1914," *Ancient Egypt*, 1915, pp. 145-53) and in Tutankhamen's tomb (see my Fig. I.46). We see evidence of the appearance of this symbol earlier than its apparent reference here in Djer's reign, in fact in the reign of Aha, who preceded Djer (see Fig. I.16, first register). Furthermore the symbol appears unequivocally two reigns later in Den's reign, still in the first dynasty (see below C-5, line 2, Nr. 3 [Cf. Fig. I.40]). Indeed U. Köhler, *Das Imiut*, 2 vols. (Wiesbaden, 1975), notes (vol. 1, p. 1) that she has found eighteen

representations of the symbol from the first dynasty alone. Her very thorough study points out that the use of the name *Imy-wt* for the cult-symbol cannot be found before the sixth dynasty, though the symbol was probably associated with Anubis as early as the first dynasty and certainly so from the third. I might add that I had already thought of the possibility that the cult-symbol of Anubis instead of *Yamet* should appear here before I had read Giustolisi's articles and so my judgment was quite independent of his earlier suggestion. Incidentally, even if this name "He who is in the bandaging room" were to be found associated with the symbol in the early dynasties (and this is not improbable since the term *wt* was connected with Anubis at least in the third dynasty when, we have seen, the symbol certainly stood for Anubis), it would not, however, ensure that mummification was already practiced by that time. In such a case it would simply reflect the Egyptian routine of bandaging limbs, a routine evident before they took up mummification.

The exact date at which mummification first began in Egypt is unknown, "but the first definite evidence of any attempt is from the beginning of the Fourth Dynasty" (see A. Lucas and J. R. Harris, *Ancient Egyptian Materials and Industries* [London, 1962], p. 271). These authors (p. 270) speak of the early history of burial practices in Egypt as follows: "During the neolithic and predynastic periods, the body was buried in a shallow grave,...generally wrapped in an animal skin or loose folds of linen, but by the early dynastic period the graves of the kings and wealthier classes had become deeper,...: and the previous loose covering on the body had given place to close-fitting linen wrappings, which in some instances eventually became elaborated into the separate wrapping of each limb, with further wrappings for the whole body, examples of which are known from the First, Second, and Third Dynasties respectively, before mummification was introduced." Chapter XII of the Lucas-Harris book is one of the best accounts of Egyptian mummification. See also the recent treatment in Spencer, *Death in Ancient Egypt*, Chaps. 2 and 5.

20. Min, the ithyphallic god of Coptos, was an early, widely venerated god, as is evident from the supposedly predynastic (but probably early dynastic) colossal statues found by Petrie at the Temple at Coptos. See H. Schäfer and W. Andrae, *Die Kunst des alten Orients* (Berlin, 1935), p. 179, for one such statue. Note that the symbol of Min appears not only on this statue but also on the mace-head of the Scorpion king (see above, Fig. I.3, first register, the middle standard). Later Amon-Re absorbs some of his attributes and is often shown in ithyphallic form. Indeed Wainwright believed Amun to be essentially Min (see below, Chap. 2, n. 60).

21. I have added here "[First Occurrence]" because of the repetition of the Festival of the Birth of Anubis in Djer's reign (see below, C-1 r, line 2, Nr. 1).

22. Here it was only necessary to select a single event because for the first time the selector of the year's name introduced the ordinal number of a festival. He tells us that this is the First Occurrence of the Feast of Djet or Wadjet (presumably in Djer's reign) and hence no other identification is necessary. Wadjet, Goddess of Buto, became the tutelary goddess for Lower Egypt.

23. Only the minutest traces of the tenth year are visible, but not enough to be read.

24. Since the preceding years are almost certainly also a part of Djer's reign, and the reading of this superscription is quite generally accepted as being the name of Djer, perhaps it would have been better to introduce this whole name where I simply have Horus Djer above note 12. The reading of the superscription is quite clear except for the Horus name, where one can see the vertical strokes of the sign for Djer but nothing else. But the name as king and Horus of Gold, namely Itet, appears to clinch the identification. I note that the reading "[Horus] of Gold" is somewhat doubtful for all we have on the fragment is *n-nbw*. If this does stand for the Golden Horus name, we would have to conclude that already in the first dynasty (at least by the time of Horus Den, the second king after Horus Djer) four of the five traditional titles for the kings of Egypt were in use: (1) the Horus title in the *serekh* or palace facade (see Fig. I.47a A), (2) the *nebti* or Two-Goddesses title (see Fig. I.47a B), (3) The Golden-Horus title, (4) the *nesu-bit* or King-of-Upper-and-Lower-Egypt title (see Fig. I.47a C). Only the Son-of-Re title was missing, it being used sporadically as an epithet or designation and not as part of a full titulary in the fourth, fifth and sixth dynasties (see Figs. I.47c-d) and formally and regularly as part of the fivefold titulary in the eleventh dynasty (see Figs. I.47e). The reader should note that the *serekh* in which the Horus name appears was also used in the first dynasty by Queens Neithhotep and Meryetneith (see Fig. I.47a D and E), with the crossed arrows of the goddess Neith surmounting the *serekh* and thus appearing where the falcon appeared in the Horus name. Similarly notice that in the second dynasty the Seth animal replaced the Horus falcon in the name of Seth Peribsen (see Fig. I.19a) and that the same animal

was used in conjunction with the Horus falcon in the name of the Horus-Seth Khasekhemuy (also see Fig. I.19a). For a discussion of the fivefold royal titulary, see Gardiner, *Egyptian Grammar*, pp. 71-74, H. Müller, *Die formale Entwicklung der Titulatur der ägyptischen Könige* (Glückstadt/Hamburg/New York, 1938), and J. von Beckerath, *Handbuch der ägyptischen Königsnamen* (Munich and Berlin, 1984), pp. 1-42. All scholars depend on the monumental work of H. Gauthier, *Le Livre des rois d'Égypte* (Cairo, 1907-17).

25. For my addition of "the Second Occurrence", see note 21 above.

26. This is unreadable in the photographs but was suggested "with reserve" by Gauthier (and I tentatively follow him). Incidentally, Daressy also gave this reading. Giustolisi adds the Festival of Sokar as a second event of this year.

27. The suggestion of the reading "Sed" is that of Daressy, who claimed to see the sign for "Birth" and a part of a vertical stroke followed by a standard. This stroke he believed to be part of "s", and on the base of the standard he hypothesized the wolf which stands on the *shedshed* standard crossed by a mace in Pr, line 3, Nr. 11 and is read "Sed" (see Fig. I.32 and *Wb*, Vol. 4, p. 365). Sed seems to have been an early form of the wolf god Wepwawet and is closely tied to the king, his (Sed's) standard accompanying the king in the king's Sed Festival (see below, note 41).

28. See note 18 above.

29. Both Gauthier and Daressy report the hill-country or foreign-land sign on a standard, which is to be read as the desert God Ha (see Gardiner, *Egyptian Grammar*, p. 488, sign N 25).

30. So reads Daressy. Gauthier suggests "Min".

31. Daressy remarks that the "Red Festival" could be a ceremony celebrated in Upper Egypt in connection with an episode in the life of Seth.

32. The sign of the particular God whose birth is being celebrated is, according to Daressy, "unreadable and partially destroyed".

33. The reading "the Great White One" derives from the seated baboon or monkey which remains on the edge of the fragment (see de Cenival, "Un nouveau fragment," p. 16). Another possible interpretation of the baboon is as a sign for Thoth. J. Černý, *Ancient Egyptian Religion* (London, 1952), p. 21, speaks of an early baboon god as follows: "Numerous small statuettes of baboons and a representation of this animal on an ivory label suggest that its cult dates from the beginning of Egyptian history; it may have been practised at Khmun (Hermopolis) where presumably it preceded the cult of the ibis of Thoth. The original reading of the name of this baboon god is uncertain; but later he was called Hedj-wer or Hedjwerew and interpreted as the 'Great White One' or 'Whitest of the Great Ones'." Cf. Petrie, *Royal Tombs*, Part I, plate XVII, 26, for a tablet of Semerkhet which seems to have a similar seated baboon (given above as Fig. I.18, right). It is interpreted tentatively (p. 42) as representing Thoth.

34. Compare the battle against the Wolf People two years hence and also that against the *Intyw* (Pr, line 3, Nr. 2). How these various people are to be distinguished is not clear. The guess that this is Year 19 of Den's reign is based on the not-too-certain assumptions that (1) there are five years between fragments C-5 and Pr, and (2) that the year reported in Pr, line 3, Nr. 3 as the year of a Sed Festival is Year 30

(see note 41 below).

35. Compare note 19. The *Senuty-Shrine*, or Double Shrines of Re, combined the two primitive shrines of Hieraconpolis (the *Pr-wr* Shrine) and Buto (the *Pr-nsr* or *Pr-nw* Shrine). See Fig. I.48 and Gardiner, *Egyptian Grammar*, pp. 494-95, signs O 19 and O 20.

36. I do not know who the enemies were in this engagement, unless they were the followers of Seth. In one of the tablets of Den, a bearded enemy (who apparently is one of the *Intyw*) has beside him a standard with a wolf symbol on it (Fig. I.18, left). See P. E. Newberry and G. A. Wainwright, "King Udy-mu and the Palermo Stone," *Ancient Egypt*, 1914, pp. 150, 152 (full article, pp. 148-55).

37. Notice that the castle called "Companion of the Gods" is still being mentioned as a place to hold ceremonies in Den's reign, though it was apparently built in Djer's reign.

38. Because the superscribed title covers the space of about seven years, there ought to be about five years between fragments C-5 and Pr.

39. I follow Schäfer in this rendering. But Giustolisi says that we should read the god Ptah and not Saw, which would make this the earliest reference to the cult of Ptah.

40. See note 36 above. The Troglodytes are described as Easterners. Newberry and Wainright call them "People of the Eastern desert and Sinai" (see *op. cit.* in n. 36, p. 152).

41. The Sed Festival is one that renews the King's rule. Tradition (still persisting at the time of the Rosetta Stone) suggests that the first Sed Festival of a king was to be held after thirty years of rule. But this

tradition was often violated, and hence the tentative assumption made here that this is the thirtieth year of Den's reign is anything but certain. For a splendid description and discussion of the Sed Festival, see Frankfort, *Kingship and the Gods*, Chap. 6. There is a fragment of a tablet of King Den (Petrie, *Royal Tombs*, Part I, plate XI, 5, cf. 14) that pictures the double-staired pavilion of the Sed Festival. Frankfort's discussion of the tradition of a 30-year period before the first Sed Festival is worth quoting in full (see *op. cit.*, p. 366, n. 2):

"The texts (e.g., at Abydos, translated by Moret, *Royauté*, [i.e. *Du caractère religieux de la royauté pharaonique* (Paris, 1902)], p. 256) leave no doubt that kingship is renewed at the Sed Festival. The Rosetta Stone, which calls the king κύριον τριακονταετηρίδων [i.e. lord of the thirty-year feasts], proves the existence of a tradition connecting the festival with a thirty-year period; and the practice of several kings (Pepi II, Senusert I, Tuthmosis III, Amenhotep III, Ramses II, Ramses III) suggests that it was normally celebrated for the first time thirty years after the king's accession. But this period was not essential, for, after the first celebration, the Sed Festival was celebrated again at two-, three-, or four-year intervals until the king's death. Moreover, some kings celebrated it before their thirtieth year (e.g., Pepi I in his eighteenth year, Ranebtaui Mentuhotep in his second year), while others, who did not reign for thirty years, celebrated Sed festivals nevertheless (Dedkare, Amenhotep II, Seti II, Psammetichos II). The assumption that the celebration took place thirty years after the admission of the king to coregency (Sethe, *ZÄS*, XXXVI, 64, n. 3) is contradicted by the known facts of the reign of Ramses

II and by the two celebrations of the Sed Festival by Tuthmosis IV, whose mummy shows that he could hardly have been more than twenty or twenty-five years old when he died. See Moret, *Royauté*, pp. 256-61, who also quotes the older literature, and Breasted, in *ZÄS*, XXXIX, 55-61.

"It seems that thirty years, or, in a more general way, 'a generation' (Edouard Naville, in *PSBA*, VII, 135), was the normal time to elapse between a king's accession and the celebration of the Sed Festival but that certain symptoms (the nature of which we cannot guess) might at any time indicate to the ancients that a renewal of kingship was due. It is possible that the king's health may have been one of the symptoms; but the widespread belief that the Sed Festival was a modification of an earlier custom which required that the incarnation of the god be replaced by a more perfect man as soon as the present king showed signs of senility or illness projects into Egypt an East African custom... which may have been adhered to, of course, but for which there is no evidence at all."

In this quotation I have added the phrases in square brackets. To the kings mentioned who celebrated their Sed Festival in the thirtieth year we can add Niuserre of the fifth dynasty (see Kees, *Ancient Egypt*, p. 156). Kees notes that among the extensive sacrificial offerings at that festival were 100,600 meals of bread, beer, and offering-cakes on New Year's Day. C. J. Bleeker, *Egyptian Festivals. Enactments of Religious Renewal* (Leiden, 1967), pp. 96-123, reviews this ceremony. E. Hornung and C. Seeber, *Studien zum Sedfest* (Geneva, 1974), evaluate in excellent fashion the historical evidence for the various Sed Festivals.

42. The event reported here is subject to many

interpretations. I have followed Sethe in interpreting it as the report of the flooding of the Delta after the unusually high Nile noted in the previous year (see note 14 above). But Sethe's full rendering is somewhat different from mine: "Flooding of the western nomes of Lower Egypt, sickness of all people." (See A. H. Gardiner, *Ancient Egyptian Onomastica*, Vol. 1, p. 104*.) Breasted and much later Giustolisi interpreted this event as the taking of a census of "all people of the nomes of the west, north, and east" (Breasted) or "of all the people of the western, northern and eastern regions of the Delta" (Giustolisi).

   43. Notice that holding of the Sokar festival has shifted from the castle called "Companion of the Gods" to this castle, now mentioned for the first time. It was this event in connection with that of the next year that caused some scholars to translate *ḥı* as the planning or designing of the castle. But I have already established the inappropriateness of such a translation (see above, note 18).

   44. Both Schäfer and Breasted simply have "Great Door" as a second item. But I believe that the castle was far enough along so that the Great Door was being added, and that this whole statement speaks of surveying the area for the Great Door. For tablets from Den's reign that show the opening of a door of a castle, see Petrie, *The Royal Tombs*, Part I, plate XI, 14, 15. It is of interest that a priest of the Goddess Seshat (a goddess of writing and learning) should be the one to perform the surveying ceremony. The role of Seshat in the foundation ceremonies of Egyptian temples is well known (see H. Kees, *Götterglaube im alten Ägypten*, 2nd ed. [Berlin, 1956], p. 212, and E. Hornung, *Conceptions of God in Ancient Egypt. The One and the*

Many [Ithaca, N. Y., 1971], p. 282). For the mention of this goddess under the special name *Sfḫt-ᶜbwy*, see W. Murnane, *United with Eternity*, Fig. 62, where she is shown participating with Tuthmosis III in the ceremony of stretching the rope during the foundation ritual of the temple at Djamet (in front of the temple of Ramesses III at Medinet Habu). She is often shown as a companion of Thoth. Such is the case of the portico of the second court in Ramesses III's temple, where north of the portal Seshat says to Ramesses: "I am inscribing for you jubilees in myriads and years like the sands of the sandbank. I am establishing your records in your august mansion eternally, and I am granting that your titulary be established forever as Re rises every day", while Thoth similarly speaks to Ramesses south of the same portal (*ibid.*, p. 40). We should also note Seshat's appearance (again under the name of *Sfḫt-ᶜbwy*) in a relief picturing the foundation ceremony of Seti I's temple at Abydos (see R. David, *A Guide to Religious Ritual at Abydos* [Warminster, England, 1981], pp. 24-25, where we read: "In the Lower Register, the king and Sefkhet-ᶜAbwy measure out the temple building in the presence of Osiris. The 'Lady of Writing, pre-eminent in the Library' says 'It is Ptah who lays out its foundations in person; it is thy father Re who establishes it like his horizon.' Osiris says '(I) cause thy mansion to abide like the sky... It is entitled: 'Stretching the cord in the Mansion of Usirmare-setepenre, near to the necropolis'"). Later (p. 173) David summarizes information on Seshat as follows: "SESHAT *(Sšᶨt)*. A very ancient goddess, the 'Mistress of Builders', whose chief centre was Memphis. Her duties included the recording of the royal names at birth, the writing of the king's name and titulary at his coronation, and the granting to him of sed-festivals. She was an account-keeper, who became associated with Thoth; she is often shown involved in the foundation ritual of temples, where her task was to measure out the ground-plan of the building. Another of her aspects was as a sky-goddess. SEFKHET-ᶜABWY was a name introduced for Seshat by Tuthmosis III, and derived from her symbol, the feathers, which came to be represented as two horns. She came to be regarded as a goddess of Fate, perhaps because of her connection with writing the life-span and with numbers and writing." This should be clarified somewhat. The name Sefkhet-ᶜAbwy literally means: "She of the Seven [Rays of the Star] and the Two Horns". It is then a description of the symbol that Seshat has on her head, which consists of a pole carrying a star with seven rays surmounted by inverted horns (see the use of this name on the east wall of the temple at Edfu: "Seshat, the Great Lady of Writing, of the Seven [rayed-star] and the Two Horns, and Mistress of the House of Books"; cf. E. Chassinat, *Le temple d'Edfou*, Vol. 3 [Cairo, 1928], p. 350, E' e. 2 g. I, lin. 2-3). See samples of Seshat's portrait in Fig. I.31: (a) on a twelfth-dynasty block where she is presiding over the House of Sacred Book(s) and recording the numbers of prisoners, cattle, and other booty; and (b) on the east wall of the Library at the Temple of Edfu. See in Fig. I.31(c) part of a limestone block from the early twelfth dynasty showing a "King of Upper and Lower Egypt" (perhaps Amenemhet I) and a divinity (Seshat?) together stretching the cord.

45. I have translated the first part of this as indicating the opening of the lake of the castle "Seats of Gods". Notice that the rectangle sign for "lake" has

some vertical strokes, and so it could be that we again have here the sign for Door of the Castle. Then we should have to translate the first part as "The Year of the Opening of the Door of the Castle". The second event, namely the shooting of the hippopotamus, may be alluded to in a seal of the time of Den (see Petrie, *The Royal Tombs*, Part II, plate VII, 5, 6) that shows a man (presumably Den) wrestling with a hippopotamus.

46. The use of the expression the "First Occurrence" refers to the first occurrence in the reign of Den. For a possible reference to an Apis Bull, see note 8 above. Apis was the sacred bull of Memphis. Frankfort, *Kingship and the Gods*, p. 167, says concerning the cults of sacred bulls: "It is generally assumed that they represent primitive cults, originally unconnected with the great gods with whom they were related in historic times. But the assumption may well be unfounded. That relationship is expressed by a significant title in the case of both the Apis bull of Memphis and the Mnevis bull of Heliopolis. The bulls are the 'heralds' of the gods. The full titles were 'the living Apis, the Herald of Ptah, who carries the truth upward to Him-with-the-lovely-face (Ptah)' and 'the Herald of Re, who carries the truth upward to Atum.'" See also Kees, *Ancient Egypt*, p. 150, who says the following regarding the report of this event in the Palermo Stone: "So too the sacred bull in the ceremony of the 'running forth of Apis' when it was led forth from the eastern door of its stall near the temple of Ptah to join the ceremonial procession, an event frequently recorded in the annals of the Thinite Period." In the Sed Festival the running of Apis also played a part by symbolizing Lower Egypt and the king's renewing his possession thereof (*ibid.*, p. 62). The bull

accompanied the king as he ran around the ceremonial track four times.

47. Seshat is the Goddess of Writing and she appears on many later monuments (see note 44 above). Concerning the goddess Mafdet, Černý, *Ancient Egyptian Religion*, p. 22, writes: "The cat- or mongoose-goddess Mafdet, 'lady of the Castle [or Mansion] of Life,' attested from the Ist Dynasty, was very early invoked as a protectress against snake bites, as both Egyptian cats and mongooses were fearless snake-killers. The centre of the cult of this goddess is still unknown." Cf. A. H. Gardiner, "The Mansion of Life and the Master of the King's Largesse," *Journal of Egyptian Archaeology*, Vol. 24 (1938), pp. 89-90.

48. I accept Kaiser's conclusion that Adjib's reign preceded the Cairo fragment on the right.

49. There is here a very small fraction of a year which lies on the right side of line 3, and its traces are completely unreadable.

50. I follow Emery in reading the priestly figure given for Semerkhet's *insibya* and *nebti* names as Semenptah (W. B. Emery, *Archaic Egypt* [Harmondsworth, 1961], p. 84). For the reading of his mother's name, see P. Kaplony, *Die Inschriften der ägyptischen Frühzeit*, Vol. I (Wiesbaden, 1963), pp. 473-74.

51. I have mostly followed the readings of Gauthier and Daressy in deciphering the readings in this line of the Cairo fragment. Here in Year 1 one would also expect notice of the Ceremony of the Circuiting of the Wall.

52. Daressy believes that the end of this year has signs for *mst*, *wp*, *r* and he further suggests that the whole reading might be *mst Ḥr wp r nṯrw*, which we

could translate as "Birth of Horus, Opening of the Mouth of the Gods". If this is a correct reading, presumably we have reference to a ceremony of the opening of the mouth of statues of gods (see above, note 6). Otherwise the ceremony of opening of the mouth in respect to gods would make little sense. I note also that this is the last year of the reign and that it must have extended through almost the whole civil year or we would have some indication of the number of months and days of the year that the king reigned before dying.

53. This is almost certainly the reign of Ḳa^{c}a, since his reign followed that of Semerkhet. His was the last reign of the first dynasty.

54. This is unreadable but it probably should read "The Year of the Appearance of the king as King of Upper Egypt and [his] Appearance as King of Lower Egypt at the Ceremony of the Union of the Two Lands".

55. I have taken the reading "Son of Nub-" from Schäfer, who credits it to Sethe. I have added "[Nufer]" since the *insibya* name of his father (Nebre) is given as Nubnufer. Presumably this would be followed here in the *Annals* by his mother's name. It could be, however, that the *nwb* sign refers not to a part of his father's name but to the king's Golden Horus name, which may be *Ren*. For the king's Horus name, Ninetjer is the simplest reading of the hieroglyphs. A. H. Gardiner in the Appendix of his *Egypt of the Pharaohs* (Oxford, 1961), p. 432, suggests as an alternate reading Nutjeren, while Sethe (*Untersuchungen*, Vol. 3, p. 40) believes it ought to be read *Ntrj-mw*. Emery, *Archaic Egypt*, p. 93, simply calls him Neteren (Netermu).

56. The bracketed material cannot be read but is

restored on the basis of the readings in Nrs. 3, 5, 7, 9, 11, 13, and 15. This is the first reign reported in the fragments in which we find the biennial "countings" mentioned. As we shall see in the later reigns, the countings are specified as either "the counting of gold and fields" or "the counting of oxen and small cattle". My suggestion that this was the sixth year of Ninetjer's reign is based on the presumed addition of "the Second Occurrence of the Counting" to this year and the conventional view that the first of the biennial countings was undertaken in the second year. It is, of course, not impossible that it took place in the first year of the reign. If so, then this would be the fifth year of Ninetjer's reign.

57. We do not know the nature of the building that is being laid out in this year. It could be a temple or a palace but is unlikely to be his tomb. In fact, Ninetjer's tomb has not yet been discovered, though there are several possible tombs which can be dated to his reign (see Emery, *Archaic Egypt*, p. 94).

58. See note 56.

59. See notes 8 and 46.

60. R. Anthes, "Egyptian Theology in the Third Millennium B.C.," *Journal of Near Eastern Studies*, Vol. 18 (1959), p. 186, translated the first part of this entry as "the first time of the sailing of the heavenly Horus, the star", which does not appear to be in character for entries in the *Annals* that concern repeated events. For the most part they represent festivals and the use of the boat determinative for such festivals is probably because the king and celebrants sailed to such a festival. The star-sign before the boat, which, following Schäfer, I have translated as "Worship" (or Adoration), Anthes translates as "the star". Even if this is correct, I think

that the proper translation would then be "the first occurrence of the festival of the heavenly Horus, the star". But frankly, I doubt even that translation. In the second part of the entry, I follow Breasted's interpretation of this event as the "hacking up" or destruction of these two mansions or cities, though Schäfer believed that the events referred to were the foundings of these two places. P. E. Newberry, "The Set Rebellion of the IInd Dynasty," *Ancient Egypt* (1922), pp. 40-46, and particularly p. 45, n. 8, believed that these events signaled "trouble in the north", prelude to the Seth rebellion of this dynasty. As the result of the civil war we notice that the later king Peribsen had a Seth title rather than a Horus title and that the last king of the dynasty, Khasekhemuy, had a Horus-Seth name. But see H. Te Velde, *Seth, God of Confusion* (Leiden, 1977), pp. 72-80.

61. I am by no means sure of this translation. One would suspect that if both Wadjet and Nekhbet were being celebrated we would have the king appearing both as King of Lower Egypt and as King of Upper Egypt. I also note that I am not sure of the reading of Nekhbet.

62. It was first thought that these two were names of the same king. But this seems unlikely. Still, perhaps the Horus Sekhemib-Perenmaat (his full name) switched allegiance and renamed himself Seth Peribsen. See Gardiner, *Egypt of the Pharaohs*, p. 417.

63. Daressy notes that only scattered signs can be seen in the fourth register, though he claims that in the first year after the division between the reigns of Ninetjer and his successor the reading is clear enough and I translate it: "The Appearance of [the king as] the King of Upper Egypt and [his] Appearance as King of

Lower Egypt....." One would suppose that this would be followed by "at the Ceremony of the Union of the Two Lands". This seems to be the ninth section of the fourth register.

64. There is considerable discussion and difference of opinion regarding the last kings of the second dynasty. See Emery, *Archaic Egypt*, pp. 99-103, and see Helck, "Bemerkungen zum Annalenstein," p. 35. Helck also assumes that there was an anonymous reign of 1 year and 8 months after that of Neferkaseker. Cf. the recent remarks of Barta, "Chronologie der 1. bis 5. Dynastie," pp. 12-13. See also von Beckerath, *Handbuch der ägyptischen Königsnamen*, pp. 48-49.

65. There is division of opinion concerning whether Nebka should be classified as the last king of the second dynasty or the first king of the third dynasty.

66. This is the first time in the *Annals* that the item or items being counted are specified. But notice that it precedes by a year the Second Occurrence of the [General] Counting. This may mean that a first occurrence of the General Counting took place in the year before (i.e. in the second year of the reign). Presumably that General Counting was of the cattle and fields and so is to be distinguished from the Counting of Gold reported here in this year. Notice that later in Years Y + 3 and Y + 5 the different counts are joined together in a General Counting of the Gold and the Fields. Note that Giustolisi assigns these four years of the London fragment and the years in the same line on the Palermo fragment to the reign of Khasekhemuy instead of to that of his successor Nebka. W. M. Stewart, *Egyptian Stelae....* Part II..., p. 6, merely says that the dimensions of the compartments on the recto

of the London fragment "match those of the fifth register of the Palermo Stone, which deals with Dynasty II". This is an incorrect statement if the fifth register of the Palermo Stone commences in the midst of the reign of Nebka, that is the first reign of Dynasty III, and continues with parts of Djoser's reign. I follow Helck in locating the London fragment.

67. Again we have mention of the Rekhyt-Folk, although it is not clear what the ceremony is. See note 17 above. Stewart interprets the birds as jabirus and translates "the souls of Pe".

68. Only the "Third" is visible, but the whole year's report is almost certainly reconstructed from the reports for Years $X + 2$, $Y + 1$, $Y + 3$, and $Y + 5$.

69. The interest here is that the temple is being built in stone. Stone was used in floors, door jambs, and stairs before the third dynasty, but we know of no large structures entirely of stone earlier than the complex of the Step Pyramid of Djoser, which was constructed in the next reign after Nebka's.

70. See note 66.

71. See K. Sethe, "Hitherto Unnoticed Evidence Regarding Copper Works of Art of the Oldest Period of Egyptian History," *Journal of Egyptian Archaeology*, Vol. 1 (1941), pp. 233-36, and particularly pp. 233-35. Presumably the making and dedication of the statue were pious acts on the part of Khasekhemuy's successor Nebka (perhaps as a step toward legitimizing the change of dynasty). However the older view, that we are concerned here with Khasekhemuy's reign, would of course interpret the builder of this statue as Khasekhemuy himself.

72. I have no idea what the first item is. But I suggest that the whole year might read "The Year of

the Fourth Occurrence of Bringing [the Gods] to the Wall [in which year took place] the Building of the Ship called 'The City of Dewadjefa'." Giustolisi suggests: "The Capture (?) of the Wall of Duagefa. The Breaking of the Red Vases."

73. As I remarked above in note 13, this last year of what is almost certainly Nebka's reign is apparently the first year of Djoser's reign, since the perpendicular indicating the end of the reign is not accompanied by a palm branch on its left, which would indicate a separate year for the new king's reign.

74. I follow Kaiser and others in believing that the new reign is that of Djoser.

75. See note 35 above.

76. It is rather interesting that in the five years of Djoser's reign reported here we find no mention of the biennial countings but simply a return to the custom of citing the Following of Horus in which some specific festival took place. Helck believes that the last three and one-half years of the reign of Djoser are on the right side of Fragment C-1r, line 4. They cannot be read. Giustolisi opines that the years we have assigned to Nebka are those of Khasekhemuy, and the years assigned to Djoser are those of Nebka (whom he calls by the Horus name Sanakht), and he (Giustolisi) believes that he can read in the first of the years on the right edge "Festa di Horo" and in the second year "The Appearance of the King of Lower Egypt. The Birth of Anubis."

77. I am assuming, along with Kaiser and Helck, that the reign of Djoser's successor, namely Djoser-tety, is completely included in the unreadable fourth line of Fragment C-1. I follow J.-P. Lauer, *Saqqara* (London, 1976), p. 137, in concluding that Djoser-tety's Horus

name was Sekhemkhet. His incomplete step-pyramid complex was discovered in the 1950s by the Egyptian Egyptologist M.Z. Ghonheim.

78. The full name of Djoser-tety's successor is not known for certain. See Helck, *Untersuchungen*, pp. 20-22.

79. This is the last reign of the third dynasty. Huny's Horus name is not known.

80. The reading of Sneferu's mother's name is that given by Černý. Compare B. Grdseloff, "Notes sur deux monuments inédits de l'ancien empire," *Annales du Service des Antiquités de l'Égypte*, Vol. 42 (1943), p. 118, full article, pp. 107-25.

81. It is possible that this specific counting is in lieu of a more general biennial counting. If this is so, then this is probably the fourth year of Sneferu's reign. From this reign onward, the stone *Annals* become true annals rather than a collection of year names, as they were in the first three dynasties.

82. See note 35 above for these shrines.

83. Compare note 71 above. The statue there appears to have been made by Khasekhemuy's successor while here the statue was made by Sneferu himself.

84. The only signs visible on the lower register of the London fragment are the top of the palm branch standing for *rnpt*, i.e. year, and the "mast" sign (Gardiner, *Egyptian Grammar*, p. 499, sign P 6) meaning "to stand" but which has been used earlier in the *Annals* to mean "a sojourn" or "staying" of the king at some place. See Pr, line 3, Nrs. 1 and 9. Cf. Stewart, *Egyptian Stelae...Part II...*, p. 6.

85. See note 16 above, and compare the vestiges here of the signs there in Pr, line 2, Nr. 5.

86. Added because two years later the *Annals*

report the Seventh Occurrence of the Counting.

87. For this type of ship in the second dynasty, see P. Lacau and J. P. Lauer, *Fouilles à Saqqara; la pyramide à degrés*, Vol. 4, fasc. 2 (Cairo, 1961), pp. 51-52. For a brief account of shipbuilding, consult Kees, *Ancient Egypt*, pp. 106-09. He notes that *meru*-wood was one of the best-known coniferous woods from Lebanon.

88. The word $c\check{s}$ has often been translated "cedar" in the early literature, though this is not precisely accurate. All that we can be sure of is that the term indicated some kind or kinds of coniferous trees.

89. These are apparently the names of two gates of the royal palace. It is not clear whether these two gates are to be distinguished from the doors of cedar mentioned immediately afterwards.

90. Notice that this eighth counting follows in the next year after the seventh so that the biennial counting seems to have been set aside in favor of an annual counting. But also notice that this does not set a trend, for the biennial counting is still being used in the fifth and sixth dynasties. See Gardiner, "Regnal Years," pp. 13-15.

91. For the reconstruction of the titulary here, see Helck, "Bemerkungen," p. 34.

92. Sethe, *Urkunden*, I, p. 238, has *ḥd* but notes that Borchardt reads *sd*, and I prefer the latter.

93. Or, less likely, the phrase *wp r nṯrw* could be rendered "except the gods". I think that the reference is to the ceremony of the opening of the mouth as applied to statues of gods. See above, note 6.

94. Bastet is the cat goddess, who was perhaps originally a lioness. She was named after her cult town Bast (in Greek Bubastis). See Černý, *Ancient Egyptian*

Religion, p. 25.

95. Only a small part of a single year is left from this line. The only thing discernible is the last part of the reading of the Nile height: "3/4" (perhaps "fingers").

96. Strictly speaking, Shepseskaf's pyramid at South Saqqara is not a pyramid but a mastaba shaped like a sarcophagus.

97. This is the first time that the expression "The Year *after* the First Counting of the Oxen" appears in these fragments. But with it, we now have a system of numbering every year of a reign, and this system appears to have remained thus through the sixth dynasty.

98. For the "Souls of Heliopolis", see Frankfort, *Kingship and the Gods*, p. 94.

99. In this number and the one succeeding it we have evidence of a primitive place-value concept. Briefly we can note that the number 44 preceding the indicated number of unit-*st'wt* or unit-arouras (i.e. 8) must count 10s. Thus 44 in this position counts 44·10 arouras (440 arouras). The same thing is true of the number 23 in the next gift of land (in III), i.e., it counts 23·10 arouras. This is true as well for the number 35 in Pv, line 2, Nr. 2 (sect. I [Schäfer has "36" instead of "35" but I have followed Sethe]. [Similar examples occur later in the Rhind Papyrus: Problems 48 and 50 (see Fig. I.49 for Problem 48, where we see in line 5 the number 8, which counts 10s, followed by the sign for *st't* with one unit below, making a total of 81)]. But where there is no indication of a distinction between 10s and units, as in the following cases: number 24 [Pv line 2, Nr. 2 (II)], 44 [*ibid.* (III)], 54 [*ibid.*, (V)], 2[*ibid.*, (VI)], etc., the numbers appear to count individual *st'wt*. Note that I have everywhere stressed in my bracketed

totals that they are in modern terms because Egyptian fractions (excepting 2/3 and 3/4) were always expressed in terms of the sum of unit fractions, as will be evident in Volume Two, Chapter 4. Note that a *stʿt* is about 2/3 of an acre.

100. This may be a reference to inventorying the estate of the pharaoh, which perhaps was carried out in the odd-numbered years, while the general counting of the oxen and other wealth of the land was made in even-numbered years. If this is so, then this surely is the year 5, which would be further confirmed by the succeeding statement that it is the year *after* the second counting. The reading "the House of Horus-Seth" was first suggested by Naville, "La Pierre de Palerme," p. 80. Afterwards Daressy made it a part of the expression I have given here. This reading is by no means certain, for in Sethe's text we find instead of the falcon (for Horus) the owl (for the letter "m"). The sign that is taken to be read as "Seth" is presumably a pig (which indeed occasionally was used for Seth in the *Book of the Dead* and elsewhere) but looks in Sethe's transcription like an anteater. The depiction of what surely must be Seth as a pig in a scene of Osiris's hall of judgment is given between the fifth gate and door in the *Book of Gates* (see Fig. II.43).

101. As Kees has noted, *Ancient Egypt*, p. 32, "a heron ruled over the legendary birthplace of the gods at Buto, corresponding to the Horus falcon of Nekhen....". Djebakherut appears to be the ancient name of Pe or Buto. By the time of the Old Kingdom this god appears as "Horus of Pe" without changing its heron form (see Kees, *Der Götterglaube im alten Ägypten*, p. 51). Hence this gift of land by Weserkaf was no doubt for Horus of Buto.

102. A form of Horus. I have given the reading of Schäfer and Breasted. Another possibility is *Dunanu*, a falcon god which is determined by a falcon on a perch (see *Wb*, Vol. 5, p. 432).

103. In this number no "hundreds" or "tens" are involved. The whole number 1804 counts individual arouras to which are added the indicated fractions. Hence in this number there is no evidence of a place-value concept. Note that only seven signs of 100 are visible, but by their placing it seems very likely that an eighth sign (now worn away) was once present. Similarly only 12 units appear with the cubit sign, but from their placing it seems likely that there was a thirteenth. I remind the reader that an area cubit was a strip 100 cubits long and 1 cubit wide and was thus 1/100 of a *st't* or aroura. See Griffith, "Notes on Egyptian Weights and Measures," pp. 410-421 and Gardiner, *Egyptian Grammar*, p. 200, for Egyptian area measurements (see my Fig. I.50).

104. See note 100 above.

105. This is Sethe's guess.

106. Perhaps intended here is the wooden statue of the goddess Mes, for the determinative is a statue. So the literal translation of this might well be "Mes in wood". Similarly the next god may well be a statue of the god Sem and thus the name here would be literally translated "Sem [in] wood".

107. In sections XI-XIV we again see evidence of a place-value concept, but in these cases the first number 2 counts 100s and precedes the signs for 10s. In the first two cases (sects. XI and XII) these signs of 10 *st'wt* are followed by the sign for a unit *st't*, of which eight and six, respectively, are indicated. Each number is completed by fractions. In the other two

cases no units are given but only fractions. There are two further cases of the apparent counting of 100s in Pv, line 4, Nr. 2 (sects. 2 and 4). They respectively produce numbers involving 110·100 and 352·100 which seem to be way out of line in comparison with the other gifts of land, so much so that one wonders if there are not errors of copying or interpretation involved. If the latter, it might mean that here we do not have cases of the use of the place-value concept.

108. I am convinced by J. R. Harris's conclusion that $\underline{d}^{c}m$-gold is indeed "electrum" (*Lexicographical Studies in Ancient Egyptian Minerals* [Berlin, 1961], pp. 48-49), although it is often translated merely as "fine gold" (see Gardiner, *Egyptian Grammar*, p. 509, signs S 40-41).

109. *Sen*-gold appears to be some alloy of gold, perhaps "2/3 gold".

110. Instead of the "Seventh Counting", as Sethe gives it in his text without question, Schäfer reads this as the "6. (?) Mal der Zahlung". Schäfer's reading may have been influenced by the fact that the Turin Canon appears to have assigned to Sahure's reign 12 years and some unknown number of months. The Year of the Sixth Counting would then be the twelfth year, and this particular year, of which Sahure served only nine months and 28 days, would be the year after the Sixth Counting and thus the thirteenth year.

111. Schäfer says that the number of months and days is very uncertain, but Borchardt and Sethe give the reading which I have translated. Indeed it is this reading which combines with that of the first year of Neferirkare's reign to produce the civil year of 12 months and five days.

112. Ceremonies devoted to the gods whose births

were associated with the five epagomenal days, i.e. the five days added to the twelve months to make the civil year of 365 days. These gods were called the children of Nut: Osiris, Horus the Elder, Seth, Isis, and Nephthys. See Kees, *Der Götterglaube*, p. 259. It is evident that since Neferirkare assumed the throne toward the end of the civil year, these ceremonies associated with the Birth of the Gods would have been among his first celebrations.

113. See note 107.

114. This town was a kind of suburb of Heliopolis. Its name means "The Place of the Battle" (i.e. the battle between Horus and Seth). It was called "Babylon" by the Greeks (e.g. Strabo). Its gods are mentioned in later texts.

115. "Great Seer" is the title of the chief priest of Heliopolis. It is evident by this reference that in the fifth dynasty there were two of them.

116. Probably a temple of thirty divine judges. Groups of thirty human judges were part of the administration of justice in the Old Kingdom.

117. Following the arrangement of the fragments proposed by both Giustolisi and Helck, I estimate that the verso of the London Fragment contains part of the second year of Neferirkare's reign. I follow the readings of Reeves, "A Fragment of the Fifth Dynasty Annals," pp. 47-51. I have, however, substituted the letters y and z as the unknown multiples of 10 and 1 arouras respectively.

118. "*Nswt Ḥn*", as this is now usually read. He was the last king of the third dynasty. Formerly read as "Setneh" and not identified. In my opinion, this is by no means certain.

Document I.2: Introduction

The "Biography" of Metjen: Inscriptions from his Tomb

As I pointed out in my general account in Chapter One, the inscriptions from the tomb of Metjen (found by Lepsius in Saqqara and now in Berlin) represent one of the earliest biographical accounts, if not the earliest, appearing on the walls of an official's tomb. Its composition was a significant step in the development of systematic writing. The inscriptions apparently date from the early years of the fourth dynasty, in the reign of Sneferu (the first king of that dynasty), and they refer to a career which in all likelihood began during the reign of Sneferu's predecessor, Huny, the last king of the third dynasty. Breasted summarizes the significance of the biography as follows:[1]

> Apart from the fact that it is our earliest document of the kind..., the biography is especially valuable because it deals with the geography and government of the North, narrating Methen's activity in the Delta, of the administration of which at this early period we otherwise know almost nothing. The narrative tells us of his gradual rise from a beginning as scribe and overseer of a

provision magazine until he governs a considerable number of towns and districts in the Delta. He also obtained in Upper Egypt the rule of the eastern part of the Fayyum[2] and the Anubis nome (Seventeenth). He was liberally awarded with gifts of lands, became master of the hunt, and tells us of the size of his house, with some account of the grounds; all of which, from an age so remote, is of especial interest. He died in the reign of Sneferu; all his affiliations were with the families preceding Sneferu, and he was naturally buried beside the terraced pyramid of Zoser [Djoser], of the earlier part of the Third dynasty.

Though it is not specifically stated in the inscriptions that Metjen began as a scribe, this is surely a correct inference by Breasted, since we are told in the document that he was to be appointed "over [or at the head of] the scribes of a provision bureau" with the title of "Administrator of the Provisionbureau" and that appointment (even if it was hereditary as it probably was) would be inconceivable if he had not himself been trained as a scribe. Such training would certainly have been undertaken or provided by his father, who was himself given the title in the document of "Judge-Scribe" (s'b-ss) which, even if it is instead translated "Elder-Scribe" or "Honorary Scribe" to indicate a pensioner,[3] betokens a scribal career before assuming that title, a career in which his son and heir was no doubt raised.

One thing of significance for us in this document is the window it offers us to view the preparation of written royal decrees, for we note quotations from such decrees interspersed in its inscriptions (and singled out below in the translation by bracketed rubrics entitled Royal Documents I-V). These quotations provide support to the belief that the royal chancery was flourishing as a document-producing organization by the end of the third dynasty (see above Chapter 1, n. 12). We can infer that these quotations were taken from copies of such royal decrees on file at either the chancery itself or a local bureau like the one that seems to be referred to in Royal Document III. From the later copies of such decrees we can judge both the physical form and epistolary style of the royal documents produced on papyrus in the chancery (see Fig. I.51). The evidence then that Document I.2 provides of the activity of the royal chancery can help us to explain the third-dynasty relief (Fig. I.29) containing the list of scribal names from the time of Djoser that we mentioned in the general account of Chapter One. The scribes organized in the chancery and elsewhere had clearly become an important element in the burgeoning governmental activity of Djoser's reign.

Though it is of no great importance for the exposition of Egyptian science, the study of the above-mentioned excerpts from the royal documents included among Metjen's inscriptions is very important in giving us some hints of the complex arrangements of private and public land division, ownership and acquisition of land, and the establishment of income-producing personal foundations in the third and fourth dynasties and of the relationships between landholding and public office (see in particular the study of K. B. Gödecken mentioned in the literature below). But surely we may conclude from the evidence of land transfers in our document (as was the case with the land donations listed in Document I.1) that full play was given to measurement, and particularly to land measurement. In this regard I cannot help but note that one of the offices held by Metjen was that of "Crier" (*nḫt-ḫrw*: lit. "Strong of Voice") who apparently evaluated the quantity and value of produce and cried out the figures to the recording scribes. It seems probable that the holder of such an office (if indeed he did anything but draw the yield or income arising from that title) would be particularly conversant with the numerical techniques used and written down by the "reckoners" in mathematical papyri like those described in Volume Two, Chapter Four. In particular, I remind the reader that one of such reckoners was the "Caller" (*nisw*), translated as "accountant" in Document IV.1, Problem 67, in Volume Two. For a pictorial representation of a "Crier" see Lepsius, *Denkmäler*, Abt. II, plate III, bottom register, where we see him depicted in the fifth-dynasty tomb of Reshepses and labeled as "Crier of the Granary" (*nḫt-ḫrw-šnwt*).

Texts and Studies

R. Lepsius, *Denkmäler aus Ägypten und Äthiopien*, Abt. I-VI (Berlin, 1849-58; photographic reprint, Geneva, 1972); see particularly Abt. II, plates III-VII. Contains reproductions of reliefs and inscriptions from Metjen's tomb.

H. Schäfer, *Ägyptische Inschriften aus den Königlichen Museen zu Berlin*, Vol. 1 (Leipzig, 1913), pp. 68, 73-87, a reproduction of the text of the inscriptions (see below, Figs. I.52-I.55).

K. Sethe, *Urkunden des Alten Reichs*, Vol. 1, 2nd ed. (Leipzig, 1933) (abbreviated *Urkunden* I; see Bibliography), pp. 1-7, another reproduction of the text.

J. H. Breasted, *Ancient Records of Egypt*, Vol. 1 (New York, 1906), pp. 76-79, an English translation of some of the inscriptions from Lepsius, Schäfer, and Sethe's first edition.

G. Maspero, "La carrière administrative de deux hauts fonctionnaires égyptiens," *Études égyptiennes*, Vol. 2 (1890), pp. 113-272, a remarkably perceptive study despite its age.

W. Helck, *Untersuchungen zu den Beamtentiteln des ägyptischen Alten Reiches* (Glückstadt / Hamburg / New York, 1954), still the most important single work on early titles, with many references to the titles of Metjen in the context of Old Kingdom titles.

H. Goedicke, "Die Laufbahn des *Mtn*," *MDAIK*, Vol. 21 (1966), pp. 1-71, a very subtle interpretation of Metjen's various titles. It is also very useful for the photographs of almost all the inscriptions. They are added at the end as Tafeln I-IX.

K. B. Gödecken, *Eine Betrachtung der Inschriften des Meten im Rahmen der sozialen und rechtlichen Stellung von Privatleuten im ägyptischen Alten Reich* (Wiesbaden, 1976). A thorough and penetrating study of the inscriptions, with references to further literature.

P. Kaplony, *Die Inschriften der ägyptischen Frühzeit*, 2 vols. (Wiesbaden, 1963), mentioning many titles of the early period; see particularly Vol. 2, pp. 1201-18, and *Supplementband* (1964), pp. 44-46; see also his *Kleine Beiträge zu den Inschriften der ägyptischen Frühzeit* (Wiesbaden, 1966), pp. 225-30.

A. Roccati, *La Littérature historique sous l'ancien*

empire égyptien (Paris, 1982), pp. 83-88.

The English Translation

My English translation often reflects Gödecken's opinions of the nature of the various titles of Metjen. For the text, I have depended principally on the works of Schäfer and Sethe, together with the photographic plates of Goedicke. The bold-faced sectional letters are those used in Schäfer's text (see Figs. I.52-I.55). Fig. I.61 from Gödecken's work includes in its legends references to the printed texts for each of the walls and sections of the cult chamber of Metjen's tomb. I have included in the footnotes the various translations of Breasted, Maspero, Goedicke, and Gödecken because of the diverse interpretations and understanding of this difficult document.

Notes to the Introduction of Document I.2

1. Breasted, *Ancient Records*, Vol. 1, p. 76.

2. This results from Breasted's misidentifying the Crocodile-District (or Nome) with the Fayyum, when it should be identified with the Dendera District. But Metjen did indeed hold a title (apparently inherited from his father) of Palace-governor of the Towns of the Southern Lake (i.e. the Fayyum), as is evident in the document below (D, line 10). By the way, the reference to the eastern part of the Crocodile-District (*ibid.*, E, line 11) is in a title that apparently belongs to the addressee of a royal document rather than to Metjen. Notice also that Breasted recounts the offices listed in what I have called Royal Document V below as if they were successively acquired by Metjen.

3. Gödecken, *Eine Betrachtung*, pp. 69-70.

Document I.2

The "Biography" of Metjen: Inscriptions from his Tomb

A   Magnate of the Ten of Upper Egypt,[1] Palace-governor, Metjen.
B   Magnate.....(of the Ten of Upper Egypt?), Palace-governor of the Great Estate of the towns of Sahu *(Sᵓḥw)*,[2] Palace-governor of Hutihet *(Ḥwt-iḥt)*,[3] Palace-governor of.....

[Royal Document III][4]

C   /1/ [To] the [Land-] Administrator, District-governor, Overseer of the [District-] Commission in the Anubis-District (i.e. the 17th nome of Upper Egypt), and Overseer of the Sinu *(snw* or *sinw)*.[5]

    /2/ [Regarding] 4 arouras of arable land in the place [named] Basahu *(Bᵓ-sᵓ-ḥw)* in the Fish-District[6] (i.e. the 16th nome of Lower Egypt), with all the [attached] people (i.e. field-workers). [This estate is the concern of] the estate-decree [addressed or pertaining to][7] the Scribe of the Provisionbureau [and its beginning is] "Behold, Give [it] to the single son (Metjen) [etc.]. Execute the royal estate-decree, for he has the [validating] document, /3/ which has been provided to him [by his father] in his lifetime."[8]

[Royal Document IV][9]
[To] the Overseer of the [District-]Commission in the   Neith-District and the West-District (i.e. the 4th

and 3rd nomes of Lower Egypt).

/4/ There shall be provided for him (i.e. Metjen) 12 "Metjen-Foundations" in the Neith-, Desert-Bull-, and Haunch-Districts (i.e. the 4th, 6th, and 2nd nomes of Lower Egypt)[10] and their yield to him at the [Provision-]Hall, /5/ [for] there has been conveyed to him in return for compensation 200 arouras of arable land by many of the king's people *(nswtyw)*, /6/ and the Columned Hall shall provide 100 rations of bread daily from the Ka-Estate (or Mortuary Temple) of the king's mother Nimaathapi, /7/ a house 200 cubits long, 200 cubits wide, built and provided with good wood, with a very large pond made there, and planted with figs and vines. /8/ The inscription here corresponds to a royal document. Their names accordingly correspond to [those in] the royal document. /9/ Let trees (or flowers) and a great number of vines be planted so that a great amount of wine can be made therefrom. /10/ Let the vineyard made for him be arable land 10 plus 2 arouras in area[11] and within the walls [of the estate], and planted with trees (or flowers). /11/ Iymers *('Iimrs)* [is] a "Metjen-Foundation" and Iatsebek *('I't-sbk)* [is] a "Metjen-Foundation".

[Royal Document V][12]

D   /1/There shall be conveyed to him (i.e. Metjen) the things of his father the Judge-Scribe (or Honorary Scribe) Anubisemankh, without barley and grain, or anything of the House, and with the [attached] people (i.e. field-workers) and small cattle, /2/ [namely,] that he be appointed at the head of (or over) the scribes of the Provisionbureau as the Administrator *(iry-iḫt)* of the Provisionbureau,[13] and /3/ that he be appointed Crier *(nḫt-ḫrw*--lit. "strong of voice") among the People of the Grindery (*or as later*, of Offerings),[14] /4/ [as] an Administrator of the Desert-Bull-District (i.e. the 6th or Xoite nome) who accompanies (*or* follows after) the Judge-Land-administrator (or Honorary Land-administrator) of that district. /5/ Let him take [the rank of] Judge-Crier (*or* Honorary Crier) and be appointed Overseer of all the Linen (*or* Flax) of the King. /6/ Let him be appointed as Estate-governor (*or* Palace-governor?) of the Towns of Per-Desu *(Pr-Dśw)* as the one having the staff (*or* in authority).[15] /7/ Let him be appointed Overseer of the People of Dep (part of Buto), /8/ being the Palace-governor of the Towns of Per-Mesedjaut *(Pr-Mśḏiwt)* and of the Towns of Per-Sepa *(Pr-Śpi)* as Administrator of the Neith-District (i.e. the 4th nome of Lower Egypt), /9/ the Governor of the Towns and Fields of the Mortuary Estate of Senet *(Śnt)* as the one having the staff (*or* in authority), /10/ the Estate-governor of the Town of Per-Shestjet *(Pr-śśṯt)*, and Palace-governor of the Towns of the Southern Lake (i.e. the Fayyum). /11/ Let one "Metjen-Foundation" be founded of that which his father Anubisemankh first gave him.

[Metjen's Titles][16]

E   /1/ Estate-governor (i.e. Palace-governor?) of the Town of Per-Desu, /2/ Estate-governor (i.e. Palace-governor?) of the Towns of Sahu, /3/ Palace-governor of the Towns of Per-Hesen *(Pr-Ḥśn)*, Administrator of the Harpoon-District (i.e. the 7th and/or 8th nome of Lower Egypt), /4/ Palace-governor of Sekhemu *(Sḥmw)*, Administrator of the Desert-Bull-District, /5/ Palace-governor of Dep, Administrator of the People of Dep, /6/ Palace-governor of the Estate of Mesdjawt,

Administrator of the Neith-District, /7/ Palace-governor of Shety *(šty)* (Two Hounds?), Administrator of the Fish-District (i.e. the nome of Mendes, that is the 16th of Lower Egypt), /8/ Palace-governor of the Heswer *(Ḥš-wr)* Canal, Governor of the Fields in the West-District and the Neith-District (i.e. the 3rd and 4th nomes of Lower Egypt), /9/ Palace-governor of Hutihet *(Ḥwt-iḫt)*, Administrator of the Desert,[17] Controller of the [wild-animal] Hunt (*or* Hunters), /10/ Governor of the Fields as one having the staff (i.e. in authority), Administrator of the Haunch-District (i.e. the 2nd nome of Lower Egypt).

[Royal Document I][18]
/11/ [To] District Governor (i.e. the nomarch), Administrator of the Land, and Overseer of the [District-] Commission in the Crocodile-District, Eastern Part (i.e. the nome of Denderah--the 6th of Upper Egypt.[19]

/12/ [Concerning] the Judge-leader (i.e. Honorary Leader) over the Grindery (*or as later*, over Offerings), the Palace-governor of the West- and Neith-Districts, and Controller of the Door of the West *(ꜥꜣ-tyw)* (*or* of the Mercenaries in the West), [Metjen].[20]

/13/ [The Content of the Decree.] There has been conveyed to him (i.e. Metjen) in return for compensation 200 arouras of arable land by many of the king's people *(nswtyw)*. /14/ He has given [for it] 50 arouras of arable land [once] belonging to his mother Nebsent, /15/ she having made a will thereof for her children; /16/ their shares were laid down according to the king's records everywhere.

[Royal Document II][21]

/17/ [To] the Governor of the Mortuary Foundation of the Property of King Huny in the Haunch District (i.e. the 2nd nome of Lower Egypt).

[Contents of the decree.] Let him (i.e. Metjen) with his son be given 12 arouras of arable land, /18/ with the [attached] people (i.e. field workers) and small cattle.

{Here I end the translation, omitting the remaining inscriptions of Schäfer's Sections F-N [see Figs. I.56-I.60], which consist largely of titles repetitious of those already mentioned and of offerings. For the notes to this document, see page 157.}

Notes to Document I.2

1. See Chap. 1, note 11. "Magnate of the Ten of Upper Egypt" *(Wr md šm^cw)* seems to be a general title of rank for Metjen, having few or no official duties attached to it. As given here, Palace-governor also seems to be a general title of rank; but notice that this title is joined to a number of specific estates and towns in the titles mentioned for Metjen in the remainder of the document below. It clearly was a district (or nome) title in the early dynastic period (see P. Kaplony, *Die Inschriften*, Vol. 1, p. 434; Vol. 2, p. 1048, Anm. 1776, and Gödecken, *Eine Betrachtung*, p. 82).

2 Maspero, "La carrière administrative," p. 169, thinks that this was a kind of feudal estate, acquired by Metjen after that of the estate of Desu (which we shall mention later). Both estates have plural town signs for a determinative, i.e. three of them. Still Maspero believes that each of the estates consisted of only one town.

3. Hutihet was to become the capital of the 3rd nome of Lower Egypt when that nome was formed. Metjen was the first to hold this title, but he also held (presumably earlier) the old title of "Administrator *(^cd-mr)* of Hutihet". He may have been the last one to hold that older title. See Gödecken, *Eine Betrachtung*, pp. 90-91, 145-46.

4. This is one of the royal decrees inserted in Metjen's inscriptions, the significance of which has been mentioned above in my Introduction. Gödecken, *Eine Betrachtung*, p. 11, calls it "Akte III" and translates it as follows:

(Adressat:) *ššm-t^j ḥ̣k^j.t* Vorsteher der

Aufträge im 17. o. ä. Gau, Vorsteher der
sjnw. (Dekrettext:) (Was angeht) den 16. u.
ä. Gau, Ort *Bȝ-sȝḥw*, 4 Aruren Feld, Leute
und alle Sachen, die enthalten sind in den
⌂-Verfügung ⟨an⟩ den Schreiber des
Versorgungsbüros: (Siehe!) 'Gib ⟨sie⟩ einem
einzigen Sohn!'-Veranlasse, dass die
⌂-Verfägung von ihm geholt werde,
(denn) er hat die Urkunde und er hat (zum
Amt?) verpflichtet (noch) zu seinen
Lebzeiten.

I note here that I have italicized Gödecken's phonetic
renderings of Egyptian words and changed her phonetic
"q" to "*ḳ*" (e.g., for Gödecken's "ḥq3" I have written "*ḥḳȝ*").
The passage has been translated twice before, by
Goedicke and Breasted. Goedicke, "Die Laufbahn des
Mṯn," pp. 64-65, translates this and the succeeding
decree (which, following Gödecken, I have called Royal
Document IV) as a single decree with interpretations of
titles that differ greatly from those later adopted by
Gödecken:

Dekret über Belehnung mit Amt und
Pfründe und Genehmigung zum Hausbau.

(Inschrift C)
Verwalter des Freilandes bei der
Landvergebung, Vorsteher der Teilung als
Vorsteher der Kolonisten aus dem
Kynopolitischen Distrikt von den 4 Aruren
Ackerland, Leuten und allen Sachen in
sȝḫt-Zr (?) im Mendetischen Distrikt.
Inhalt des Dekrets an den Schreiber
der Speisenverwaltung sowie (an) einen

Sohn. Veranlassen, dass das Königsdekret
zu ihm gebracht werde: berantwortet ist
ihm auf Lebenszeit (das Amt eines)
Vorstehers der Teilung im 4./5. und 3.
unterägyptischen Distrikt. Gegrändet
werden für ihn 12 *Mtn*-Gründungen im
4./5., 6. und 2. unterägyptischen Distrikt.

Der Diener des (Königshauses), der
die Speisenhalle unterhält, gebracht werde
ihm die Pacht von 200 Aruren Ackerland
von zahlreichen Königsleuten und eine
Belieferung der Werkhalle von 100
Rationen täglich von dem Stiftungsgut der
Königsmutter *Nj-m^ct-Hp*: ein Haus von
200 Ellen Länge, 200 Ellen Breite,
gemauert und ausgestattet, belegt mit
gutem Holz; angelegt werde ein sehr
grosser Teich darin, (sowie) Feigen und
Weinstöcke.

Die Inschrift hier entspricht einer
königlichen Urkunde, ihre Namen
entsprechen vollauf der königlichen
Urkunde. Gepflanzt werden Bäume und gar
viel Weinstöcke und gar viel Wein werde
davon gemacht. bertragen werde ihm ein
Weingarten von *1 ḥ³ + 2 t³* und 1 Arure
umwallt, bepflanzt mit Bäumen: das
Mtn-Gut von *'Ij-mr.s* und das *Mtn*-Gut von

T³t-.

Breasted did not cast these two passages as a decree
but translated them together as a simple historical
narrative (*Ancient Records*, Vol. 1, pp. 77-78):

Honors and Gifts

⌐Administrator,¬ nomarch, and overseer of commissions in the Anubis nome, overseer of ⌐-¬ of the Mendesian nome, ⌐--¬ 4 ⌐stat¬ of land, (with) people and everything..........There were founded for him the 12 towns of Shet-Methen *(št-Mtn)* in the Saitic nome, in the Xoite nome, and the Sekhemite nome....., There were conveyed to him as a reward 200 stat of lands by numerous royal ⌐--¬; a [mortuary] offering of 100 loaves every day from the mortuary temple of the mother of the king's children, Nemathap *(N-m'ᶜ.t-ḥ'p)*; a house 200 cubits long and 200 cubits wide, built and equipped; fine trees were set out, a very large lake was made therein, figs and vines were set out. It was recorded therein according to the king's writings; their names were according to the decree *(sr)* of the king's writings. Very plentiful trees and vines were set out, a great quantity of wine was made therein. A vineyard was made for him: 2,000 stat of land within the wall; trees were set out, ([in]) Imeres *(Yy-mrs)*, Sheret-Methen *(šr-Mtn)*, Yat-Sebek *(Ï't-Sbk)*, Shet-Methen *(št-Mtn)*.

For Breasted the half-brackets used above did not indicate additions to the text but rather uncertainties of translation. I have eliminated the line numbers and Breasted's notes and their references in the text.

5. The addressee here is the one to bear these titles, if indeed it is a correct conclusion ·that this is part of a royal decree. For the nature of these titles

and particularly that of Overseer of the [Land-] Commission *(mr-wpwt)* see Gödecken, *Eine Betrachtung*, pp. 53-71. Maspero, "La carrière administrative," p. 212, suggests *sounou* and translates it as "coureurs".

6. Kees identifies the deity of this district as the "First-of-the-Fish" in his *Ancient Egypt* (Phoenix ed., Chicago and London, 1977), p. 92. The hieroglyph of this district, the fish with the descending tail *(ḥ꜂)*, appears as a representation for marshy or swampy land. Hence we could perhaps translate the name of this district as the "Swampy-District". The principal town in this district was Mendes.

7. My added phrase suggests two possibilities, either the estate-decree was addressed to an unknown Scribe of a Provisionbureau or the decree concerned a specific Scribe of a Provisionbureau, who could then be Metjen's father Anubisemankh. Gödecken believes the latter to be true (see *Eine Betrachtung*, p. 35).

8. My understanding of this sentence differs from that of Gödecken. See her translation in note 4 above.

9. Gödecken labeled this as "Akte IV" and translated it as follows (*Eine Betrachtung*, p. 12):

(Adressat:) Vorsteher der Aufträge im 3. und 4. u. ä. Gau. (Dekrettext:) Man soll einrichten für ihn 12 "*Grg.t-Mṯn*" in den u. ä. Gauen vier, sechs und zwei und ihre "Belieferung" für ihn in die Speisehalle - (denn/indem) er hat gekauft (geholt) gegen Entgelt 200 Aruren Feld von/bei mehreren *nśwtjw* und die Grabvorhalle 'liefert' 100 Portionen Brot (und) aus dem *Ḳś*-Gut der Königsmutter *Nj-mꜣꜥt-Ḥꜥpj* täglich - (dazu) ein Haus / Anwesen, 200 Ellenlang, 200

Ellen breit, bedeckt mit gutem Holz, indem ein Teich darin angelegt ist, sehr gut, und mit Feigen und Weinstöcken angepflanzt. Es sei eine Urkunde darüber in der königlichen Akte und ihre Namen dazu in der königlichen Akte. Man pflanze die Bäume und Weinstöcke sehr ordentlich, damit daraus sehr guter Wein gemacht wird. Man mache für ihn einen Weingarten von 1 $\underline{h}^{j}$ und 2 t^{j} innerhalb der Mauer, bepflanzt mit Bäumen. *'Ij-mr.š* (ist ein) *"Grg.t-Mṯn"*, *iʲ.t-Šbk* (ist ein) *"Grg.t-Mṯn"*.

This should be compared with the translations made by Goedicke and Breasted given in note 4 above. In Goedicke's translation the title given here as belonging to the addressee of the decree was assigned to Metjen for his lifetime. In Breasted's translation, the part containing this title was omitted.

10. For an illuminating treatment of the various kinds of personal foundations in this period, see Gödecken, *Eine Betrachtung*, pp. 95-113. She distinguishes three kinds of "Metjen-Foundations". The first kind was put together from property that he had personal ownership of, property that he developed from the property that his mother left him, as is the case with the 12 "Metjen-Foundations" mentioned here in Royal Document IV. The second kind is that provided for him during a specified time he held some royal office, the foundation supplying a yield from the land or towns that were bound to the office which he occupied. Perhaps this kind of "Metjen-Foundation" is represented by Iymers and Iatsebek mentioned in C, line 11. A third kind is somewhat like the second but in fact

results from the property bound to the offices he inherited from his father and therefore retained during his lifetime. The last kind is illustrated in Royal Document V below.

11. All of the translations of the size of the land provided for the vineyard are incorrect in some respect. The correct figure is 1 $\underline{h}^{j}$ (= 10 $st^{j}wt$) + 2 $st^{j}wt$, making a total of 12 $st^{j}wt$, or in translation 12 arouras. For the correct rendering of areas, see Document I.1: Introduction, paragraph (9). See also Fig. I.50.

12. Gödecken does not number this document but notes that it is a new Decree-text (*Eine Betrachtung*, pp. 12-13):

> (Neuer Dekrettext:) Man soll ihm geben die Dinge des Vaters, des $s^{j}b$-$s\check{s}$ '$Inpw$-m-^{c}nh ohne it und $bd.t.$ irgendwelche Sachen des Hauses, (Feldarbeiter-)Leute und Kleinvieh! Indem man ..

> ... ihn einsetzt über die Schreiber des Versorgungsbüros als irj-iht des Versorgungsbüros.

> ... ihn einsetzt als $n\underline{h}t$-$\underline{h}rw$ unter den Leuten der Reibanlage (?), indem der $^{c}\underline{d}$-mr des 6. u. ä. Gaues hinter dem $s^{j}b$-$\underline{h}rj$-$\check{s}\underline{k}r$ des 6. u. ä. Gaues ist (nachfolgt), welcher das Amt eines $s^{j}b$-$n\underline{h}t$-$\underline{h}rw$ einnehemen wird!

> ... ihn einsetzt als Vorsteher aller Flachsarbeiten des Königs!

> ... ihn einsetzt als $\underline{h}\underline{k}^{j}$ von pr-$d\check{s}w$ als einer mit Amtsstab! ... ihn einsetzt als $^{c}\underline{d}$-mr der Leute von Dep, $\underline{h}\underline{k}^{j}$-$\underline{h}w.t$-$^{c}j.t$ von pr-$m\check{s}\underline{d}^{j}wt$ und pr-$\check{s}p^{j}$ und (gleichzeitig) $^{c}\underline{d}$-mr vom Neithgau, als $\underline{h}\underline{k}^{j}$ der Döfer und Äcker des

Totenstiftungsgutes der *Šn.t*, die unter dem
Amtsstab sind, als *ḥḳⁱ* von *pr-šštt* und als
ḥḳⁱ der Dörfer des Gutes vom Fajjum!
Man gründe ein "*Grg.t-Mṯn* von dem, was
ihm der Vater *Ỉnpw-m-ᶜnḫ* gegeben hat.
Goedicke had translated the same passage as follows
("Die Laufbahn des *Mṯn*," pp. 65-66):
Dekret für Übertragung des väterlichen
Besitzes

(Inschrift D)
Gegeben werde ihm das
Eigentum seines Vaters, des *Zⁱb-Zš*
Ỉnpw-m-ᶜnḫ, und nicht falle Weizen und
Emmer oder irgendwelche Sachen an das
Königshaus, oder Leute unde Kleinvieh.
Er erlasse Vorschriften der
Speisenverwaltung als Verantwortlicher
der Speisenverwaltung.
Er lege fest den Beuteanteil unter
den Militärkolonisten, die im Kataster des
6. unterägyptischen Distrikts sind, und
das-für-das-Opfer-des-verstorbenen-Königs-
Bestimmte der Leute des 6.
unterägyptischen Distrikts.
Er nehme die Beute des Königs in
Empfang.
Er bestimme ⟨als⟩ Vorsteher allen
Flachses (?) des Königs.
Er bestimme als Verwalter der
Gründungen des Königs der
(Königs)verwaltung im unterworfenen
(Gebiet).
Er bestimme im Gebiet von Dep (und

als) Verwalter des *msd'wt*-Landes der Königstotenstiftung und des Königsverwaltung und des Freilandes der Königsverwaltung im 4./5. unterägyptischen Distrikt (und als) Verwalter der Liegenschaften und des unterworfenen Freilandes der Grenzverwaltung (und als) Verwalter der Liegenschaften der Deltaresidenz der Königsverwaltung (und als) Verwalter der Liegenschaften der Königstotenstiftung der südlichen Residenz.

Mtn gründe ein Gut von dem, was ihm sein Vater *Inpw-m-Cnh* gegeben hat.

Breasted's translation again was narrative in form since he did not consider the inscriptions to be part of or paraphrasing decrees (*Ancient Records of Egypt*, Vol. 1, p. 77):

Death of Methen's Father

171. There were presented to him the things of his father, the judge and scribe Anubisemonekh; there was no grain or anything of the house, (⌈but⌉) there were people and small cattle.

Methen's Career

172. He was made chief scribe of the provision magazine, and overseer of the things of the provision magazine. He was made ⌈____⌉ becoming local governor of Xois (Ox-nome), and inferior field-judge of Xois. He was appointed ⌈_____⌉ judge, he was made overseer of all flax of the king,

he was made ruler of Southern Perked
(Pr-ḳd), and ⌐deputy⌐, he was made local
governor of the people of Dep, palace-ruler
of Miper (⌐My⌐-pr) and Persepa (Pr-spⁱ),
and local governor of the Saitic nome, ruler
of the stronghold of Sent (Snt), [deputy] of
nomes, ruler of Pershesthet (Pr-šsṯt), ruler
of the towns of the palace, of the Southern
Lake. Sheret-Methen (šrt-Mṯn) was
founded, [and the domain which] his father
Anubisemonekh presented to him.

I should remark that Maspero, "La carrière
administrative," p. 167, gives a translation of the first
part of this passage that is also in narrative form:

Le maitre-scribe Anoupoumânkhi lui
donna sur son bien les choses nécessaires à
sa vie, quand il n'avait encore ni blé, ni
orge, ni aucune autre chose, ni maison, ni
domestiques mâles et femelles, ni
troupeaux, ânes et porcs. Il fut mis
premièrement scribe de place
d'approvisionnement, directeur responsable
des biens d'une place d'approvisionnement.
Il fut mis crieur, taxateur des colons; puis,
étant détaché à la suite du curateur du
nome Xote et matre-chef des chaouiches du
nome Xote, il fut pris comme matre-crieur.
Il fut mis directeur de tout le lin du roi. Il
fut mis régent de Pidosou et eut le droit de
porter la canne de commandement.

13. I have followed Gödecken in translating this
paragraph, containing this and other titles, as if these
various offices were a part of Metjen's inheritance from
his father. If this is correct, they indeed did constitute

the "things of his father" mentioned in line 1. And, as I said in my introduction to this document, I believe that even though Metjen does not list "Scribe" as one of his titles in the various inscriptions devoted entirely to his titles, we almost certainly should assume that his father taught him the craft, knowing that he would take over his office of Administrator of the Provisionbureau, where presumably he would have to supervise the scribes.

14. The nature of this office was discussed at length by Maspero, "La carrière administrative," pp. 134-39. He concluded that the Crier is one who oversees operations of measurements and evaluation and reports the results to the scribes. We know of cases where the Crier is called a Crier of the Granary (see p. 120 above). Presumably his duties were not unlike Metjen's. It is of course possible that the title already entailed supervising offerings as it apparently did later or even that it was a title without any duties. Further on in the list we note that Metjen was to be appointed "Judge-Crier" (i.e. Honorary Crier?), which title is immediately followed by that of Overseer of all the Linen (or Flax) of the King. It seems likely that the title of Judge-Crier would not pass to him until he was ready to hand over the "things of his father" to his son. Or it could be that Breasted and Maspero were correct in simply reporting this list of offices as if they were offices successively acquired by Metjen. Where I have "People of the Grindery" Jonckheere, *Les médecins de l'Égypt pharaonique* (Brussels, 1958), pp. 117-18, reads *sinw grgt* and he seems to approve the translation "Médecin des colons". He also discusses the various other possibilities. I note that there is no other indication among the titles that Metjen was a physician.

15. I am not sure of the translation of the phrase *ḥr mḏ* in this context. Presumably it refers to Metjen's position as "having authority" and thus is specifying that this is not merely an income-producing position without official duties. Notice that the phrase is repeated in sect. D, line 9, and sect. E, line 10 below.

16. It will be noticed that the first ten lines of sect. E contain titles that are clearly those belonging to Metjen, and for the most part they are repeated in other sections of the inscriptions where they are followed by Metjen's name. With line 11 we find titles which appear to be those of the addressee of Royal Document I.

17. This title and the one succeeding it give us hints of the role that Metjen probably played in the Libyan border region.

18. Gödecken labels this document as "Akte I" and translates it as follows (*Eine Betrachtung*, p. 11):

> (Adressat:) *Ḥḳ³-sp³.t sšm-t³* Vorsteher der Aufträge im 6. u. ä. Gau, Ostteil. (Betrifft:) (Den) *s³b-ḫrj-sḳr, ḥḳ³-ḥw.t-ᶜ³t* im 3. und 4. u. ä. Gau, Leiter der *ᶜ³.tjw.* (Dekrettext:) Er hat gekauft (geholt) ⟨gegen⟩ Entgelt 200 Aruren Feld bei mehreren *nswtjw*. Er hat (dafür) gegeben die 50 Aruren Feld der Mutter *Nb.s*-Neith, da sie ein *imj.t-pr* darüber gemacht hat für die Kinder, indem ihre Anteile gelegt wurden (d. h. eingetragen wurden) zu den königlichen Akten eines jeden Büros.

Goedicke's earlier translation ("Die Laufbahn des *Mṯn*," pp. 66-67) includes the titles I have given in the preceding paragraph (often differently interpreted) and the texts of both Royal Documents I and II without

any break (thus not distinguishing Metjen's titles from
those of the addressees of both royal documents):

Dekret für die bertragung des mütterlichen
Besitzes

(Inschrift E)

Verwalter der Gründungen des
Königs der Königsverwaltung, Verwalter
der Lehen des oberägyptischen
Reichsheiligtums, Verwalter der
Liegenschaften der Grenzverwaltung im
Küstendistrikt, Verwalter der
Opferstiftungen der Königstotenstiftung im
Distrikt von Xois, Verwalter (der
Liegenschaften von) Dep der
Königstotenstiftung im Distrikt von Dep,
Verwalter des *msdꜣwt*-Landes der
Königstotenstiftung im Satischen Distrikt,
Verwalter (der Liegenschaften) der
Königstotenstiftung von *štwj* im
Mendetischen Distrikt, Verwalter (der
Liegenschaften des) Marschlandes der
Königstotenstiftung, Verwalter des
ꜥẖt-Besitzes der Königstotenstiftung im
West- und Satischen Distrikt, Verwalter
(der Liegenschaften der)
Königstotenstiftung von *Ḥwt-iẖt*, Leiter der
Jäger des Wüsten-distrikts, Verwalter des
ꜥẖt-Besitzes des unterworfenen Landes im
Mendetischen Distrikt, Verwalter des
Freilandes in der Landvergebung und
Vorsteher der Verteilung (für die Leute)
aus dem Distrikt von Dendera (im) Ostland,
Verwalter der Ablebensgabe der
Königstotenstiftung im West- und

Satischen Distrikt, Leiter der Söldner des Westens, dem die Pacht von 200 Aruren Ackerland durch viele Königsleute gebracht wird:

Gegeben werde ihm die 50 Aruren Ackerland der Mutter *Nbsnt*, indem sie ein Testament darüber machte fr die Kinder. Festgelegt werde ihr (pl.) Besitz durch Königsurkunde <in> allen Stellen.

Der Verwalter des Stiftungsgutes (Königs) *Nj-swtḥ* im Letopolitischen Distrikt gebe ihm 12 Aruren Ackerland mit seinen Kindern, sowie Leute und Vieh.

Breasted (like Goedicke later) has the two documents together as a single section, which he precedes by Metjen's titles (*Ancient Records of Egypt*, Vol. 1, pp. 78-79):

Methen's Offices

174. Ruler of Southern Perked *(Pr-ḳd)*; Ruler of Perwersah *(Pr-wr-sʾḫ)*; Ruler and local governor of the stronghold, Hesen *(Ḥsn)*; in the Harpoon nome; Palace-ruler and local governor in Sekhemu *(Sḫmw)* of Xois (Ox-nome); Palace-ruler and local governor in Dep (Buto); Palace-ruler and local governor in Miper *(ʿMyʾ-pr)*, of the Saite nome; Palace-ruler and local governor in Two hounds, of the Mendesian nome; Palace-ruler in Heswer *(Ḥs-wr)*; Ruler of fields in the west of the Saitic nome; Palace-ruler of the Cow stronghold; local governor in the desert, and master of the hunt; Ruler of fields,

[deputy] and local governor in the Sekhemite nome; Nomarch, [administrator], and deputy in the eastern Fayum; Field-judge, palace-ruler of the west of the Saitic nome, leader of ⌜___⌝.

Gifts of Land

175. There were conveyed to him, as a reward, 200 stat of land by the numerous royal ⌜___⌝.

There were conveyed to him 50 stat of land by (his) mother Nebsent (*Nb-snt*); she made a will thereof to (her) children; it was placed in their possession by the king's writings (in) every place.

Ruler of ⌜___⌝ of the Sekhemite nome. There were given to him 12 stat of land, with his children; there were people and small cattle.

As before, I have eliminated Breasted's inclusion of the line numbers and notes.

19. Presumably these titles were all held by a single person who was expected to see that the decree was executed. It is not clear why the chief official of the Denderah nome should be addressed in connection with this decree unless the original 50 arouras of Metjen's mother were located in that district.

20. This last title is further evidence of the role played by Metjen in the Libyan border area. The translation "Controller of the Door of the West" is found in Kees, *Ancient Egypt*, p. 185; for the alternate translation, see Goedicke's translation given in note 18.

21. This document was entitled "Akte II" by Gödecken, who translates it as follows (*Eine*

Betrachtung, p. 11):
>   (Adressat:) Leiter des Totenstiftungsgutes
>   des Königs Hwnj im 2. u. ä. Gau.
>   (Dekrettext:) Man gebe ihm 12 Aruren Feld
>   zusammen mit seinem Sohn, dazu Leute und
>   Kleinvieh.

Translations of it by Goedicke and Breasted are included in note 18.

Document I.3: Introduction

Inscriptions from the Tomb of Niankhsekhmet

This short document contained on a well-produced stela illustrates one of the ways in which the king could reward the successful career of one of his physicians (in fact any one of his competent courtiers), namely by providing the stone for and the decoration of the false door of the retainer's tomb. The ruler in question in this document is Sahure, the second king of the fifth dynasty, while the honored physician is Niankhsekhmet. The tomb is at Saqqara. It was excavated and first published by Mariette (see the literature below).

Note that Niankhsekhmet is designated as a Chief of Physicians. Jonckheere claims that we can detect three further ranks above this one in the Old Kingdom: Inspector of Physicians, Overseer of Physicians, and Controller of Physicians.[1] Hence it appears that when the false door was decorated Niankhsekhmet was on the lowest rung of the senior medical personnel. Jonckheere points out that Niankhsekhmet also bore the titles of Chief of Physicians of the Palace and Chief of Dentists of the Palace, that he had a brother named Anubishotep *(Inpw-ḥtp)* and two daughters named Hetepheres *(Ḥtp-ḥr-s̄)* and Mersankh *(Mr.s̄-ꜥnḫ)*, and that the names of his wife and sons were effaced.[2]

ANCIENT EGYPTIAN SCIENCE

Texts and Studies

For a bibliography on Niankhsekhmet's tomb, see the second edition of B. Porter and R. L. B. Moss, *Topographical Bibliography of Ancient Egyptian Hieroglyphic Texts, Reliefs, and Paintings*, Vol. 3, Part 2 (Oxford, 1978), pp. 482-83.

The texts which I have used for my translation are those of K. Sethe, *Urkunden des Alten Reichs*, Vol. 1, 2nd ed. (Leipzig, 1933) (=*Urkunden* I), pp. 38-40, and L. Borchardt, *Denkmäler des Alten Reiches (=Catalogue général des antiquités égyptiennes du Musée du Caire)*, Vol. 1 (Berlin, 1937), pp. 169-73 (and particularly pp. 172-73 for my extracts), and plate 39 (No. 1482).

I note also the early publication by A. Mariette, *Les mastabas de l'Ancien Empire*, edited by G. Maspero (Paris, 1882-89), pp. 203-05 (and especially pp. 204-05).

Consult the English translation of J. H. Breasted, *Ancient Records of Egypt*, Vol. 1 (New York, 1906), pp. 108-09, and the French translation of A. Roccati, *La Littérature historique sous l'ancien empire égyptien* (Paris, 1982), pp. 96-98.

See also P. Ghalioungui, *The House of Life: Per Ankh. Magic and Medical Science in Ancient Egypt* (Amsterdam, 1963; 2nd ed. 1973), plate 8; F. Jonckheere, *Les médecins de l'Égypte pharaonique* (Brussels, 1958), pp. 49-50; and P. Ghalioungui, *The Physicians of Pharaonic Egypt* (Cairo, 1983), pp. 19-20.

See further the still useful article of G. Maspero (with Mariette's text and a French translation), "De quelques termes d'architecture égyptienne," *PSBA*, Vol. 11 (1889), pp. 304-17.

The English Translation

In my translation I have kept a close eye on Breasted's translation, though I have several times departed from it. I have translated only the passages to the left and right of the false door which recount the exchanges between Niankhsekhmet and the king.

Notes to the Introduction of Document I.3

1. Jonckheere, *Les médecins*, p. 96.
2. *Ibid.*, pp. 49-50.

Document I.3

Inscriptions from the Tomb of Niankhsekhmet

[A. Inscriptions on the Left]

/1/ The Chief of Physicians Niankhsekhmet spoke before his majesty: "Would that your ka (k^j =double or vital force), which is beloved of Re, would command that there be given to [me] a false door of stone /2/ for the tomb of mine in the cemetery." Thereupon his majesty caused that there be brought for him two false doors[1] of limestone from Tura[2] /3/ to be set [initially] in the audience-hall of the House [called] "The White Crown of Sahure shines forth"[3] and that there be appointed for them the two chief-controllers of the crafts (i.e. the two high priests of Memphis?)[4] /4/ and w^cb-priests of the House of the Craftsmen so that the work might be done on them in the presence of the king himself. The stone cutting continued every day. That which was done on them was inspected in the court daily. His majesty had inscriptions (?)[5] placed on them and had them painted in lapis lazuli.[6]

[B. Inscriptions on the Right]

/1/ His majesty said to the Chief of Physicians Niankhsekhmet: "As these nostrils are healthy, as the gods love me, may you depart to the cemetery /2/ at a very old age as one honored." I gave adoration to the king greatly and worshiped every god for the sake of

Sahure, /3/ for he knows the desires of [his] entire Following. Now as for everything which goes forth from the mouth of his majesty (i.e. when he commands or expresses something), it immediately happens, /4/ for the god has given him knowledge of everything which is in the body [i.e. in the heart of anyone else][7] because he is more august than every god. If you love Re, you will worship every god for the sake of Sahure who did this [for me]. I was one honored by him; never did I do anything evil to any person.[8]

Notes to Document I.3

1.   According to Breasted, Erman has suggested that the text is concerned here with a double false door rather than with two false doors.   As P. Spencer, *The Egyptian Temple: A Lexicographical Study* (London, 1984), p. 223 (nn. 210, 211), notes, the forms of the determinatives in this and the succeeding writing of *rwt* in line 2 given by Sethe in his text were incorrectly drawn.   She gives the corrected forms on page 196.

2.   The limestone quarries opposite Memphis.

3.   This may well have been the name of one of Sahure's residences.   We are not to conclude that the false doors were to be set up there permanently but only while the work on them proceeded.   They were transported to Niankhsekhmet's tomb after their completion.

4.   The title *wr ḥrp ḥm(wt)*, translated here as "chief-controller of the crafts", is the title of the High Priest of Ptah at Memphis, but it may be that at this early period it simply meant "master-craftsman".   See R. O. Faulkner, *A Concise Dictionary of Middle Egyptian* (Oxford, 1962), p. 170.   M. S. Holmberg, *The God Ptah* (Lund and Copenhagen, 1946), pp. 51-55, translates it as "supreme leader of handicraft" and says (p. 53): "not until we come to texts from the fifth and sixth dynasties, all of which may be of a later date than the above cited text in the tomb of Niankhsekhmet, is the *wr ḥrp ḥmw.t*-title regularly associated with the designations 'the hem-priest of Ptah, the hem-priest of Sokaris'."   That he was also the High-Priest of Ptah cannot be surely affirmed before the sixth dynasty (*ibid.*, p. 54).   See also A. H. Gardiner, *Ancient Egyptian*

Onomastica Vol. 1 (Oxford, 1947), p. 38*, for other examples where architects were assisted by the two high priests of Memphis. This matches the existence of two high priests of Heliopolis (see Document I.1, n. 115). At any rate the king appointed two such master-craftsmen to this project of preparing the false doors along with a number of lesser craftsmen.

5. The word here questioned ("inscriptions") seems appropriate to the context, but I confess that I have not seen *ḫr-ᶜw* (followed by three circles) so translated. I have written *ᶜw* by assuming that the three circles are signs of the plural. See Gardiner, *Egyptian Grammar*, p. 490, sign N 33. Breasted suggested "color" as a possible translation, and Maspero, "De quelques termes," p. 309, wrote "sculptures (?)" following it by "dont la peinture est bleue".

6. Breasted and Maspero translated this as "blue". With the determinative of three circles (which Sethe's text omits but which are clearly present in Ghalioungui, *The House of Life*, pl. 8, and are given by Borchardt, *Denkmäler*, Vol. 1, p. 172), we would expect the rendering "lapis lazuli" (perhaps not the stone itself or its pigment but some blue pigment imitating it; see J. R. Harris, *Lexicographical Studies in Ancient Egyptian Minerals* [Berlin, 1961], pp. 148-49).

7. My bracketed phrase follows the remarks given by Breasted in *Ancient Records*, Vol. 1, p. 109, n. e. This is another way of saying that the king was sensitive to the desires of his followers.

8. This is a commonplace refrain in tomb biographies throughout Egyptian history, a refrain that becomes expanded as Spell 125 of the *Book of the Dead* (see Doc. II.3, Spell 125, S 2).

Document I.4: Introduction

Inscriptions from the Entrance to the Tomb of Washptah

The two inscriptions here translated give us an intimate picture of the relationship between a favorite official and the king, i.e. between the Architect, Judge, and Vizier Washptah and his king Neferirkare (the third king of the fifth dynasty). The most interesting feature of these extracts from the point of view of this volume is the reference to the sudden illness and death of Washptah in the course of his showing the king a new building for which he (Washptah) was responsible and the facts recorded in connection with this event, namely that the king summoned not only the chief of physicians but also a king's companion (or companions) and a lector-priest, and that he caused to be brought to the scene a chest of writings. We can guess with some confidence that this chest contained one or more medical papyri like those which we have included in Volume Three, Chapter Five, and that it perhaps also contained collections of spells which the lector-priest would have found useful if the illness turned out to be a case of possession. Alas, neither books nor attendants were of any use. Washptah's condition was hopeless, as the attendants informed the king, no doubt delivering their prognosis in the customary way, "an ailment not to be treated" (e.g. see Volume Three, Document V.1, case 8). Following this prognostication the king prayed mightily to Re promising to do everything for the deceased that he had desired. In fact he ordered the event recorded in writing in Washptah's tomb, demonstrating once more the favors that kings were wont to bestow on favorite officials in connection with their burials.

Texts and Studies

See the bibliography concerning Washptah's tomb in Porter and Moss, *Topographical Bibliography* Vol. 3, Part 2, p. 456. To this add P. Ghalioungui, *The Physicians of Pharaonic Egypt* (Cairo, 1983), pp. 73-74. The full titles of all the works cited below are given in the Introduction to Document I.3.

For the early publication of the tomb, see Mariette, *Mastabas*, pp. 267-71. The later texts, which I have used in my translation, are Sethe, *Urkunden* I (2nd ed.), pp. 40-45, and Borchardt, *Denkmäler*, Vol. 2, pp. 40-42, 129, 144, and plates 69, 70.

See Breasted's *Ancient Records*, Vol. 1, pp. 111-13, for an English translation and Roccati's *La Littérature historique*, pp. 108-111, for a French translation.

The English Translation

My English translation demands little comment except to note that the text is in poor shape. I have, of course, paid special attention to the translation by Breasted, as well as that of Roccati. I have included Breasted's headings since they are helpful to the reader. As usual my footnotes constitute a brief commentary on the text and my translation.

Document I.4

Inscriptions from the Entrance to the Tomb of Washptah

[Inscription A]
Erection of the Tomb by His Son
/1/ It was his eldest son, King's First Deputy[1] having the Authority over the Rekhyt-Folk,[2] Merneternesut, who made [this] for him (Washptah) when he was in his tomb in the cemetery.
The King Visits a New Building
/2/..... Neferirkare came to see the beauty of ....[3] /3/.... when his majesty came forth upon them.... /4/ His majesty caused that it be.... /5/....the royal children saw /6/ ....and they marveled greatly /7/ ....Then, lo, his majesty praised him (i.e. his architect Washptah) because of it.
Washptah's Sudden Illness
But his majesty saw him [Washptah] [attempting to?] kiss the ground [in obeisance] (i.e. to respond properly).[4] /8/ His majesty said ".... Do not kiss the ground (i.e. do not bend over so far?), but rather kiss my foot." When the royal children and the companions [of the King] [who] were in the court [heard this exchange], fear beyond everything (i.e. exceedingly great fear) was in their hearts.

[Inscription B]
He is Conveyed to Court and Dies

/1/ [His majesty had him taken] to rest in the residence. His majesty had the royal children, the companions [of the king], the lector-priest, and the chief of the physicians[5] go [into Washptah]. /2/ They said before his majesty....His majesty had brought for him (the sick Washptah) a chest of writings.[6] /3/ ....They said before his majesty that he (Washptah) was helpless.[7] [Then his majesty] prayed to Re on the [sacred?] lake ....exceedingly beyond everything. His majesty said that he would do everything according to [Washptah's] desire. Then he returned to the Residence. /5/ ....Never was it done for the likes of him before.[8] He prayed to Re every day /6 / ....in the heart of his majesty beyond anything (i.e. exceedingly). Then his majesty ordered [this event] put into writing on his (Washptah's) tomb.[9]

Notes to Document I.4

1. By the time of Washptah this had become a title of rank. See W. Helck, *Untersuchungen zu den Beamtentiteln des ägyptischen Alten Reiches* (Glückstadt / Hamburg/New York, 1954), p. 60.

2. For the *Rḥyt*-Folk, see Document I.1, n. 17.

3. This was obviously a reference to the building which Washptah was erecting for the king.

4. That is, Washptah, stricken with his illness, had not made the expected deferential response. In giving this sense to the passage, namely that Washptah did not acknowledge the king because he was stricken, I am following what I believe to be the sense of the passage. I suppose the king urges Washptah not to kiss the ground but rather his foot because that would be easier if the king were on a raised chair or throne. The state of the text is particularly bad here and an examination of Borchhardt's plates is not very fruitful.

5. As I pointed out in the introduction, it is of interest that the lector-priest was called in along with the chief of physicians so that there could be magical as well as medical help for the stricken architect.

6. No doubt this chest contained medical papyri. It could well be that both Documents V.1 and V.2, in Volume Three, were based on medical papyri that themselves went back to the Old Kingdom. At any rate, it appears certain that some such books were kept in the chest of writings made accessible to the physician at Washptah's bedside. A similar case can be made for the existence of some collection of spells, which would be useful to the lector-priest. Examples of each type of book to be consulted are evident in the

two parts of the Edwin Smith Papyrus given as Document V.1.

7. As I have suggested in the Introduction to this document, this is probably a reference to a negative diagnosis like that found occasionally in Document V.1.

8. This is a standard phrase that appears in tomb biographies throughout Egyptian history, to the effect that the king has treated the deceased in an exceptional way.

9. We have already noticed in the preceding biography that it was the custom of the king to assist in the preparation of the tombs of his favored officials. Here we are specifically told that this event was to be recorded in the deceased's tomb.

Document I.5: Introduction

Inscriptions from the Entrance of the Tomb of Senedjemib

These extracts from inscriptions that appear on Senedjemib's tomb at Giza near the Great Pyramid of Cheops (Khufu) present a warm picture of King Djedkare Issy (*or* Izezi), the penultimate king of the fifth dynasty, and of his talented architect and official Senedjemib. It will not surprise readers of Chapter One above that Senedjemib was one of the royal officials who was trained as a scribe and rose through a series of extremely important positions, not the least of which for our interest was his position as Overseer of the Scribes of the King's Records (*or* Writings). The first list of positions in Inscription A records his titles of Overseer of the Treasury, Overseer of the King's Palace, Overseer of the Armory, and Overseer of the Southern Estates. In the course of the events described in that inscription it is noted that Senedjemib was honored before the king as a Master of the Secret Things of the King and as a Favorite of the King. Then we are told that when the king was at the Place of Records (presumably to examine the plans drawn up by Senedjemib for some building or other), he sent a servant to fetch his official so that he might honor Senedjemib by having him anointed and washed in the presence of the king. The king's visit to the Place of Records reminds us that a large number of papyrus fragments (among the earliest discovered) date from the reign of Issy.[1]

This inscription contains a striking bit of evidence of the king's education and interest in writing. It is said here that the king wrote "with his own fingers in order to praise" Senedjemib. Presumably Issy learned to write as a boy along with other princes and sons of officials.

Another point of interest in these inscriptions is the inclusion among them of two royal letters (one in each inscription) addressed to Senedjemib, continuing a tradition that began at least as early as the time of Metjen (see Document I.2). It should be realized that royal letters (particularly if they confirmed the reception of honors bestowed by the king) represented high points in the lives of the officials. One of the most celebrated of such letters is that inscribed on the entrance of the tomb of the Overseer of Scouts or Caravan-leader Harkhuf in the cliffs across the river from Aswan, a letter written by King Pepi II (end of the sixth dynasty) when he first came to the throne as a boy. The letter expresses the young king's enthusiasm concerning the news that Harkhuf was bringing back a dancing pygmy (or dwarf) from his fourth voyage. It is worth quoting almost in full:[2]

> Seal of the king himself: Year of the second occurrence (=Year 4, *or perhaps* Year 2),[3] Month 3 of Akhet (i.e. the first season), Day 15. Decree of the king to the Sole Companion, Lector-priest, Overseer of Scouts, Harkhuf.
>
> I have taken notice of the matter of this letter of yours, which

you sent to the king at the palace to inform him that you had come down safely from Yam with the army that was with you. You said in this letter of yours that you have brought all kinds of great and good gifts, which Hathor, Lady of Immaau, has given to the *ka* of the King of Upper and Lower Egypt Neferkare, living forever unto eternity. You said in this letter of yours that you have brought a pygmy of the god's dances (i.e. one who dances) from the Land of the Horizon-dwellers like the pygmy brought back by the God's Seal-bearer Bawerded from Punt in the time of Issy. You have said to my majesty that no one like him (the pygmy) has ever been brought by anyone else who has visited Yam before. Truly you know how to do everything your lord desires and praises. Truly you spend days and nights planning and executing what your lord desires, praises, and commands. His majesty will provide you with many excellent honors for the benefit of the son of your son forever, so that all the people will say when they hear what [his] majesty has done for you: "Is there anything like what was done for the Sole Companion Harkhuf when he came down from Yam on account of the vigilance he showed in doing what his lord desired, praised, and commanded?" Come north to the [royal] Residence immediately. Hurry and bring with you this pygmy which you have brought back from the Land of the Horizon-dwellers, live, hale, and healthy, for the dances of the god, to rejoice and gladden the heart of the King of Upper and Lower Egypt Neferkare, living forever. When he (the pygmy) embarks on the ship with you, station trustworthy people around him on both sides of the ship to prevent him from falling into the water. When he lies down at night, have trustworthy people lie down around him in his tent and have them make an inspection ten times in the night. [His] majesty wishes to see this pygmy more than all the gifts (or tribute) from the Mine-Land and Punt. If you arrive at the Residence with this pygmy in tow, live, hale, and healthy, [his] majesty will do great things for you, more than was done for the God's Seal-bearer Bawerded in the days of Issy....

The first inscription (A) comes from the early period of Issy's reign, i.e. the fifth year (or less likely, the tenth year; see note 3 to the document below). And the second inscription (B) is dated from the end of the reign, i.e. the sixteenth occurrence [of the counting] (equal to Year 32 of the reign; see note 12 to the document below). If the transcriptions of these numbers are correct, and this seems likely, then we have in these two inscriptions evidence of the use of two different systems of numbering regnal years, one annual and the other biennial.

The second inscription (B), in its letter from the king, lists the following titles for Senedjemib: Chief Judge, Vizier, and Overseer of the Scribes of the King's Records (*or* Writings), all very important positions, showing us how far Senedjemib had advanced in the years between the dates of the composing of the two inscriptions. This second letter from the king has a remarkably sophisticated conclusion for a document arising from ca. 2356 B.C.: "O, Senedjemib, what you desire, you have, for assuredly knowledge is what you desire." This statement epitomizes the best attitude of a society confident in the power of its scribal activity and of the knowledge it would bring.

In a third inscription (Sethe's C), which I have not included in my translation below, Sebedjemib-Inty's son, Senedjem-Mehy, remarks that a royal command was issued to assemble the princes and other people (Sethe, *Urkunden* I, 2nd ed., Vol. 1, p. 64, line 1), no doubt for the purpose of endowing his father's tomb. He notes that the tomb was completed in one year and three months (*ibid.*, line 5). The king appointed mortuary priests (lit. "servants of the *ka*") for the endowment (*ibid.*, p. 65, line 3), and the endowment was put in writing and engraved on the tomb by sculptors (*ibid.*, line 4). All of this tells us once more what an important part writing played in the burial procedures of the Old Kingdom.

Texts and Studies

Porter and Moss, *Topographical Bibliography*, Vol. 3 (2nd ed.), pp. 85-87. Lepsius, *Denkmäler*, Abt. II, plate 76c-f (especially 76d and f) was the earliest publication of the tomb.

For my extracts I have used Sethe, *Urkunden* I (2nd ed.), pp. 59-63 (which includes the additional fragments found by G. A. Reisner and C. S. Fischer, "Preliminary Report on the Work of the Harvard-Boston Expedition in 1911-13," *Annales du Service des Antiquités de l'Égypte*, Vol. 13 [1914], pp. 227-52, and particularly p. 248, nos. 1 and 2).

Breasted, *Ancient Records*, Vol. 1, pp. 121-25, has an English translation based on the first edition of Sethe's *Urkunden* and hence without the additions discovered by Reisner and Fischer. See also the French translation of Roccati, *La Littérature historique*, pp. 122-28.

The English Translation

My English translation has been made from the revised text of Sethe's (see literature above) and thus is more extensive than Breasted's translation. Again observe that the headings are taken from either Breasted or Sethe (or both). The line numbers are those indicated in the text of Sethe.

Notes to the Introduction of Document I.5

1.   A. H. Gardiner, *Egypt of the Pharaohs* (Oxford, 1961), pp. 86-87.

2.   Sethe, *Urkunden* I (2nd ed.), pp. 128-31. Compare the translations of Breasted, *Ancient Records*, Vol. 1, pp. 160-61; Gardiner, *Egypt of the Pharaohs*, pp. 58-59; and M. Lichtheim, *Ancient Egyptian Literature*, Vol. 1 (Berkeley/Los Angeles/London, 1975), pp. 26-27.

3.   We have here the question of whether the Egyptian expression *rnpt-sp* 2 (perhaps to be read as *ḫ' t-sp* 2) at this time still meant "The second occurrence" of the counting of the cattle that took place biennially or whether it simply meant "Regnal year 2", the biennial counting having been abandoned or changed to an annual affair.   In this translation I prefer to assume that the biennial count is referred to.

Document I.5

Inscriptions from the Entrance of the Tomb of Senedjemib, Pet-named Inty[1]

[Inscription A]

/1/....Overseer of the Two Houses of Silver (i.e. the Treasury),[2] /2/ Overseer of the King's Palace, /3/ Overseer of the Armory, Overseer of Every Seat of the Residence, Overseer of the Southern Estates, [Senedjemib]. /4/ Year 5, Month 4, Day 3, today, under Issy,[3] /5/ when I was honored before Issy, more than anyone like me, as the Master of the Secret Things of the King [and] as a Favorite of His Majesty. /6/ What his majesty wished was done. Indeed, his majesty praised me for every project which his majesty commanded to be done. I did it according to the desire of his majesty. /7/ ...his majesty while he was in the Place of Records (or Writings).[4] When it came to pass /8/ that a servant was standing by the house and his majesty had ordered him to hasten....and his majesty caused that I be anointed with unguent /9/ and that my flesh be cleaned in the presence of his majesty.[5] Never before was the like done in the presence of the king for anybody, /10/ because of [my being] more noble, trustworthy, and loved before Issy than the likes of anybody.... His majesty himself wrote with his own fingers[6] in order to praise [me] /11/ because I did everything.... (he commanded?) well and excellently and according to the desire of his majesty concerning it.

Letter by the King's Own Hand[7]

/12/ Royal Command [to] the Chief Judge, Vizier, and Overseer of the Scribes of the King's Records (i.e. Writings), /13/ Overseer of All the Works of the King, Senedjemib. /14/ My majesty has seen this letter of yours which you have written to inform his majesty of everything you have done....the writing (i.e. plan) /15/ for the building [called] "Beloved of Issy" which will be upon the lake of the palace.... Now you are rightly [named] Senedjemib (i.e. He Who Makes the Heart Rejoice), for can it not be said: "Lo, it is a thing (i.e. a building) /16/ which makes the heart of Issy rejoice?" His majesty causes the truth to be known immediately. For assuredly it happens that you /17/ say what Issy loves (i.e. desires) better than any noble who is in the land.... /18/ when indeed his majesty knows that every vessel (?) is for his good.....of the statement (i.e. plan) of the Overseer of All the Works of the King. /19/ It rejoices the heart of Issy very truly....

[Inscription B]

A Statement of the King to Senedjemib[8]

/1/ ....was brought to you a command of the king....[when] you said to his majesty that you would make a lake according to what was said in the palace.... /2/ when you said that you would .... Sed Festival[9], my majesty greatly liked these words of yours ....

A Further Letter from the King[10]

/7/ Royal Command [to] Chief Judge, Vizier, Overseer of All the Works of the King, /8/ Overseer of the Scribes of the King's Records (i.e. Writings), Senedjemib.

/9/ His majesty has seen that plan which you caused to be brought forth according to the understanding [reached] in the palace, [the plan] for the lake of the mansion Hutmehwasekh *(Ḥwt-mḥ-wsḥ)* [11] and /10/ for the Palace of Issy [called] "Nekhbet...." .....of the [Sed?] Festival; when you said to his majesty: "This will be done for you.... /11/ [the building or lake?] 1220 cubits [in length] and 220+.... cubits [in width] as was commanded of you in the palace.... /12/ Assuredly the god has made you a favorite of Issy.   His majesty knows that you are more skilled than the overseers of all the works /13/ produced in the whole land. I will do for you more than I have done for anybody. /14/ For I shall give you the strength unto eternity.... You will be made [forever?] Overseer of All the Works of the King. /15/ O, Senedjemib, what you desire (*or* love) you [already] have, for assuredly knowledge *(rḫt)* is what you desire (*or* love)."   /16/ Year[12] of the sixteenth occurrence [of the counting?], Month 4 of Shemu (i.e. the third season), Day 28.

{For the notes to this document, see page 199.}

Notes to Document I.5

1. Pet-name" is my translation of Egyptian *rn-nfr* (lit. "good name"). It is often a shortened name that contrasts with *rn-wr* ("great name"), which latter in this case is Senedjemib. *Wb.*, Vol. 2, p. 428, suggests that *rn-nfr* is equivalent to the rarer expression *rn-nds* ("small name"). For a full discussion of these various name forms, see H. Ranke, *Die ägyptischen Personennamen*, Vol. 2 (Glückstadt/Hamburg/New York, 1952), pp. 6-8. See also "Name,"*Lexikon der Ägyptologie*, Vol. 4, c. 322.

2. For this title, see A. H. Gardiner, *Ancient Egyptian Onomastica*, Vol. 1, p. 26" (and for the next title, see *ibid.*, p. 27").

3. As the text stands we have [glyph] (i.e. [glyph]) (=*rnpt 5*), which literally is "Year 5". If this is the correct reading, it surely looks as if the biennial system was not being employed. Of course it could simply be that the glyph ☉ (meaning "time" or "occurrence") has accidentally been omitted from the text. If so, the text should have been [glyph] (i.e. [glyph]). If this glyph was meant to be there, as it was in the later date discussed in note 12, the meaning would then be the "Year of the fifth occurrence" [of the counting]. Consequently this would imply that the date given here was "Year 10", as would be expected if the biennial count was being followed. See Document I.1: Introduction, notes 6 and 7.

4. My guess is that Senedjemib's description and plans of the building whose construction was agreed upon in the palace were deposited in the Place of Records, where the king went to study them.

5.   It was apparently a signal honor to be anointed and washed in the presence of the king.

6.   I have already mentioned the significance of this statement for estimating the king's education.

7.   This is Breasted's heading, which he took substantially from Sethe, and of course it is not in the document (nor indeed are any of the headings in my translations).

8.   This heading comes from Sethe's text.

9.   Senedjemib seems to have been entrusted with some part of the preparations for the king's Sed Festival (see Document I.1, n. 41). If this was to be celebrated in the thirtieth year of the king's reign, as it often was, then it means that the events described in this paragraph took place at least two years before the apparent end of Issy's reign (see note 12 below).

10.   Again I reproduce Sethe's heading.

11.   This is a sheer guess since I have not located any reference to this mansion.

12.   The date given here seems to be in the biennial system of dating and should be understood as the "Year of the sixteenth occurrence" [of the counting], which would accordingly be Year 32 of Issy's reign. Of course it is not impossible that the *rnpt sp* used by itself here simply means regnal year, which, if Sethe's reading of the number is correct, would then mean "Regnal year 16". There is one further complication. According to Sethe, Reisner believed "26" instead of "16" was a possible reading. In this case, if the biennial system was being employed, we would then have at least 52 years in Issy's reign, but there is no other evidence that he reigned so long. In fact, the latest year to which we have a reference (aside from the date here) is also the "year of the sixteenth time (*or*

occurrence)" found in one of the papyrus fragments mentioned in my introduction to this document (see Gardiner, *Egypt of the Pharaohs*, p. 435, n. 2), which, in the biennial system, would again be a reference to the Year 32. Needless to say, "Year 26" (interpreting the expression "26th occurrence" as simply meaning "Regnal year 26") would present no problem of falling outside of Issy's probable reign length of 32 years. On the whole, I prefer accepting the number "16" and referring it to a biennial system.

Document I.6: Introduction

Tales of Wonder at the Court of King Cheops (Khufu)

I have included as this document two from a series of at least five tales of magical acts performed by lector-priests. These tales are present in a single manuscript, the Westcar Papyrus (Papyrus 3033 of Berlin), which appears to date from the time of the Hyksos (ca. 1640-1532 B.C.). They were probably composed in the twelfth dynasty (1991-1783 B.C.). The form of the narrative is that of tales told by the sons of King Cheops (the second king of the fourth dynasty) to their father.

Of the five tales, the third and the fourth have been given here. The entire narrative part of the first tale is missing and only the end persists, but enough to show that it concerned a magical wonder supposedly performed in the third dynasty during the reign of King Djoser, the builder of the great complex of the step pyramid at Saqqara.

The second story, a tale of adultery, was laid in the reign of Djoser's predecessor, King Nebka. The magical act performed by the lector-priest named Webaoner was the manufacture of a wax crocodile seven fingers(?)[1] long, over which the lector-priest spoke magical words, so that when thrown in the water in which the adulterer was bathing it grew to life-size (seven cubits in length) and seized the offender, holding him for seven days until the lector-priest (accompanied by the king) told the crocodile to bring him forth. At this point the lector-priest picked up the crocodile and once more it became a crocodile of wax in his hand.

The third and fourth stories may be entitled "The Boating Party" and "The Deeds of the Magician Djedi". The third takes place in the time of King Sneferu, the father of Cheops and the first king of the fourth dynasty, while the fourth is laid in the reign of Cheops himself.

Toward the end of the fourth tale there is a reference (which I have not translated here) that provides a connecting link with the fifth tale. After the account of Djedi's magical acts of restoring the severed heads of two birds (a goose and a water fowl) and that of an ox, there is an omission, followed by a passage in which Djedi is asked by the king whether he knows the number of the sacred chambers of the sanctuary of Thoth. Djedi says that he does not but that he does know where that number may be found, namely in a chest of flint in a building or chamber in On (Heliopolis) called "Inventory". When the king then asks Djedi to fetch the chest for him, Djedi replies that he cannot. But, he says, the eldest of the three children who are in the womb of Ruddedet, the wife of a priest of Re, will be able to get it for him. The children in the pregnant woman's womb are declared to be the sons of Re, Lord of Sakhbu, and they are further said to be the future rulers of the land after the reigns of Cheops's son and grandson, the eldest serving first as the "Great Seer" (i.e. High Priest) of Heliopolis. This then is a fanciful, historical account of the origin of the first three kings of the fifth dynasty: Weserkaf, Sahure, and Neferirkare.

As I said earlier, this dynasty was particularly devoted to Re and the priests of Heliopolis must have exerted considerable influence on it. This story, then, telescopes the rest of the fourth dynasty into two reigns, those of Cheops's son (Chephren) and his grandson (Mycerinus), to be followed by those of the first three kings of the fifth dynasty.

The fifth and last story, which I have not included here, concerns the birth of the three children of Ruddedet and the assistance provided by the goddesses Isis, Nephthys, Meskhenet, and Heket as midwives. Re says to the goddesses and to Khnum, who accompanies them as a porter and the one who "gave health" to the bodies of each child as he was born: "Please go and deliver Ruddedet of the three children who are in her womb, those who will exercise this potent office (i.e. the kingship) in this entire land." One last point to be made in connection with this bit of fictional history is that it had Re as the father of the future kings. This was no doubt a rationalization of the fact that "Son of Re" occasionally appears as a title of the king in the fifth dynasty (see Document I.1, n. 24). In a way this prefigures the accounts by Hatshepsut and Amenhotep III in the eighteenth dynasty of the impregnation of their mothers by Amon-Re. I can mention finally that this last story is replete with magical tricks and devices.

The main reason I have included the third and fourth tales here is to indicate how strongly in the minds of literary artists (and presumably the people at large) the lector-priest was connected with magic. As I said in Chapter One, the title itself, *hry-hbt*, literally means "the one who carries the festival roll". Indeed the tomb reliefs often depict a lector-priest as one carrying a papyrus roll. He was primarily concerned with the magical spells and incantations uttered during the funeral and temple rites. One tomb of the Old Kingdom describes the role which the lector-priest was to play in the burial of the deceased: "Beloved of the King and of · Anubis is the lector-priest ...who shall perform for me [the deceased] the things beneficial to a blessed spirit according to that secret writing of the lector-priest's craft."[2] Furthermore, he is shown on occasion as "reciting incantations with upraised arms".[3] In view of these activities it should not surprise the reader that he was called in on medical cases where possession or the like was suspected, as we saw happen at the illness of Washptah recounted in Document I.4, or that the lector-priest was described as the discoverer of semi-magical spells,[4] or indeed that the author of these tales of the fantastic took him as the magician par excellence. We shall see in the next chapter how magic pervaded the whole religious fabric of Egyptian society (at least at its top), how Egyptians attempted to achieve afterlife by means that were fundamentally magical, and further how they were concerned with preserving the cosmic order by those means.

Texts and Studies

For the text, see A. Erman, *Die Märchen des Papyrus Westcar (Mittheilungen aus den orientalischen Sammlungen*, Hefte 5-6) (Berlin, 1890). This includes not only plates of the hieratic text, but also a hieroglyphic transcription of the text, a transcription of it in the Roman alphabet, and a German translation. The hieroglyphic transcription was also published by K. Sethe, *Ägyptische Lesestücke* (Leipzig, 1924; 2nd ed. 1928), pp. 26-36.

See also Sethe, *Erläuterungen zu den ägyptischen Lesestücken* (Leipzig, 1927), pp. 32-45.

Of the many translations of these tales available, that of M. Lichtheim, *Ancient Egyptian Literature*, Vol. 1 (Berkeley / Los Angeles / London, 1975), pp. 215-22, appeals to me the most because it is highly accurate and literary at the same time. Also useful is the translation of W. K. Simpson in *The Literature of Ancient Egypt*, new ed. (New Haven and London, 1973), pp. 15-30. For some of the extensive literature, see the introductions to the translations of Lichtheim and Simpson.

The English Translation

My English translation follows closely (but not literally) the translations of Simpson and Lichtheim. The plate and line numbers are those of Erman's edition.

Notes to the Introduction of Document I.6

1. The measure "fingers" is a guess, since it is not readable in the hieratic text. All that we know is that the wax crocodile was small enough to fit in the magician's hand. In Blackman's translation of A. Erman, *The Ancient Egyptians: A Sourcebook of their Writings*, Torchbook ed. (New York, 1966), p. 37, we find "spans" instead of "fingers", reflecting Erman's German translation in the original (*Die Märchen*, p. 8) where he wrote "sieben Spannen". But in the commentary in the same volume (p. 25) we find "7 [Zollen lang war?]", that is to say "7 fingers" rather than "7 spans".

2. Gardiner, *Ancient Egyptian Onomastica*, Vol. 1,

p. 55*.

      3. *Ibid.*, p. 56*.

      4. *Ibid.*, cites the London Medical Papyrus (8,12).

Document I.6

Tales of Wonder at the Court of King Cheops (Khufu)[1]

The Boating Party

/4,17/ Baufre stood up to speak and said: I shall let your majesty hear of a wonder produced in the time of your father Sneferu, justified (i.e. deceased), by the chief lector-priest (*ḥry-ḥbt* /4,20/ *ḥry-tp*) Djadjaemankh, [an event] that illuminates the past.....[2]

[One day King Sneferu wandered through] all [the rooms] of the palace, L.P.H.,[3] in search of [something refreshing (i.e. a diversion) without finding it. Thereupon he said:][4] "Go and bring me the chief lector-priest and scribe of books, Djadjaemankh." He was brought to him immediately. Then his majesty said: "I have [wandered through all the rooms] of the palace, L.P.H., in search of something /5,1/ refreshing without finding it." Then Djadjaemankh said: "May your majesty proceed to the lake of the palace, L.P.H., and equip a boat with [a crew of] all the beautiful girls from inside your palace. Then your majesty's heart will be refreshed by seeing them row up and down /5,5/ [the lake]. As you see the beautiful nestings of your lake and you see its beautiful fields and banks, your heart will be refreshed on account of it." [His majesty said:] "Indeed I shall go boating. Let there be brought to me twenty oars of ebony worked (i.e. decorated) with gold, their grips of sandal-wood (?) worked with electrum. Let there be brought to me twenty women /5,10/ with the most beautiful bodies, breasts, and braids who have not yet given birth (i.e., who are virgins). Also let there be brought to me twenty nets and let these nets be given to those women in place of their clothes." Everything was done as his majesty commanded.

Thereupon they rowed up and down. The heart of his majesty was happy on account of /5,15/ seeing them rowing. Then the one who was at the stroke-oar became entangled with her braids, and a fish-shaped pendant of new turquoise fell into the water. Then she stopped rowing and so the rowers on her side stopped rowing. His majesty said: "Why are you not rowing?" Then they said: "The stroke-rower /5,20/ has stopped rowing." So his majesty said to her: "Why are you not rowing?" She replied: "My fish-shaped pendant of new turquoise has fallen into the water." [Then his majesty said to her: "Row! I shall replace it for you."] Then she said: "I like my own better than one like it." Then his majesty said: "Go and bring me the chief lector-priest Djadjaemankh." and he was brought immediately. Then said /6,1/ his majesty: "Djadjaemankh, my brother. I did what you said. The heart of his majesty was refreshed by seeing them row. Then the fish-shaped pendant of new turquoise belonging to one of the lead-rowers fell into the water. So she stopped rowing, upsetting the rowers on her side. Then I said to her /6,5/ 'Why are you not rowing?' And she said to me: 'My fish-shaped pendant of new turquoise has fallen into the water.' So I said to her: 'Row! I shall replace it.' Then she said: 'I like my own better than one like it.'"

Then the chief lector-priest Djadjaemankh spoke his words of magic. Then he put one side of the lake's water on top of the other, and he found the fish-shaped pendant /6,10/ lying on a potsherd. Then he brought it and gave it to its owner. But now the water which had been 12 cubits deep in the middle[5] ended up as 24 cubits deep when folded back. So he spoke his words of magic and brought back the waters of the lake to their [former] position. His majesty spent the day in holiday with his entire palace, L.P.H. Then he rewarded the chief lector-priest /6,15/ Djadjaemankh with all good things.

Behold the wonderous act that took place in the time of your father, the King of Upper and Lower Egypt Sneferu, justified, by the chief lector-priest and scribe of books Djadjaemankh.[6]

His majesty, the King of Upper and Lower Egypt, Cheops, justified, said: "Go and give an offering of 1000 loaves of bread, 100 jugs of beer, an ox, two measures of incense to the majesty of the King of Upper and Lower Egypt Sneferu, justified. Further let there be given one loaf, one jug of beer, one measure of incense to the chief lector-priest and scribe of books Djadjaemankh, for I have seen his deed (*sp*) of knowledge (*or* skill: *rḫt*)."[7] Everything his majesty commanded was done.

The Deeds of the Magician Djedi

Then Hardedef, the son of the king, stood up to speak. He said: "[So far you have heard] about the knowledge (*rḫt*) of those who have passed away and [so] one does not know the things that are true from those that are false [concerning them].[8] [But there is a subject][9] of your majesty in your very own time /6,25/ whom you do not know [but who is a great magician]." His majesty said: "What is this, Hardedef, my son?" Then Prince Hardedef said: "There is a man /7,1/ whose name is Djedi. He resides in Djed-Sneferu, justified. He is a man 110 years old. He eats 500 loaves of bread and one half an oxen as his meat, and drinks 100 jugs of beer up to this very day. He knows how to join a severed head, and he knows how to make a lion /7,5/ follow behind him, even though its leash is on the ground. He knows the number of secret chambers of the Sanctuary of Thoth." Now his majesty, King of Upper and Lower Egypt Khufu, justified,[10] had spent a long time seeking the secret chambers of the Sanctuary of Thoth in order to make a copy for his tomb.[11]

Then his majesty said: "You yourself Hardedef, my son, bring him to me." Then ships were readied for Prince Hardedef. He traveled /7,10/ upstream to Djed-Sneferu, justified. Then after the ships were moored to the riverbank, he traveled by land, seated in a sedan chair of ebony, its poles being of *senedjem-*wood mounted with gold. When he reached Djedi, the sedan chair was set down. He (Hardedef) got up to greet him (Djedi) and found /7,15/ him lying on a mat on the threshold[12] of his house. One person beside his head was smearing him [with unguent?] and another was wiping his feet.

Then Prince Hardedef said: "Your condition is like one who has not reached old age (for old age is the state [lit. 'seat'] of dying, the state of [being ready for] burial, and the state of [being ready for] interment)--you who sleeps until dawn free of illness and without a hacking cough. Greetings /7,20/ to an honored man. I have come here commissioned by my father, Khufu, justified,[13] to summon you [to the court where] you will eat delicacies which the king gives, the food of those who are in his service. He will convey you in good time to your fathers (i.e. ancestors) who are in the necropolis."[14] Then Djedi said: "In peace! In peace! Hardedef, king's son, beloved of his father. May your father Khufu, justified,[15] praise you. May he advance /7,25/ your rank [to be] among the elders. May your ka[16] prevail over your enemy. May your ba[17] know the ways leading to the portal which conceals the weary-ones (i.e. the dead).[18] So greetings /8,1/ to a prince."

Then Prince Hardedef extended his hands to him, helped him stand up, and proceeded with him to the riverbank, while giving him his arm. Then Djedi said: "Let me have one of [those] transport barges *(k'k'w)* to transport for me my children[19] and my books." Then two ships with their crews were given to him. /8,5/ Djedi journeyed downstream in the ship in which Prince Hardedef was. After he arrived at the Residence, Prince Hardedef entered to report to the majesty of the King of Upper and Lower Egypt Khufu, justified.[20] Prince Hardedef then said: "O, sovereign, L.P.H., my lord, I have brought Djedi." Thereupon his majesty said: "Go and bring him to me." His majesty proceeded to the Forecourt (*or* Great Hall) of the /8,10/ palace, L.P.H. Djedi was ushered into him.

His majesty then said: "What is this, Djedi, I have not seen you [before]?" Djedi then said: "It is [only] he who is summoned who comes, O sovereign. I have been summoned, and, lo, I have come." His majesty then said: "Is it true, what they say, that you know how to join a severed head?" Djedi said: "Yes, I know how, O sovereign, L.P.H., my lord." /8,15/ Then his majesty said: "Let there be brought to me a prisoner who is in the prison that he may be executed." Then Djedi said: "But not to people (i.e. this may not be done to a human being), O sovereign, my lord, for surely the doing of such a thing to the august cattle (i.e. man) is forbidden." Then a goose was brought to him and his head was cut off. Then the goose was placed on the west side of the Forecourt, its head on the east /8,20/ side of the Forecourt. Thereupon Djedi spoke his words of magic and the goose stood and waddled, as did also his head. When the one part reached the other [and they became joined], the goose stood up cackling. Then he had a waterfowl[21] brought to him, and the same thing was done to it. Then his majesty caused an ox to be brought to him /8,25/ and his head was felled to the ground. Then Djedi spoke his words of magic and the ox arose[22]....

Notes to Document I.6

1. The title is approximately that given by Sethe in his edition.

2. The narrative is announced as if it were an historical account. Literally the fragment says: "illuminating its yesterday".

3. "L.P.H." stands for "Life, Prosperity, and Health" (or perhaps better, "May it live, prosper, and be in health"). By the time of the Middle Kingdom it became conventional to speak of the palace as a kind of royal entity and hence to append to it "L.P.H.". Then later the palace came to be more directly identified with the king. Thus "palace", when translating "*pr-ꜥꜣ* ", i.e. "pharaoh", became the designation of the king himself, perhaps for the first time in the reign of Amenhotep IV (i.e. Akhenaten) in the eighteenth dynasty and more often from the nineteenth dynasty onwards (see Gardiner, *Egyptian Grammar*, 3rd ed., p. 75). Notice also that throughout this document the epithet "justified" follows the mention of a king's name. This literally may be rendered "true of voice", with the probable meaning "acclaimed as right or true". It was an epithet applied to dead kings (and later, from the Middle Kingdom, to dead persons of any rank). As Gardiner (*ibid.*, pp. 50-51) says, it was "often practically equivalent to our 'deceased'. Originally applied to Osiris with reference to the occasion when his legal rights, being disputed by Seth, were vindicated before the divine tribunal in Heliopolis. The same epithet is also used in connexion with Horus as the 'triumphant' avenger of the wrongs done to Osiris". Indeed it was apparently Horus rather than Osiris who first bore the

epithet. For its applications to Horus and Osiris, and its various interpretations, see R. Anthes, "The Original Meaning of *m³ᶜ-ḫrw*," *Journal of Near Eastern Studies*, Vol. 13 (1954), pp. 21-51. Cf. J. G. Griffiths, *The Origins of Osiris and his Cult*, 2nd ed. (Leiden, 1980), pp. 178-80. The point to notice here in my translation is that the epithet is applied not only to Kings Djoser, Nebka, and Sneferu, all of whom are already deceased when the tales are being told to King Cheops, but also to King Cheops himself, even though he is alive as the stories are being told. The reason for this apparent inconsistency seems to be that the author (or scribe) who was composing (or writing down) these tales lived long after all of these kings were dead and by his time it was conventional, when any dead king was mentioned, to describe him as "justified" regardless of the period depicted in the story.

4. The reconstructions in brackets are possible because of the narrative practice in these stories of having the speaker who has been engaged in some activity which the author has just recounted repeat aloud his action when he encounters the person to whom he is speaking. Notice that the phrase *st ḳbt*, which I have translated "something refreshing", literally means "a place of refreshment". In the context here it surely means that the king was seeking some sort of diversion.

5. Lichtheim prefers "across" to "in the middle".

6. Throughout the document these two titles are linked to guarantee that the person producing the magical deeds has the best possible credentials for such deeds.

7. Again notice the stress on *rḫt*, i.e. knowledge, learning, or skill, so admired in Egyptian society.

8.   The prince is emphasizing here the difficulty of determining the truth of past events when the participants are no longer alive. He offers in contrast examples of deeds in Cheops's time.

9.   So Lichtheim would restore the text of the lacuna.   The next bracketed phrase also comes from Lichtheim's translation.   Something like these restorations was no doubt in the original text.

10.   See note 3 for an explanation of why the term "justified" is used here even though Cheops is still alive in the narrative.

11.   The Egyptian term is *ꜣḫt*, meaning "horizon" or "tomb".   Lichtheim translates it as "temple", which is probably more specific than is intended in this place. Of course, in the time of Cheops, the interior burial chambers of the king's pyramid were not decorated or engraved, though the mortuary temple on the east side of the pyramid had some decoration.

12.   Lichtheim translated this as "forecourt of his house".

13.   See note 3.

14.   That is to say, the king will give a good burial to Djedi when his time comes.   This would have been a decisive argument to an Egyptian, namely, to be guaranteed a good burial among his ancestors.

15.   See note 3.

16.   That is, may your ka (vital force), which is in control after you are deceased, overcome opposition in the afterlife.   For the concept of the ka, see S. Morenz, *Egyptian Religion* (Ithaca, 1973), p. 170, and U. Schweitzer, *Das Wesen des Ka im Diesseits und Jenseits der alten Ägypter (Ägyptologische Forschungen*, Heft 19) (Glückstadt/Hamburg/New York, 1956).

17.   The ba as early as the Old Kingdom was

analogized as a bird in flight and later in the New Kingdom was depicted as a bird with a human head (and sometimes with human hands) which sat near the coffin of the deceased. It is usually translated as "soul", but not without ambiguity since by the time of this document the ba seems to have developed from a manifestation of the power of the deceased (as it was in the Old Kingdom) into a personified agent of the deceased. At any rate, it was thought to be able to fly back to the living world left by the deceased. The wish, then, in this passage is that Hardedef's ba may know the correct way to fly. See Morenz, *Egyptian Religion*, pp. 157-58, and, above all, L. V. Žabkar, *A Study of the Ba Concept in Ancient Egyptian Texts* (Chicago, 1968), particularly p. 116.

18. Blackman-Erman and Simpson would associate this portal with an individual, Blackman-Erman translating the phrase as "the portal of Him-that-hideth-weakness" who is identified as "a door-keeper in the underworld" and Simpson translating it as "the Portal of One Who Clothes the Weary One", whom he identifies in a note as the embalmer.

19. So the text says, but in the Blackman-Erman translation a note is added: "His pupils?". Simpson simply says in the text "students" instead of "children".

20. See note 3.

21. So Simpson translates $\underline{h}t$-$^{c}\!\jmath$. The Blackman-Erman translation has "duck" and Lichtheim "'long-leg'-bird" for it.

22. At this point in the text the scribe has omitted the account of how Djedi was able to make a lion follow him without a leash and only the very last words of that account are here added directly after the story of the severed ox's head.

Document I.7: Introduction

Scribal Immortality

As I have remarked in the first chapter, Egyptian scribes were unusually conscious of the significance and desirability of their profession. This document from the end of the nineteenth dynasty or a little later stresses that the scribe's writing was a more efficacious route to immortality than his building of tombs. His books are read and remembered long after his tombs and those of others have crumbled and are forgotten. In brief, "their names are [still] proclaimed on account of the books which they produced since they (the books) were good, and the memory of him who made them will last to the limits of eternity". The document goes on to cite the names of a number of sages whose fame was still present in the author's time: Hardedef, Imhotep, Nefry, Khety, Ptahemdjehuty, Khakheper[re]seneb, Ptahhotep, and Kaires (four of whom are pictured on the wall of a Ramesside tomb at Saqqara; see Fig. I.62).

Gardiner, the editor of this piece, has suggested that the rather skeptical tone of its author toward the efficacy of building tombs may well reflect the famous Song of the Harper that probably goes back to an original carved in a Middle Kingdom royal tomb:[1]

Song which is in the tomb of King Intef, the
justified, in front of the singer with the harp.
He is happy, this good prince!
Death is a kindly fate.

ANCIENT EGYPTIAN SCIENCE

A generation passes,
Another stays,
Since the time of the ancestors.
The gods who were before
        rest in their tombs,
Blessed nobles too are
        buried in their tombs.
(Yet) those who built tombs,
Their places are gone.
What has become of them?
I have heard the words of
        Imhotep and Hardedef,
Whose sayings are recited whole.
What of their places?
Their walls have crumbled,
Their places are gone,
As though they had never been!
None comes from there,
To tell of their state,
To tell of their needs,
To calm our hearts,
Until we go where they have gone!
Hence rejoice in your heart!
Forgetfulness profits you,
Follow your heart as long
        as you live!
Put myrrh on your head,
Dress in fine linen,
Anoint yourself with oils
        fit for a god.
Heap up your joys,
Let your heart not sink!
Follow your heart and your
        happiness,

Do your things on earth as
    your heart commands!
When there comes to you that
    day of mourning,
The Weary-hearted (i.e. Osiris)
    hears not their mourning.
Wailing saves no man from the pit!
Make holiday
Do not weary of it!
Lo, none is allowed to take his
    goods with him,
Lo, none who departs comes back
    again!

It was the mention of the sages Hardedef and Imhotep here that alerted Gardiner to the possibility that this was a source for our document.

This document is a part of a student's miscellany in Beatty Papyrus IV (Brit. Mus. 10684). According to its editor, it is "one of those miscellanies or collections of edifying writings which formed the staple of a Ramesside scribe's education".[2] Another section of this miscellany tells the student: "Be a scribe. It will save you from taxation and will protect you from all labours",[3] a theme stressed in our next document, which is concerned with the value of the profession in this world. This section goes on to compare the scribal profession to menial occupations, to the great benefit of the scribe's. Not only are the physical conditions of his work better than those of other occupations, since he is ordinarily in charge of those engaged in hard work, but the scribe may rise "step by step until he has reached (the position of) magistrate".[4]

Another motive for assuming the scribal calling to set beside those already mentioned is the contribution that writing makes to the furtherance of knowledge. This is briefly alluded to in a well-known instruction-book, ostensibly (but not certainly) composed by a king of the First Intermediate Period (ca. 2075 B.C.) for his son Merikare:[5]

> Copy your fathers who were before you; (achievement?) is determined by knowing. See! Their words are made lasting in writing. Open (the writings) that you may read and emulate what is known. So the expert becomes the one who is instructed.

Text and Study

The Egyptian text and English translation of this document are included in A. H. Gardiner, *Hieratic Papyri in the British Museum. Third Series. Chester Beatty Gift*, 2 vols. (London, 1935). For the text see Vol. 2, plates 18-19. The translation occupies Vol. 1, pp. 38-39, and a discussion of Beatty Papyrus IV appears on pp. 28-44 of the same volume. See also the English translation given by John A. Wilson in J. Pritchard, ed., *Ancient Near Eastern Texts Relating to the Old Testament* (Princeton, 1950), pp. 431-32.

The English Translation

I have kept an eye on both of the earlier translations but have not followed them slavishly. The italicized beginnings of the paragraphs represent words that are rubricated. The references in parentheses are to Gardiner's text as noted above.

Notes to the Introduction of Document I.7

1.   Gardiner, *Hieratic Papyri...Third Series*, Vol. 1, p. 41, cites the well-known Song of the Harper in A. Erman's version as translated by A. M. Blackman, *The Literature of the Ancient Egyptians*, p. 133. I have given here the fine and sensitive translation of Lichtheim, *Ancient Egyptian Literature*, Vol. 1, pp. 196-97.

2.   Gardiner, *op. cit.*, p. 37. Compare the various texts edited by Gardiner, *Late-Egyptian Miscellanies* (Brussels, 1937), and translated and commented upon by Caminos, *Late-Egyptian Miscellanies* (London, 1954).

3.   Gardiner, *Hieratic Papyri....Third Series*, Vol. 1, p. 41. I have changed Gardiner's "thee" forms to "you" to make them conform with the procedure I have followed in translating this document.

4.   *Ibid.*

5.   T.G.H. James, *Pharaoh's People. Scenes from Life in Imperial Egypt* (Chicago and London, 1984), p. 25.

Document I.7

Scribal Immortality

(18, vers. 2,5) *Now then if you do these things, you are* skilled in [what is needed to produce] writings. As for knowledgeable scribes since the age of those who came after the gods--those who were able to foretell the future--their names have endured for eternity though they have completed their life-spans and all their relatives are forgotten.

They did not make for themselves pyramids of copper[1] and tombstones of iron.[2] They did not know how to leave heirs in the form of children [who would] pronounce their names. [Rather] they made for themselves heirs in the form of the writings and instruction-books they produced.

They gave to themselves [the papyrus-roll] as a lector-priest, the writing-board as a son-whom-he-loves, [the instruction-books] as their pyramids; /10/ the reed-pen was a child, and the back of a stone as a wife. They transformed the great and the humble into their children by being their [writing] supervisor.

Though [mortuary] doors and houses were made [for them], these are [now] in ruins, their *ka*-servants are [gone],[3] their tombstones are covered with dirt, and their tombs are forgotten. [But] their names are [still] proclaimed (*lit.* pronounced) on account of the books which they produced since they (the books) were good, and the memory of him who made them (i.e. the books) will last to the limits of eternity.

Be a scribe; put it in your heart that your name /19,1/ may fare similarly. A book is more effective [in keeping your name alive] than is a decorated tombstone or an established tomb-wall. These houses (i.e. chapels) and pyramids are made so that their names (i.e. those of the deceased) will be pronounced. Surely it is beneficial in the necropolis for a name to be on people's lips (*lit.* in the mouth of men).

A man has perished and his corpse has become dirt. All of his kindred have gone to ground (i.e. crumbled into dust). But it is writing which causes him to be remembered in the mouth of the reciter. More effective is a book than the builder's house (i.e. chapel?) or tombs in the West. It is better than an established estate or than a stela /5/ in a temple.

Is there anyone here like Hardedef?[4] Is there another like Imhotep?[5] No one has appeared among our kin like Nefry[6] and Khety,[7] that chief one of them. I recall to you (*lit.* I cause you to know) the name of Ptahemdjehuty[8] and of Khakheper[re]seneb.[9] Is there another like Ptahhotep[10] or similary Kaires?[11]

Those learned men who foretold what was to come. That which came forth from their mouths happened, [for] it is found as a pronouncement written in their (*lit.* his) books. The children of other people are given to them to be heirs like their own children. Though their magic [in practice] was concealed /10/ from the whole world, it can be read in an instruction-book. Though they are gone and their names forgotten, yet writing causes them to be remembered.

Notes to Document I.7

1. J. R. Harris, *Lexicographical Studies in Ancient Egyptian Minerals* (Berlin, 1961), pp. 50-62.

2. *Ibid.*, pp. 59-60. Though *bi᾽ n pt* may originally have been meteoric iron (i.e. "iron of heaven"), it became the general expression for iron however obtained.

3. That is to say, the mortuary services established in the will of the deceased had by this time petered out and the attendants ("the *ka*-servants") were no longer taking care of the deserted tomb, an inevitable eventuality sooner or later.

4. We have already seen that Hardedef was the son of Cheops who recounted the tale of the magician Djedi (see above, Document I.6). He was also considered to be the author of an instruction-book, of which a fragment is extant (see the English translation in Simpson, ed., *The Literature of Ancient Egypt*, p. 340).

5. Imhotep, the vizier and architect of King Djoser, was responsible for building the mortuary complex of the Step Pyramid at Saqqara. He was not only considered as a traditional sage and patron of scribes during the course of Egyptian history (see M. Weber, *Beiträge zur Kenntnis des Schrift- und Buchwesens der alten Ägypter* [Cologne, 1969], p. 43), but in the later period was deified and became a god of healing like Asclepius (see J. B. Hurry, *Imhotep, the Vizier and Physician of King Zoser and afterwards the Egyptian God of Medicine* [Oxford, 1926], passim, and particularly pp. 27-28 and 29-73).

6. Nefry is written here as *Nfrii*. But Gardiner

thinks that the first *i* may well be *t*. If so, perhaps the Neferti who results is the author of a well-known book, the *Prophecies of Neferti*, an account of future events supposedly told to King Sneferu but undoubtedly written in the reign of Amenemhet I (1991-1962 B.C.) since it is propaganda for that monarch. For a translation of the *Prophecies*, see Lichtheim, *Ancient Egyptian Literature*, Vol. 1, pp. 139-45.

7. Khety is read by Gardiner as Akhthoy, whom he believes to be not only the author of the *The Satire of the Trades* (Document I.8 below) but probably as well the author of *The Instruction-book of Amenemes I for his Son Sesostris I*, since a later section of Beatty Papyrus IV mentions an Akhthoy who is said to be the author of this instruction-book (see *Hieratic Papyri....Third Series*, Vol. 1, p. 43).

8. Ptahemdjehuty is not known. Gardiner suggests the possibility that it was an error for Djedihuty, mentioned in another papyrus, apparently as an ancient sage (*ibid.*, p. 40).

9. Khakheperreseneb was, according to Gardiner (*ibid.*), "the native poetaster who, on a writing-board in the British Museum, bemoans the difficulty of finding new things to say".

10. This is apparently the author of the so-called *Instruction-book of Ptahhotep*, a work of which the oldest copy (the Papyrus Prisse) dates from the Middle Kingdom. It has been much studied and often translated (see Lichtheim, *Ancient Egyptian Literature*, Vol. 1, pp. 61-80).

11. Kaires was a sage whose work is not extant. See Fig. I.62, where he is pictured along with other famous men.

Document I.8: Introduction

The Satire of the Trades

The tone of praise for scribal life in this document is more worldly than that found in the preceding document. The setting for this instruction-book, which was composed by one Dua-Khety (*or perhaps*, Khety, son of Duauf), is a boat plying upstream to the Royal Residence, where the author's son Pepy is to be enrolled in the writing-school. Composed in the Middle Kingdom, the document has two purposes: (1) to "sell" the scribal profession to the young Pepy (and presumably to all of the readers of the work) by comparing it very favorably with other callings, and (2) to offer the boy the usual advice concerning manners and conduct found in many instruction-books. It is quite evident that the father and son are not themselves of the "upper class", which in the Old Kingdom probably supplied the overwhelming majority of students to scribal schools, for otherwise the father would scarcely have compared the scribal profession with so many menial professions like those of washermen, reed-cutters, cobblers, and the like. Furthermore, in the very first paragraph the author seems to be stressing that many of the students at the schools were the sons of the elite officials of the Residence. A similar remark was made (no doubt by another father to his son) later in Ramesside times:[1]

I have placed you at school (*t³-ᶜt sb³*)

> along with the children of dignitaries (*or* nobles; *srw*) in order to instruct you concerning this surpassing office (i.e. scribedom).

He goes on to give the usual advice as to how to get ahead:

> See! I shall tell you the way of the scribe in his [saying] "Early to your place! Write in front of your associates! Tidy (*lit.* put your hand on) your clothes and attend to your sandals!" You bring your papyrus roll daily with good intention. Do not be idle. They [say: recite diligently the tables like?] "Three plus three" .... You will make your calculations quickly .... Write with your hand, recite with your mouth, and take advice. Be not weary, pass no day in idleness, or woe to your limbs (i.e. expect a beating). Fall in with the ways of your instructor and obey his teachings. Be a scribe!

Many other Ramesside documents offer similar advice, and still others indicate to us that often the advice was not taken, as the students were reported to be inattentive or spending their time carousing.[2] The same Ramesside documents also follow *The Satire of the Trades* in comparing the scribal calling favorably to other trades.[3]

Texts and Studies

For the text of *The Satire of the Trades*, see

especially H. Brunner, *Die Lehre des Cheti, Sohnes des Duauf (Ägyptologische Forschungen*, 13) (Glückstadt and Hamburg, 1944), and W. Helck, *Die Lehre des Dwꜣ-Ḫtjj* (Wiesbaden, 1970). Both have extensive notes and German translations.

The three most recent English translations are worth perusing: those of J. Wilson in J. B. Pritchard, *Ancient Near Eastern Texts Relating to the Old Testament* (Princeton, 1950), pp. 432-34; W. K. Simpson, in *The Literature of Ancient Egypt* (New Haven and London, 1973), pp. 329-36; and M. Lichtheim, *Ancient Egyptian Literature*, Vol. 1 (Berkeley/Los Angeles/London, 1975), pp. 184-92. Lichtheim cites earlier translations and several key works of commentary.

English Translation

The two German and three English translations mentioned above have all proved useful to me in making my own translation. On the whole I have followed Helck's text closely. The use of italics at the beginning of some of the paragraphs represents rubricated phrases.

Notes to the Introduction of Document I.8

1. Gardiner, *Late-Egyptian Miscellanies*, pp. 68-69. Cf. Caminos, *Late-Egyptian Miscellanies*, pp. 262-63.
2. Gardiner, *ibid.*, pp. 3-4, 23-24, 36-37, 47-48, 59-60, 64-65, 65-66, 83, 101, 102, 106-07; Caminos, *ibid.*, pp. 13, 83, 131-32, 182, 231-32, 247, 250-51, 315-16,

377-78, 381-82, 395-96.
        3.   Gardiner, *ibid.*, pp. 44-45, 60-61, 64-65, 83,
84-85, 103-04, 107-09; Caminos, *ibid.*, pp. 169, 235, 247,
315-16, 317-18, 384-85, 400-02.

Document I.8

The Satire of the Trades

Beginning of the Instruction-book which a man from Sile named Dua-Khety[1] made for his son named Pepy when he was traveling upstream to the Residence to put him into writing-school *(pr sbʲ nt sšw)* among the sons of the officials belonging to (*or* of the elite of) the Residence.[2]

Then he said to him: I have seen beatings [applied to laborers]. Set your heart on books. I have observed those who were taken off for [forced] labors (i.e. the corvée). There is nothing better than books. It (i.e. the profession of writing) is like a boat in water (i.e., it keeps one safe from the dangerous or uncomfortable depths ever present in other professions).

Read then the end of the *Kemyt*-Book[3] where you will find this sentence: "As for a scribe in any position in the Residence City, he will not be poor in it (i.e., he will be well-off in such a position)." For he fulfills the need of another man and [hence] he will not go forth [dis]contented (i.e. unrewarded).[4] I do not see [another] office of which this statement could be made.

I shall cause you to love writing more than your mother. I shall cause its beauty to come before you. For it is the greatest of all professions. There is none like it in this land. When he (i.e. the young scribe) grows sturdy but still is a child he is hailed [with respect] and sent to perform missions. On returning, he is begowned [like an adult].

I have never seen a sculptor [acting as] an envoy, nor a goldsmith sent [on a mission]. But I have seen a smith at work before his furnace door, his fingers like [the claws of] crocodiles. He stinks more than fish roe....

{Then follows a description of sixteen trades with their difficulties and hardships described, presumably for a comparison with the less physically demanding profession of the scribe: carpenter, jewel-maker, barber, reed-cutter, potter, mason, gardener, farmhand, weaver, arrow-maker, courier, furnace-tender, cobbler, washerman, bird-catcher, and fisherman.}

Behold, there is no profession free of a boss except [that of] a scribe; he is the boss.

If you know writing, it will be better for you than [it is] in the professions which I have set out before you.... Behold what I do [for you] when traveling upstream to the Residence. Behold I do it for the love of you. Advantageous to you is a day in school (*lit.* House of Instruction). Its works last forever [like?] a mountain....

Let me speak to you of other matters which you should know...[5]

Behold I have set you on the way of god. The fortune (i.e. the Goddess Renenet)[6] of a scribe is on his shoulder from the day of his birth. [By this] he reaches the Halls of Magistrates, which the people have made. Behold there is no scribe who lacks food and provisions from the King's Palace, L.P.H. The destiny (*lit.* The Goddess Meskhenet)[7] allotted to the scribe promotes him before the Magistrates. Praise god for your father and your mother who set you on the way of life. This is what I set before you and the children of your children.

It (i.e. this work) has come to an end in peace (i.e., it has come to a happy conclusion).

Notes to Document I.8

1.   Note that Brunner's earlier text of this work used the reading of three manuscripts to give the names as Khety, son of Duauf, while Helck in his later edition followed Seibert in adopting the reading given in two manuscripts: Dua-Khety.

2.   See Weber, *Beiträge zur Kenntnis des Schrift- und Buchwesens*, pp. 92-93, where he notes that the relative exclusiveness of the schools in the Old Kingdom began to break down by the time of this document and seems to have disappeared in the New Kingdom. It seems to have returned in the Late Period, when a reformer of the House of Life notes he has staffed the Houses with "persons of rank, not a poor man's son among them" (see the text above note 31 in Chapter One). Cf. also the discussion given by Weber.

3.   The *Kemyt*-Book was an apparently popular instruction-book, of which many fragments remain (G. Posener, *Ostraca hiératiques littéraires de Deir el Medineh*, Vol. 2 [Cairo, 1951], Plates 1-25). T. G. H. James believes that the *Kemyt's* simple, prosaic text, written in vertical columns, played a role in the elementary teaching of scribes (*Pharaoh's People*, pp. 148-50).

4.   I have given a translation which embraces the meaning suggested for this passage by Lichtheim in her translation but not her exact words.

5.   The passages that follow, and which I have

omitted, include the kind of wisdom and advice found in many of the instruction-books, e.g. be respectful, cautious, dignified, accurate in delivering messages, truthful in what you say about your mother, restrained in the quantity of bread and beer you ingest, and so on.

6. Renenet ("She-Who-Nourishes") is a goddess personifying fate and fortune. See Hornung, *Conceptions of God in Ancient Egypt*, p. 281. The statement in our document means that a scribe's fate is fixed at the time of his birth.

7. Meskhenet is another goddess personifying destiny. She was one of the goddesses acting as a midwife at the birth of the three kings in the last story told in the Westcar Papyrus (see above, Document I.6: Introduction). In the birth-scenes at Hatshepsut's temple at Deir el-Bahri, Meskhenet makes a speech, ordaining many good things for Hatshepsut (see Sethe, *Urkunden* IV, p. 227).

Document I.9: Introduction

The Onomasticon of Amenope

In my general account of the House of Life in Chapter One above, I mentioned the encyclopedic name-list probably prepared at the very end of the twentieth dynasty by one Amenope, son of Amenope, "scribe of the sacred books in the House of Life". Following its editor, I have characterized it as a list of things that exist rather than as a dictionary or collection of glosses. The author himself makes this abundantly clear at the beginning of the treatise when he says that this instruction-book is for "learning all things that exist: what Ptah has created and what Thoth copied down". This was of course not a unique composition. Gardiner discussed and edited two further onomastica in his edition of Amenope's work. The first is the Ramesseum Onomasticon, which is a list probably from the thirteenth dynasty (i.e. ca. 1750 B.C.).[1] It contains the remains of a list that ought to have included 343 items but in fact has only 323 items, among which are names of liquids, oils, plants, birds, fish, quadrupeds, southern fortresses, cities of Upper Egypt (a list of twenty-nine that extends from Elephantine in the south to a little beyond Akhmin in the north), loaves or cakes, cereals, a butcher's list of parts of oxen (as sacrificial joints or parts), condiments, and fruits (or products of trees). To this list is added a supplement that contains varieties of cattle (the distinction being based on color). The second onomasticon is a very short piece found on a University College Writing-Board, which is to be dated about the twenty-first or twenty-second dynasty.[2] On the recto read:

> (1) I acquaint you with the occupations that are in a temple: guardian of the Treasury, guardian of the Granary, (2) maker of *bit*-loaves, baker, maker of *Ḳꞌw*-cakes(?), baker of *sꜥy(t)*-cakes, butcher, confectioner, (3) maker of *psn*-loaves, shaper of incense, basket-weaver (?), dyer of red cloth, (4) maker of rush mats (?), bouquet-maker, gardener, bearer of floral offerings....

On the verso we find:

> (1) I acquaint you with the work of a (wood-)carver *(gnwty?)* and initiate you into what he makes: chapel, (2) divine bark, carrying stands for gods, sanctuary, ..., doors, poles, poles (3) for uraei, statue in its chapel, beds, palanquins, footstools (4) (for the) feet, boxes,..., coffers, chests, receptacles, coffins (*the rest is lost*).

Much the earliest list of this kind is found on a writing-board of the fifth or sixth dynasty which contains (in those parts which are readable) the names of kings, gods, and cities.[3]

In fact, the listing of words, signs, and names for other purposes was widespread. For example, there are more than twelve lists of the parts of human bodies.[4]

Notice also the list of parts of ships found in the *Coffin Texts* (not included in my extracts in Doc. II.2; but see Spell 398 in the edition and translation mentioned there). Of interest likewise is the list of seventy-five names of Re appearing in the *Litany of Re* (see Document II.5), a list which reflects the varied mythological accounts surrounding the creator god, his passage at night, his activities, and his attributes.

I should stress that often lists of names are given with the express purpose of bringing into existence that which is named. Surely this is the purpose of the lists of offerings that appear on the walls of the tombs, the names of which were to be pronounced in the "invocation-offerings" there specified, and particularly the food offerings arranged before the deceased as he sits at an offering table in the stela above the false door in his tomb. We shall have occasion in Chapter Two to see how important for magical spells and acts (both those connected with funerary practices and those involved in ordinary human relations) was the pronouncing or writing of names.

This ancient view, that to name is to bring forth what is named, is reflected in the remarkable Memphite Theology (see Document II.9), where it is said that the gods of the Ennead and indeed everything were conceived in the heart of Ptah and came into being by spoken command. Even if this document was the product of the scribes of King Shabaka in the twenty-fifth dynasty rather than being of great antiquity as used to be assumed,[5] a similar kind of creation by the word appears in numerous other documents from all periods, e.g. in the *Book of the Divine Cow*, in the cosmogonic part of which Re brings into being by spoken command: Nut as the sky (i.e. the raising of Nut to become the sky), the celebrated Field of Offering and Field of Rushes, the Heh gods, which support the sky, and the stars themselves (see Document II.6).

Though the Onomasticon of Amenope (and works like it) are not dictionaries since they contain no definitions, there are evidences of some quite late dictionary-like lists of words. For example, we note the fragments of a hieroglyphic dictionary in the Papyrus Carlsberg No. VII (copied in the first century A.D. and probably composed not too long before that time).

On its first page it includes words that begin with the hieroglyph □ (=h), of which I give the first two along with the introduction:[6]

> Explanation of the employment of signs, explanation of the difficulties. Disclosure of the things hidden, explanation of the obscure passages.... by their noble protection.

> Explanation of what emanated from the Gods, the noble ancestors, the sacred traditions from the nomes of Upper and Lower Egypt ....(found on) a leather-roll in the temple of Osiris, the first of the Westerners, the great God, Lord of Abydos, in....

> I.e. An Ibis (hbw). I.e. "A heart descends", in accordance with what Re said about it: "It descended from the body." I.e. A Ba descends. I.e.... Everything is perceived[7] through him. It is a hjn, 5....? It is the

ancient one, who emerged from the box. It is the palette.... Everything in this land is perceived through the treatises and the utensils, which came into existence through him. It is his finger .... Thot[h], the chief of the marvels in the house of clothing, who regulates the entire land, the ...? comes into existence through him.

I.e. The Day *(hrw)*, I.e. Re in his rise in the morning, by means of whom everything is perceived. I.e. the Ennead.... The eye is called the Ennead. The sun-disk came into existence from the right eye of Re. It is the Vulture-Goddess who binds(?) the bows, and who binds.... It is Ta-tenen, the male one. The Uraeus came into existence from the right eye of Re; it is the crown of Lower Egypt who unites it with her body.

It is evident in this treatise that we have no ordinary dictionary but rather a mythological exposition, which shows in part how the mythological associations originated in punning or the use of words that sounded like those being discussed. Returning to the Onomasticon of Amenope, we can observe that it is not complete in its longest copy (G) but breaks off at the 610th item. It seems probable, in view of the additional items in the copy known as the Ramesseum fragments and in other such lists, that plants, fish, birds, and quadrupeds were included or were projected for inclusion.

One section of our document is particularly noteworthy, the list of towns in Egypt. The principal copy contains 80 place-names, of which I have included only a few of the more important to illustrate this category. This is surely one of the most useful extant lists of Egyptian towns and the editor in his commentary has made splendid use of it, integrating it into other lists of towns, such as that given in the Ramesseum Onomasticon mentioned above.[8] The table of towns which Gardiner included in his last volume, the one devoted to plates, is of great interest to the student of ancient Egyptian geography.

Text and Study

A. H. Gardiner, *Ancient Egyptian Onomastica*, 3 vols. (Oxford, 1947).

English Translation

I have followed Gardiner's translations of the names except in a few instances. Needless to say, I have omitted the long commentary by which Gardiner so expertly explicates the text, but the interested reader will certainly want to examine some of the long essays included therein. I have occasionally modified the modern spellings of the transliterations of the Arabic names of towns included in Section V (for example, I use Dendera instead of Denderah in No. 313). The item numbers given in brackets are those assigned by the editor, for there are no such numbers in the Egyptian text. When an "A" appears with a number this indicates that the item is not in the principal manuscript (G) but comes from one or more of the copies.

The reader interested in the town-list of Section V will want to consult the very useful sketch-maps included by the editor but which I have omitted here since I used so few of the town names. In this connection the reader will also find of use the maps in Baedecker's guide, *Egypt and the Sûdân*, as well as those in J. Baines and J. Málek, *Atlas of Ancient Egypt*, (Oxford, 1980).

I have included some of Gardiner's comments in the notes to the document without page references but always within quotation marks. The reader will readily locate them in Gardiner's text by turning to the item numbers to which they apply. If a quotation appears in a footnote without attribution, the source is Gardiner.

Notes to the Introduction of Document I.9

1. Gardiner, *Ancient Egyptian Onomastica*, Vol. 1, pp. 6-24.

2. *Ibid.*, pp. 64-68.

3. G. A. Reisner, "A Scribe's Tablet found by the Hearst Expedition at Giza," *ZÄS*, Vol. 48 (1911), pp. 113-14. Reisner dates it as fifth dynasty, but Grapow and Westendorf date it "6. Dynastie" in the *Handbuch der Orientalistik*, Abt. 1, Vol. 1, Part 2 (Leiden, 1970), p. 221.

4. H. Grapow, *Grundriss der Medizin der alten Ägypter*, Vol. 1: *Anatomie und Physiologie* (Berlin, 1934), p. 12, and G. Lefebvre, *Tableau des parties du corps humain mentionnées par les égyptiens*

(*Supplément aux Annales du Service des Antiquités*, 17) (Cairo, 1952).

     5.   See F. Junge, "Zur Fehldatierung des sog. Denkmals memphitischer Theologie oder Der Beitrag der ägyptischen Theologie zur Geistesgeschichte der Spätzeit," *MDAIK*, Vol. 29 (1973), pp. 195-204 and S. Morenz, *Egyptian Religion* (Ithaca, 1973), pp. 154-55. See the remarks reflecting the view that "das Hervorbringen ist die Konsequenz des Sprechens" in Weber, *Beiträge zur Kenntnis des Schrift- und Buchwesens der alten Ägypter*, pp. 68-70, and the rich collection of passages on the creating word from all periods of Egyptian history in J. Zandee, "Das Schöperwort im alten Ägypten," *Verbum: Essays on Some Aspects of the Religious Function of Words dedicated to Dr. H. W. Obbink* (*Rheno-Traiectina*, Vol. 6, 1964), pp. 33-66. I find reasonable the view of H. A. Schlögel, *Der Gott Tatenen* (Freiburg, Switz., and Göttingen, 1980), pp. 110-17, that the Memphite Theology had a more probable origin in the nineteenth dynasty. This concept of the creative word is treated quite thoroughly in Chapter Two below.

     6.   E. Iversen, *Papyrus Carlsberg Nr. VII: Fragments of a Hieroglyphic Dictionary* (Copenhagen, 1958), pp. 13-21. Iversen's general comment (p. 7) on the nature of this dictionary is of interest: "If, however, we consider the commentary, it will be seen that the first page contains 11 separate catch-words [introduced in the right margin by hieroglyphic signs, as is evident in Fig. I.63], the reading of which are given respectively *hꜣbw hrw hnm.t h hꜣb hmhm hn hmj hnw*. As it is obvious that these words have nothing in common except the fact that they all begin with *h* [*hnm.t* being no exception owing to the assimilation of *ḥ* by *ḥ*], it

would be most tempting to conclude that alphabetic considerations had determined their arrangement. Unfortunately, the condition of the second page does not permit us to draw any definite conclusions as to the arrangement of the signs there, as all the original readings of the catch-words except *kʲ* have been lost, and the phonetic value of several signs is ambiguous and doubtful. The sequence of the first readable signs of the page does not speak for an alphabetic arrangement but the four last ones...might probably be read as *kʲ* *kʲrj* *km*, and *km*." For the much longer sign-list (arranged in no discernible order) edited by F. Ll. Griffith, see *Two Hieroglyphic Papyri from Tanis* (London, 1889).

7. I have usually translated *rḫ* as "known" in this volume, but I let stand Iversen's "perceived" both times that he uses it.

8. See the neat summary of other kinds of geographic lists and inventories in Sauneron, *Les prêtres de l'ancienne Égypte*, pp. 144-50.

Document I.9

The Onomasticon of Amenope

I. *Introductory Heading*

Beginning of the teaching for clearing the mind, for instruction of the ignorant, and for learning all things that exist: what Ptah created, what Thoth copied down, heaven with its designs, earth and what is in it, what the mountains belch forth, what is watered by the flood, all things upon which Re has shone, all that is grown on the back of earth, excogitated by the scribe of the sacred books in the House of Life, Amenope, son of Amenope. He said:

II. *Sky, Water, Earth*

[1] sky [2] sun [3] moon [4] star [5] Orion [6] the Foreleg (i.e. the Great Bear or Big Dipper) [7] Cynocephalus Ape (a constellation) [8] the Strong one (a constellation) [9] the Hippopotamus (also a constellation) [10] storm-cloud, storm [11] tempest [12] dawn [13] darkness [14] sun, light *(šw)* [15] shade, shadow [16] sunlight *(kḥ)* [17] rays of the sun *(sty itn)* [17A] storm-cloud *(šnᶜ)* [18] dew [19] *ꜣwdt* (? meaning unknown) [20] snow (?) [21] *srmt* (meaning unknown, but perhaps something to do with a body of water) [22] primeval waters, Nile *(nw)* [23] flood (i.e. Nile) *(mtr)* [24] river, Nile *(itrw)* [25] sea *(ym)* [26] wave [27] swampy lake *(ḥnw)* [28] pond, lake *(š)* [29] well (in desert; *ḫnm(t)*) [30] *ḫnm(t)* (basin?) [31] *ḫnini* (some

sort of irrigation basin or canal?) [32] waters *(nwy(t))*
[33] pool *(brkt)* [34] frontier, front *or* southern part
[35] back *or* northern part [36] well *(šdt)* [37] cleft?
(for water) [38] *d'bb* (meaning unknown) [39] river
bank (?) [40] *šgr* (meaning unknown) [41] watercourse
[42] place for drawing water [43] runnel [44] flood
(wdnw) [45] *wg'(t)* (meaning unknown) [46] current
[47] water-hole [48] *db(w)* (meaning uncertain) [49]
shores, river-banks [50] *rn(w?)* (meaning doubtful) [51]
standing water? *(ishm* or *shm(t))* [52] island [53] fresh
land *(nhb)* ¹ [54] tired land *(tni)* [55] (normal)
agricultural land (*lit.* "high land"; *k'yt)* [56] mud, clay,
mud-flat [57] low-lying shoal (*lit.* "it comes in the
return of the year"?; *iw.f-n(*or *-m)-nri)* [58] woodland
[59] sand [60] new land [61] *pᶜt* (some kind of land)
[62] riparian land *(idb).*

   III. *Persons, Court, Offices, Occupations*
   [63] god *(ntr)* [64] goddess *(ntrt)* [65] (male)
spirit *('h) (or* Blessed Dead) [66] female spirit *('ht)* [67]
King *(nsw)* ² [68] Queen *(nsyt)* [69] King's Wife
(hmt-nsw) [70] King's Mother *(mwt-nsw)* [71] King's
Child *(msw-nsw)* [72] Crown-prince *(r-pᶜt* or *iry-pᶜt)*
[73] Vizier [74] Sole Friend (the commonest title of
courtiers) [75] Eldest King's Son [76], [77] Overseer of
the Hosts, (even) the Greatest Ones of the Courtiers (*or
possibly two separate titles:* Overseer of the Army *and*
the Great Ones of the Courtiers)³ [78] Dispatch-writer
of Horus, Mighty Bull (i.e. of the King) *(sš šᶜt n Hr k'
nht)* [79] Chief of Department of the Good God (i.e. of
the King) [80] First King's Herald of His Majesty [81]
Fan-bearer on the Right of the King [82] performing
excellent works for the Lord of the Two Lands (an
epithet not a title) [83] Superintendent of the

Chamberlains of the Victorious King [84] Chief of Bureau (Diwân) of his Lord [85] Royal Scribe within the Palace [86] the Vizier and Overseer of the Cities of Egypt[4] [87] General (*lit.* Overseer of a [Military] Expedition) [88] Scribe of the Infantry [89] Lieutenant Commander of the Army [90] Overseer of the Treasury of Silver and Gold [91] King's Envoy to Every Foreign Land [92] Overseer of cattle [93] Overseer of the Palace (lit. "King's House") [94] Overseer of Horses[5] [95] Lieutenant Commander of Chariotry [96] Charioteer [97] Chariot-warrior [98] Standard-bearer[6] [99] Chief (or Chiefs?) of the Scribe(s) Who Place(s) Offerings before All the Gods [100] Overseer (or Overseers?) of the Prophets of Upper and Lower Egypt [101] The Mayors of the Towns and Villages [102] the Great Controllers of His Majesty [103] in command of the secrets of the palace (less a title than an epithet) [104] at the head of the entire land (an epithet of viziers) [105] Deputy of the Fortress-Commander of the Sea [106] Intendant(s) of Foreign Lands of Syria and Cush [107] Scribe of Distribution [108] Scribe of Assemblage [109] Overseer of the River-mouths of the Hinterland [110] Chief taxing-master of the Entire Land [111] Major-domo of the ruler of Egypt [112] Chief of Scribes of the Mat (?) of the Great Court [113] Chief of the Record-keepers of the House of the Sea [114] Royal Scribe and Lector-priest as? (*or* of?) Horus[7] [115] Scribe of the House of Life, skilled in his profession [116] Lector-priest of the Royal Couch [117] First Prophet of Amun in Thebes [118] Greatest of Seers of Re-Atum (high priest of Heliopolis) [119] Greatest of Artificers of Him who is South of His Wall (i.e. of Ptah, title of the high priest of Memphis) [120] *Setem*-priest of Kindly of Face (i.e. Ptah, a second title of the high-priest of

Memphis) [121] Overseer of the Granaries of Upper and Lower Egypt [122] King's Butler in the Palace [123] Chamberlain of the Palace [124] Great Steward of the Lord of the Two Lands [125] Scribe Who Places Offerings before All the Gods[8] [126] Prophets (*lit.* "god's servants") [127] God's Fathers [128] (ordinary) Priests (*lit.* "pure or clean ones"; $w^c bw$) [129] Lector-priests [130] Temple scribe [131] Scribe of the God's Book (*or* Books) [132] Porter (*lit.* [Builder's] "Workman") [133] Elder of the Portal (*or* Forecourt)[9] [134] Hour-watcher, Astronomer [135] Bringer of Offerings [136] Bearer of the Wine-jar Stand [137] Maker of Runners(?) (*lit.* "a way of rushes?") [138] Milker (of cows) [139] Butcher [140] Preparer (*lit.* "turner over") of Tripe [141] Baker of $s^c y(t)$-cakes [142] Baker of rhs-cakes [143] Maker of *bit*-loaves [144] Maker of *psn*-loaves [145] Brewer [146] Baker *(rthty)* [147] Shaper of Incense [148] Cooker (*or* baker) of *trr* [149] Maker of Sweetmeats [150] Confectioner *(bnrty)* [151] Maker of Baskets of Date-cakes (?) [152] Herdsman [153] Milkman (*lit.* "carrier of milk-jug(s)") [154] Carpenter *(hmw)* [155] Sculptor *(gnwty?)* [156] Carpenter, shipbuilder *(mdhw)* [157] (Portrait) sculptor (*lit.* "He who makes to live"; $s^c nh(y)$) [158] Coppersmith [159] Goldsmith [160] Worker in Precious Stones [161] Maker of Faience [162] Purveyor of Precious Stones [163] King's Sandal-maker [164] Corselet-maker [165] Chariot-maker [166] Arrow-maker [167] Bow-maker [168] Maker of Necklaces (?) [169] Stone-worker (*lit.* "Wielder of the $b\check{s}^i$ -tool") [170] Bead-maker [171] Rope-maker [172] Fan-maker [173] Barber *(ss̆ⁱ)* [174] Barber *(h^c kw)* [175] Hairdresser (? *nbdy)* [176] Maker of....(?) *(irw tkt)* [177] Miner[10] [178] Quarryman (*lit.* "necropolis-man") [179] Demolisher [180] Draughtsman (*lit.* "the scribe of contours"; *sš ḳdy*) [181] Sculptor (in relief; *lit.* "wielder of the chisel"; *ṯỉy mḏỉt*) [182] Gypsum-worker [183] Bringer of Stone [184] Potter [185] Potter of *hin*-measures (i.e. of the measures containing about 1/2 litre) [186] Builder of Walls [187] Patcher(?) of Stonework [188] Medjay (here, desert police or troops) [189] hunter [190] diver [190A] Harpooners (of hippopotami) [191] Master of the ....(?) (*ḥry miỉt*) [192] Master of the Cowhouse [193] Doorkeeper [194] Guardian [195], [196] Measurer; land-administrator (?) (*ḥỉy n(?) rmnyw*) [11] [197] (Military) Herald[12] [198] an officer of some sort (*sk(ỉ)*) [199] Transport Officer (?) (*mškb*) [200] Policeman, Guard (*sᶜšỉ*) [201] Bearer of Weapons [202] *sw*(??) (meaning unknown) [203] Groom [204] Guardian of Crops [205] Sailor[13] [206] Pilot (*lit.* "he who is in the front") [207] Steersman [208] Bird-catcher [209] Fisherman [210] Trader, Merchant [211] Buyer(?) (*mhr*) [212] Seller [213] Female (?) Singer[14] [214], [215] Male and Female Musicians [216] ᶜ*wy* (?) (reading and meaning unknown) [217] Libyan Dancers [218] *kmr* (dancers of some kind) [219] *dpk* (or *dpg*) (dancers of some kind) [219A] Dancers (*ksks*) [220] Leader [221] Servants (*lit.* "hearers") [222] Porter of....(*kỉ(w))ty*.... [223] Clothes-porter [224] Vineyard-keeper[15] [225] Gardener [226] Tenant Farmers, Agricultural laborers (*iḫty* (ᶜ*ḫwty*)) [227] Vegetable-dealer(?) [228] Herdsman (repeated from No. 152 above) [229] Keeper of Cattle-pens.

IV. *Classes, Tribes, and Types of Human Beings*
[230] men (*or* man *rmṯ*) [231] patricians (*or* mankind; *pᶜt*) [232] plebeians (*or* mankind; *rḥyt*)[16] [233] sun-folk (*ḥmm(t)*) [234], [235] commander(s) of

troops (probably a single category but could be two)
[236] infantry [237] chariotry [238] *Tmḥw*-people (i.e.
Libyans)[17] [239] *Tḥnw*-people (Libyan people to the
west of the N. W. corner of the Delta?) [240]
Meswesh (Libyan of some sort) [241] Libu (Libyan, i.e.
North African land and people).... [243] Keshkesh (one
of the peoples of the Hittite confederacy at Kadesh....
[245] Khatti (the land of the Hittites) .... [250]
Carchemish (the well-known city on the Upper
Euphrates).... [252] Kadesh (on the Orontes).... [257]
Byblus.... [260] Nahrin (the country near and mainly to
the east of the Euphrates).... [262] Ascalon (on the coast
N. of Gaza).... [264] Gaza [265] Isr (Assyria or, perhaps
less probably, Asher) .... [268] Sherden (a Mediterranean
people, whose identity is much discussed) [269] Tjekker
(one of the Sea Peoples who attacked Syria and Egypt
in the reign of Ramesses III) [270] Pelesti, Philistines....
[276] *Ḥ'(i)w-nbw(t)* (Mediterranean islanders or perhaps
occasionally the islands themselves).... [286] Sangar
(quite probably Babylonia).... [294] Begrek (an unknown
locality) [295] man *(s)* [18] [296] stripling *(mnḥ)* [297]
old man *(i'w)* [298] woman *(st)* [299] young woman
(*lit.* "beautiful one"; *nfr(t)*) [300] various person(s) *(tp
šbn)* [301] boy [302] child (from infancy upwards;
nḥn) [303] lad *(rnn)* [304] maiden *(rnnt)* [305] weaver
[306] subordinate, assistant [307] *d'ty* (meaning
unknown) [308] Overseer of Carpenters (*var.* Carpenter
of the Dockyard) [309] sailor (*or* ship's hand) [309A]
boat-builder [310] a goer forth *(pry)* (meaning not
clear) [311] (male) slaves *(ḥmy(w))* [312] female slaves
(ḥmy(wt)).

V. *The Towns of Egypt*
[313] town *(dmi)* [19] [314] Senmet (i.e. the island

of Bigga or Biga opposite Philae) [315] Elephantine (the
island opposite Aswan) [316] Ombi (the modern Kom
Ombo) [317] Silsilis [318], [319] Edfu [320]
Hieraconpolis (here *Mḫn*, but the older form is *Nḫn*, i.e.
Nekhen) [321] Nekheb (the modern El-Kab on the right
bank opposite Nekhen).... [323] Inyet (modern Esna)....
[332], [333] Hermonthis.... [335], [336] Waset, the City of
Amun, mistress of every town (Thebes, the main town
being between the modern Luxor and Karnak).... [340]
Coptus [341] Ombos (Nebet, included the modern town
of Naqada).... [343] Dendera.... [350] Abydos.... [353] This
(*Tn(i)*, old writing *Ṯni*) (exact site unknown) [354]
Akhmin.... [371] Asyut.... [374] Kos *(Ḳis)*.... [377] Khmun
(Hermopolis, the modern Ashmunein).... [389]
Heracleopolis *(Nn-nsw)* (modern Ihnasya el-Medina)....
[392] Mi-wer (Moeris; Kom Medinet Ghurab).... [394]
Memphis (normal writing is *Mn-nfr* but here *Mnf*)[20]
[395] Troia (the Modern Tura, the site of the limestone
quarries).... [400] On of Re (Heliopolis; *Iwnw-Rˁ*)....
[404] Mendes (*lit.* "House of the Soul" [earlier and better
'Ram'], lord of Djedet; *Pr-Bꜣ-nb-Ḏdt*).... [410] Piramesses
(*lit.* "The House of Ramesses, Beloved of Amun,
L.P.H.")[21].... [412] Andjet (alternate name for Djedw, i.e.
Busiris).... [415] Buto (*lit.* "House of the goddess Edjo")....
[417] Tanis.... [419] The fortress of Tjel *(Ṯꜣrw)*....

VI. *Buildings, Their Parts, and Types of Land* [22]
    [420] castle, pylon *(bḫn)* [23] [421] settlement,
village *(wḥt)* [422] house *(pr)* [423] room (later "house";
ˁt) [424] living room [425] side room (?) [426] lower
part, basement [427] outer chamber [428] broad hall
(wsḫt) [24] [429] alcove, moon-shaped recess [430]
ergastulum, storehouse [431] colonnade(?) *(wḥꜣy(t))* [25]
[432] upper chamber [433] ceiling, roof *(ḥꜣtyw)* [26]

[434] stairway [435] tomb chapel, tomb *(ḥwt-kʲ)* [27] [436] a hidden place [437] magazine (for corn and the like; *mḥr*) [438] container (for corn; *sʲꜥ*)[28] [439] garner *(sꜥyt)* [440] chest [441] storehouse *(wḏʲ)* [442] window [443] chink, crack [444] surrounding wall *(sbty)* [29] [445] rampart *(or* bastion)[30] [446] wall *(inb)*[31] [447] street [448] ankh (meaning unknown) [449] guard-house [450] fortress [451] prison *(kri)* [452] corner, angle *(ḳnbt)* [453] angle *(ḳꜥḥ)* [454] granary *(šnwt)* [cf. No. 439] [455] Treasury *(lit.* "White House") [456] *miʲt* (probably a farm building) [457] cow-house [458] vineyard [459] a name whose meaning and reading are unknown [460] garden *(ḥsb,* a late writing of *ḥsp)* [461] avenue, promenade [462] roof *(tp-ḥwt)* [463] ground-floor [464] *rbn* (unknown) [465] ...*rt* (unidentified) [465A] demolition (? or rubble?) [466] *mḫn* (exact meaning unknown) [467] hillock [468] vein (? of rock; *ḏꜥt)* [469] *srft* (perhaps a kind of earth or building material) [470] caves (? *mgrt?)* [471] (destroyed) [472] ruin (? *sḫnn)* [473] flood *(nt)*.[32]

VII. *Agricultural Land, Cereals, and their Products*[33]

[474] ploughland *(skʲ(t))* [475] hillock (a repetition of No. 467 above) [476] mud-flat (repeated from No. 56) [477], [478] (lost words) [479] *pḥʲ* (meaning unknown) [480] *ꜥmd* (meaning unknown) [481] *whm-ṯmḫ* (meaning unknown) [482] vegetables [483] cucumber-beds [484] *ꜥmt* (?) (unrecognizable word) [485-7] (several words that cannot be divided) [488] *ḫt* (doubtless for *ḫtiw,* "threshing-floor") [489] *npt* (?) (doubtful, perhaps to be taken with the next word) [490] winnow [491] *pis* (a cereal of some kind) [492] *sꜥḳ* (a cereal) [493] (lost)[34] [494] white emmer [495]

black emmer [496] red emmer [497] ....emmer [498] *hrnt* emmer [499] orange-red(?) emmer [500] emmer of Ptah [501] (unknown) [502] (unknown) [503] country wheat (? *stwt? n sht*) [504] *bš¹* (a cereal of some kind) [505] dates (*bnr* or *bnrt?*) [506] flour [507] *mᶜr* (probably grain from a plant *mᶜr*)....35

VIII. *Beverages*36

[556] beer (*ḥ(n)ḳt*) [557] *trk* (some kind of intoxicating drink) [558] *ḥmt* (apparently a kind of beer in the process of making).... [565] new wine, must [566] wine of Egypt (*irp n Ḳmt*) [567] wine of Khor (i.e. Syria) [568] wine of the Oases [569] wine of Andjet (i.e. Busiris) [570] wine of Hardai (i.e. Cynopolis) [571] wine of Amor [572] vinegar [573] *ipwr* (a wine of second-rate quality) [574] *ᶜḏ* (? fat?, but this does not fit in with this series) [575] *ᶜw¹y(t)* (a fermented beverage of some sort, found in medical sources) [576] dregs (or lees; *g¹š*) [577] *dnd* (meaning unknown) [578] *brbs* (meaning unknown).

IX. *Parts of an Ox and Kinds of Meat*37

[579] meat (*iwf* or *if*) [580] head (*ḏ¹ḏ¹*) [581] neck.... [584] breast [585] vertebra of the upper back [586] back [587] rib [588] thighs (or the like; *m¹st*).... [590] foreleg [591] under part of foreleg (? *ḥry-ḥpš?*) [592] loins [593] *ḳnḳn* (a joint of some sort) [594] tail [595] *ḏnḥ* (perhaps the upper part of the foreleg).... [598] liver [599] lungs [600] spleen [601] heart (*ḥ¹ty*) [602] intestines (*imy-ḫt*, apparently identical with *mḫtw*) [603] *rᶜm* (meaning unknown) [604] *shn* (? perhaps the pancreas or alternatively the mass of fat in which the kidneys are enveloped) [605] flank, side [606] *ṯrst* (an undetermined part of an ox) [607] *ḳbḥ*

(part of the leg or foot) [608] raw meat [609] cooked meat [610] spiced meat.

Notes to Document I.9

1. Gardiner comments on this and the next two kinds of land: "The three next kinds of land appear from P. Wilbour, Text B, to have formed a recognized administrative classification and to have been assessed (for what purpose is obscure) in the proportions 10: 7 1/2: 5 respectively."

2. I am capitalizing all the titles; Gardiner is somewhat inconsistent in his capitalization.

3. Gardiner finally settles for this title as equivalent to Generalissimo of the Army.

4. Here Gardiner writes: "At this point we pass from the grandees in the immediate entourage of the King to his military staff, but after only three essential members of this have been named (Nos. 87-9) five high administrative officials intervene (Nos. 90-4). Then the list of army officers is continued in Nos. 95-8. Nos. 107-8 deal with scribes concerned with the organization of the army, and later on there are some references to soldiers of lower rank (Nos. 197-8, 201, 202(?), 234-5) and to certain types of troop (Nos. 236-7)...."

5. Again Gardiner says: "The mention of horses recalled to Amenope's mind several other titles connected with chariots; of these all are exclusively military except No. 96, so that the way is paved for the 'standard bearer' of No. 98...."

6. "The next two entries, which name personages concerned with executing the duties owed by the King to the gods, were possibly meant to link up with Nos. 90-4, after which the military or semi-military titles Nos. 95-8 formed a digression."

7. Gardiner adds: "Nos. 114-20 refer to priestly

persons of relatively high rank, the lower ones being dealt with below in Nos. 125ff. In Nos. 117-20 we have the designations of the high priests of the three great cities of Thebes, Heliopolis and Memphis respectively."

8.   At this point Gardiner says: "Priests and temple-employments follow, starting with the general terms, in the plural, for the higher grades and thence descending to menial occupations like those of confectioners and the like (Nos. 148-51).... The remaining employments from Nos. 152-229 may also have belonged to the temple service."

9.   To the references given by Gardiner, add Spencer, *The Egyptian Temple*, p. 157.

10.   Gardiner says here: "Nos. 177-87 enumerate quarry-workers, builders and the like."

11.   Combined because of the presence of the *n*, so that it might be a measurer of an administrative domain instead of the two titles given. As usual, Gardiner's commentary is instructive.

12.   Gardiner writes here: "Some degree of homogeneity is discernible in Nos. 197-204, all of them implying coercion of one kind or another. Nos. 197, 198, 201, 202 are military titles, of which the higher ones occurred earlier, Nos. 77, 87-9, 95-8."

13.   This and the next two "deal with boatmen, after which Nos. 208-9 refer to callings in which a boat would naturally be used...."

14.   "Nos. 213-9 are all concerned with music and dancing."

15.   "Nos. 224-9, concluding the enumeration of human employments, deal exclusively with agricultural callings. A few more military terms occur near the beginning of the next section (Nos. 234-7) and two nautical occupations near the end of it (Nos. 308-9), the

the latter very much out of place."

16. This entry had these meanings at this time, but see Document I.1, n. 17. Gardiner's long commentary (pp. 98*-112*) on the meaning of Nos. 230-33 is of particular interest.

17. "The list of foreign peoples that follows (Nos. 238-94), insofar as the names are identifiable, mostly reflects the external relations of Egypt in the Ramesside period." I have given here some of the more important names that can be identified. The reader should consult Gardiner's rich commentary for these various names.

18. "The remaining words of this section (Nos. 295-312) refer to differences of age, sex and status among human beings, though Nos. 305, 307, 308, 309 do not fit well with this formulation; the last three, together with No. 309A, are all connected with boats; a sailor's life was perhaps regarded as a slavish occupation."

19. After this general word for town "follows a long enumeration of the towns of Upper Egypt, followed by a shorter one of those in Lower Egypt." This list is "arranged consecutively from South to North." Important as this list (Nos. 314-419) is for students of ancient Egyptian geography, I have included only some of the better known towns to illustrate this category of entities in Amenope's work.

20. This name has its origin in the name of the pyramid of Pepi I (or the settlement around it), i.e. *Mn-nfr-Ppii* (or more commonly *Mn-nfr-Mryrᶜ*). As usual, Gardiner gives an interesting essay on this entry. He notes that this name for the city around modern Mit Rahina "occurs perhaps no earlier than Dyn. XVIII (cf. *Urk.* IV,3)...." (p. 123*).

21. The following conclusion of Gardiner's (pp. 174*-75*) is no longer accepted: "My final verdict must, accordingly, be that the case for Tanis [being identical to Pi-Ramesse], though of considerable strength, is not yet strong enough to put Kantir entirely out of court; much confirmatory evidence in favour of Tanis is required to outweigh completely the separate mentions of Pi-Ramesse and Tanis in On[omasticon] Am[enope]; for Kantir, on the other hand, there is as yet little to be said except that the place possessed a palace of Ramesses II of some magnificence." This opinion is further modified in the succeeding postscript. Gardiner in an earlier article had identified Pi-Ramesse not only with Tanis but also with the Hyksos town of Avaris. Baines and Málek, *Atlas of Ancient Egypt*, distinguish the three cities, suggesting that Avaris may have been located at Tell el-Dab^ca and Pi-Ramesse at Qantir. See also E. P. Uphill, *The Temple of Per Ramesses* (Warminster, Eng., 1984), pp. 1-3. The key to the recent rejection of the identification of Tanis with either Avaris or Pi-Ramesse is that none of the foundations of Tanis appears to be earlier than the twenty-first dynasty.

22. "The new category that begins here shows both a continuity and a discontinuity with what precedes: we are still concerned with habitations of men, these passing into parts of buildings and types of land where human occupations were carried on; on the other hand specific localities distinguished by proper names are at an end, and we now embark on a series of general names."

23. For a discussion of the feminine form (the normal word for a pylon), see Spencer, *The Egyptian Temple*, pp. 192-96. She notes that *bḫn* "was used, from

the New Kingdom onwards, for a large estate, and the two terms can be written in virtually identical ways."

24. *Ibid.*, pp. 71-80. Spencer concludes that both "hall" and "court" are sound translations and we need to know the context before we can decide which translation is appropriate.

25. *Ibid.*, pp. 243-47, discussing *wḥ*.

26. *Ibid.*, pp. 155-61.

27. *Ibid.*, p. 23. It was used as a "funerary temple" as early as the first dynasty.

28. For our purposes Gardiner's comment is worth quoting: "in the Rhind mathematical papyrus either 'circular'.... or 'square'....; in *JEA* XII, 131 Gunn cites an example where the sense may be more abstractly 'volume'."

29. Spencer, *The Egyptian Temple*, pp. 270-78.

30. *Ibid.*, pp. 281-83.

31. *Ibid.*, pp. 260-64.

32. "This entry seems incongruous here, and would have been more in place in Section II, where there are two more or less closely synonymous and possibly related words, namely No. 22 ...*nw* and No. 32 ...*nwy(t?)*."

33. "In spite of the rubric there is but little distinction of subject between Nos. 474ff. and the preceding numbers. The new section might more fitly have opened with the cereals, Nos. 491ff."

34. Gardiner suggests that perhaps "barley" *(it)* was given here. Then follow seven kinds of *bty* (emmer or spelt).

35. The next forty-seven items "doubtless name all kinds of pastry, bread or cake made from the previously mentioned cereals."

36. Gardiner indicates that there is no rubric

here and he gives the heading as a convenience for his edition.

      37. "That parts of an ox are here intended, not parts of the human body, seems clear...."

Section Two

Order

CREATION AND COSMOLOGY

Chapter Two

The World and Its Creation: Cosmogony and Cosmology

Even the briefest glance at the extraordinary volume of ancient Egyptian literature that touches upon the nature of the world and how it came into being will convince a reader that during the three thousand years of Pharaonic Egypt there was no natural philosophy or physics that was separate from religion, myth, and magic.[1] Hence it is not very surprising that the documents presented in this section for the description of the various cosmogonies and the general view of the world are all religious documents. They include: (1) funerary spells, like those that make up the first three documents: the *Pyramid Texts*, the *Coffin Texts*, and the *Book of the Dead*; (2) books concerned with one or more gods that are partly mythological and partly ritualistic, like the *Litany of Re* (Doc. II.5) and the *Book of the Divine Cow* (Doc. II.6); (3) books that describe the underworld and the passage of the solar bark through it at night, e.g. the *Book of Amduat (Amdat)* (Doc. II.4); (4) hymns (Doc. II.7) and ritual accounts, like the *Destruction of Apep* (Doc. II.8); (5) miscellaneous inscriptions and texts found in graves, temples, and on separate stones, like the *Memphite Theology* (Doc. II.9); and (6) magical papyri filled with references to the gods (Docs. II.10-II.11).

A convenient manner of arranging the various

cosmogonies is by the locales in which they developed:[2] (1) the Heliopolitan scheme composed at On (i.e. Heliopolis) in the Old Kingdom, a scheme emphasizing creation by the solar deity; (2) the Hermopolitan system, a creation devised in Khmun (i.e. Hermopolis), in which eight primitive gods (the so-called Ogdoad) play the important role; they were the chaos-gods who in later times were thought of as the associates of Thoth, the patron of learning, who himself became a creator god; (3) a Memphite cosmogony, arising at the original capital city of ancient Egypt, Memphis, and featuring Ptah the Creator identified with the creative activity of Tatenen ("the land which rises"). From these three important systems arose synthetic accounts which make use of various features of the three main accounts: (4) a synthesis of (1) and (2) featuring the solar creator assisted by the Ogdoad; (5) a synthesis of (1) and (3) in which Ptah is differentiated into eight hypostases, of which the principal one is Atum (the sun-god), and sunlight is introduced with the emerging land; (6) the Theban cosmogony (or cosmogonies) centering on the syncretic god Amon-Re, "King of the Gods", as the demiurge; (7) later systems like those of Edfu (featuring Horus) and Esna (with Khnum and Neith as the creators).

Before giving the details of the main systems and referring to the various documents for supporting authority, we should note that some features of the diverse systems are shared. For example, all of the systems reject initial creation *ex nihilo* by indicating that before creation at the "first time" the amorphous "Abyss" or "Deep" existed under the name of Nun, described everywhere as the primitive waters in which the creator god, whoever he was, lay formless, and no land, no sky, no light, no life, no time, no birth, no death or strife existed (in fact no entity that formed a part of the later created cosmos existed) (see Doc. II.l, Sects. 1040, 1463, 1466; Doc. II.7d, D.6-7). So creation was to be a process of giving form to the primitive Abyss and separating entities from it. In all systems the creator god, whether he was the sun, or the primitive Eight (the Ogdoad), or Ptah, or any other god or goddess, created himself, that is, first fashioned his form. As the one being who was alone after his self-creation, the creator god is often called the Sole One or the Unique One, with no monotheistic implications. In many systems the creator god after creating himself created an emerging mound of land or an island on which to stand and many a city later held that the original mound emerged in its area (indeed each of the great temples was conceived as being built on the original mound and included the original sanctuary of the creator god).[3] After creating himself and the emerging land he created other gods and then (with or without the help of one or more of these gods) he formed man and the rest of the entities of the ordered world. In all of the systems a principal creation was that of world order or maat $(m^{j}t)$, which so much of Egyptian religious ritual and magic strove to preserve from the ever-present danger of the still-existing waters of Nun lying on the edges of and even within the ordered world. Accordingly the creator god is usually called Lord of Maat. We see that early spells tended to identify the king with the creator god (see Doc. II.l, Sect. 1040).

The various cosmogonical systems also share, no doubt, their primitive origins in the two pervading natural features of Egypt: the overwhelming importance of the Nile and its annual flooding and the ever-present sun as a continuing source of light and heat. The first surely accounts for both the insistence on the origin of everything in the primitive waters of Nun and the emergence of the mound or island of creation. The second stimulated, in all likelihood, the appearance of the sun as either the creator god or his principal creature in the Egyptian cosmogonic schemes. Nor is it surprising that an early stage in some of the schemes is the appearance of a lotus on the emerged mound as the first step toward life. For each year when the flood subsided and land rose from the receding waters plant shoots were evident on the emerging land. And it is equally understandable how the Egyptian cosmologist might have conceived the daily rising of the sun following the cold, dark night as repeating again and again the creation of the "first time", the time when the sun first appeared shining at creation. A naturalistic analogy for the rising sun is found in the mythological-cosmological accounts which show a great dung-beetle pushing the sun along (Fig. II.1) like its earthly counterpart, which can be seen to roll the ball of dung and mud in which it lays its egg (and it may be that the beetlelike image for the rising sun resulted from the fact that the words for "beetle" and "become" or "come into being" share the same consonants, namely *h̲*, *p*, and *r*, the word for "beetle" originally being distinguished by having double *r*).

Though the various systems diverge on the procedure of creation by the demiurge (e.g. by spitting, by masturbation, by conception in the heart and speech on the tongue, or by craftwork), as we shall see, they all fail to elucidate the mysterious autogenesis in the Abyss of the creator god. The word *kheper* used for

this generation on the "first day of time" corresponds, as
Sauneron remarks,[4]

> to a notion very difficult to
> grasp....According to the contexts in
> which the word figures, a modern
> occidental is forced to translate it in
> very different ways: "to be born", "to
> come into existence", or "to exist", "to
> be in existence" or better "to
> become", "to be transformed (into)",
> "to be manifest (under such a form)",
> while the noun *kheperu* will
> sometimes be rendered by "(mode of)
> existence" and sometimes by
> "transformation". Only a better
> appreciation of the fundamental
> sense of this root, *kheper*, now static
> and now dynamic depending on the
> case, will permit us to determine the
> true metaphysical conceptions of the
> Egyptians on the matter of the
> genesis of the creator (and of the
> creatures).

Finally, as we shall see later when discussing
general cosmological features, all systems of cosmogony
emphasized the creation of many gods except that of
Akhenaten (Doc. II.7c). This last was the lone example
of a truly monotheistic system, as Hornung has
convincingly shown in refuting the efforts of many
scholars to find a single great god of which the many
gods are mere manifestations.[5] To put it briefly, all
Egyptian schemes but Akhenaten's were polytheistic.

Before passing to the first of the cosmogonic
systems, I should remark on the bewildering complexity

and the contradictory nature of many of the concepts accepted without apparent demur or concern on the part of the ancient Egyptians. A syncretic god like Amon-Re could exist as an entity with a life and a history of its own without the component gods losing their individualities. Bonnet has put it nicely:[6]

> The formula Amon-Re does not signify that Amun is subsumed in Re or Re in Amun. Nor does it establish that they are identical; Amun does not equal Re. It observes that Re is in Amun in such a way that he is not lost in Amun, but remains himself just as much as Amun does, so that both gods can again be manifest separately or in other combinations.

Syncretism was carried to more than two gods: e.g. in Ptah-Sokar-Osiris, Osiris-Apis-Atum-Horus, Amon-Re-Harakhti-Atum, and Harmachis-Khepri-Re-Atum. It is of interest that the Great Sphinx at Giza was considered by the Egyptians to be a representation of the last of these syncretic gods, consisting of the three daily forms of the solar god (Khepri in the morning, Re at midday, and Atum in the evening) present in Harmachis (the sphinx itself).

In one scheme Re may be the creator, while in another he is created by Ptah, and both schemes seem to prevail simultaneously. Similarly the Ogdoad may be the primary creator or simply an agent of another creator, again without apparent concern for consistency (see below, note 66). Older scholars like Erman expressed disdain or even horror at the wholesale inconsistency:[7]

A strange curse lay on the Egyptians: they could not forget. At the earliest period writing had been discovered by them and had placed them in the front rank of the nations, but the price of this remained to be paid. Every fresh epoch of their long existence brought them new ideas, but the earlier ideas did not disappear in consequence. It is possible that the latter might fall into temporary neglect, but they were still treasured as sacred possessions, and in another century would once more assume a prominent position. Or again, a book that lay dormant in some temple library would one day become a living influence. In this way the confusion of ideas, national and local, old and new, increased with every successive period, and added to the mass of religious details that rejoiced the Egyptian theologians, but which we regard with horror.

More recent scholars reject the use of modern rational evaluation of Egyptian thought and attempt to explain its rather different approach to reality. Thus Frankfort tells us:[8]

We find, then, in Egyptian religion a number of doctrines which strike us as contradictory; but it is sheer presumption to accuse the ancients of muddleheadedness on this score .... The ancients did not attempt to solve the ultimate problems confronting man by a single and coherent theory; that has been the method of approach since the time of the Greeks. Ancient thought —mythopoeic, "myth-making" thought— admitted side by side certain *limited* insights, which were held to be *simultaneously* valid, each in its own proper context, each corresponding to a definite avenue of approach. I have called this "multiplicity of approaches," and we shall find many examples of it as we proceed. At the moment I want to point out that this habit of thought agrees with the basic experience of polytheism.

Rudolf Anthes takes an approach somewhat different from that of Frankfort's.[9] He holds that the Egyptians possessed common sense and so did not take varying pictorial representations of concepts (and indeed the concepts themselves) at their face value but only as symbols. As an example he discusses the various concepts of the sky represented in the *Book of the Divine Cow* (our Doc. II.6) and its picture of the cow (see Fig. II.2a). In it the goddess Nut is shown as the Divine Cow, whose underbelly constitutes the sky as seen, and on it appear some stars that lie in the line of the underbelly. It is also quite obviously considered as a waterway on which the solar bark is seen twice (once at the beginning and once at the end of its passage), and furthermore the legs of the cow are obviously considered as the supports of the vault of the cow and each of them is in turn supported by a pair of support gods, the so-called Heh-gods. Anthes further points out that the idea of Nut's carrying the boats of the gods with her when she was raised as the sky, with the gods becoming stars, is attested by the *Pyramid Texts* (Doc. II.1, sect. 785, 909 [and 802, not included in Doc. II.1]), and indeed "in these texts a cow, an ocean, a vulture, and the woman Nut appear among the other concepts of heaven".[10] Regarding this diversity he concludes:[11]

> Nobody in Egypt was supposed to believe in one single concept of the sky, since all the concepts were accepted to be valid by the same theologians. Furthermore, since the Egyptians had as much common sense as we have ourselves, we may conclude with certainty that no one, except perhaps a very unsophisticated mind, took the composite picture of the heavenly cow at its face value. This conclusion is supported by the fact that there exist, in the same royal tombs about 1300 B.C., other pictures of the sky, e.g., in the form of the human figure of Nut and with the sun disk in place of the sun boats. Whoever might have sought for a replica of the actual shape of the sky in these pictures would have become completely confused. Consequently, they were meant to be symbolic of

the sky. The picture under
discussion is an artistic combination
of symbols, each of which stands for
the sky or heaven. We have seen
that the composite pictures of
heaven in the royal tombs about
1300 B.C. have their counterparts in
a drawing of about 2900 B.C. [where
the sky is simply depicted as the
wings of a vulture or a falcon
perhaps supported by two *w!s*-staffs;
see Fig. II.3] and in the Pyramid
Texts. There is no question that at
the very beginning of their history,
about 3000 B.C., the Egyptians were
aware that the concept of the sky
could not be understood directly by
means of reason and sensual
experience. They were conscious of
the fact that they were employing
symbols to make it understandable in
human terms. As no symbol can
possibly encompass the whole
essence of what it stands for, an
increase in the number of symbols
might well have appeared
enlightening rather than confusing.

A somewhat different method of "saving"
Egyptian thought, but which points in the same
direction as Frankfort's "multiplicity of approaches", is
Hornung's suggested possible use of a "principle of
complementarity" to confirm the view that the divine in
Egyptian thought is both "one and many".[12]

In the act of worship, whether

it be in prayer, hymn of praise, or ethical attachment and obligation, the Egyptians single out one god, who for them at that moment signifies everything; the limited yet colossal might and greatness of god is concentrated in and focused on the deity who is addressed, beside whom all other gods vanish into insignificance and may even be deliberately devalued .... The god who is addressed is superior to the gods, he is more than they are.... However one describes the emphasizing of the one among the many, the phenomenon itself leads us straight to the problem of logical thought. According to the principles of western logic it would be an impossible contradiction for the divine to appear to the believer as one and almost absolute, and then again as a bewildering multiplicity; we find it surprising that in Egyptian thought these two fundamentally different formulations are evidently not mutually exclusive but complementary [descriptions of reality]. Did the Egyptians think wrongly, imprecisely, or simply in a different way?

This question about Egyptian thought, which we must consider here, has been answered in the most various ways. Egyptian thought has long been said to be "illogical" or at the least "prelogical," and in this way the contradictions that are encountered have been set aside as imperfections in its structure. Edouard Naville's remarks about Egyptian "soul" concepts, published in 1906, are typical of many judgments: "All these doctrines are very vague and ill-defined; here, as with all Egyptian ideas, there is an absolute lack of system and logic."

In sharp contrast, Rudolf Anthes points to the "undeniable role that rational thought and action played in public and private life in Egypt". He wishes to find this "rational" (*vernünftig*) thought, which he relates to timeless "common sense" (*gesunder Menschenverstand*), in Egyptian religion and mythology, and he rejects the assumption that there is a different mode of thought which is "mythopoeic," as Henri Frankfort termed it .... But formal thought in theology, philosophy and science, which is governed by well-defined calculi, is quite another matter. Here problems cannot be solved by "common sense" [as were the problems of social mores and conduct in Egyptian wisdom literature reported by Anthes], and this is just as true of ancient Egypt. The highly systematic theology of the New Kingdom is a formal conceptual structure, which must be studied according to strict, formal criteria that cannot be derived from a loose concept of "reason" or "common sense".

Any application of a two-valued logic, which is based on *a* / not-*a* distinctions and on the law of the excluded middle, to Egyptian philosophical and theological thought leads at once to insoluble contradictions .... Either we equate truly logical thought with two-valued logic, in which case Egyptian thought is undeniably "illogical" or "prelogical"; or we admit the possibility of a different type of logic which is not self-contradictory, which can only be a many-valued logic....

So long as the intellectual basis of a many-valued logic remains uncertain, we can indicate only possibilities, not definite solutions. If the basis is not established, Egyptian thought and all "pre-Greek" thought will continue to be open to charges of arbitrariness or confusion. If it is found, we shall be able to comprehend the one and the many [both with respect to the divine and to existence and non-existence in the world] as complementary propositions, whose truth values within a many-valued logic are not mutually exclusive, but contribute together to the whole truth: god is a unity in worship and revelation, and multiple in nature and manifestation.

Hornung had already said that the Egyptologist is not competent to decide the validity of the concept of many-valued logic, but he also had said that the Egyptians did not move carelessly in their thought and that the Egyptologist can "sense that their system of thought has a coherence of its own which can often convince the emotions, even though it cannot be analyzed without contradiction according to western criteria, or defined in formal terms".[13]   In spite of Hornung's criticism of previous efforts to isolate the characteristics of Egyptian thought as being too concerned with the "general 'cast of mind' of the Egyptians and not enough with the formal side of their thought", his own feeling or sense of the coherence of Egyptian thought, which I have just quoted, is not so far removed from the opinions expressed by those he criticizes.   Furthermore one can surely doubt that the Egyptians themselves intentionally used or realized they were using anything so subtle as the modern Principle of Complementarity used in physics, as seems to follow from Hornung's analysis.

One last feature common to the various cosmogonic systems may be alluded to, namely the use of the doctrine of the creative word, that is, the view that to name something and then to pronounce the name can bring it into existence. This was the central view of creation in the *Memphite Theology* (Doc. II.9), but it played at least some role in other systems, as we shall see. Indeed this doctrine accounts for the extraordinary use of punning in almost all Egyptian theological accounts, as is evident for example in the statements by which Re creates the sky, the Field of Offering, the Field of Rushes, and the evershining stars in the *Book of the Divine Cow* (see Doc. II.6). Sauneron describes this doctrine of the creative word and its relationship to punning in a very lucid statement:[14]

> The Creation of the world has been imagined by the Egyptians in many fashions. Each was wont to conceive it on the basis of his own ideas but, as is logical, left the principal part in it to his own local god. One creative "technique", however, seems to have brought together a unanimity among the theologians: namely, that the agent is the *word*. The initial god, in order to create, had only *to speak* and the beings or things evoked were born at the sound of his voice. Speech in the Egyptian mind is not in effect a simple social tool facilitating human relations but is the audible expression of the intimate essence of things. It remains what it was at the origin of the world, the divine act which brought the matter forth. In the articulation of the syllables resides the secret of the existence of

the things evoked. To pronounce a word, a name, is not only a technique allowing an image to be born in the mind of the listener which reflects that of the speaker, it is a procedure of acting on the thing or the being which was mentioned in order to reproduce the initial act of the creator....

The Egyptians never considered language--namely that which corresponds to the hieroglyphs--as a social tool. It always remained for them a sonorous echo of the essential energy which gave rise to the universe, in fact a *cosmic force*. Also the study of this language allowed them an "explication" of the world. This explication was the "play on words" which furnished it to them. From the moment that one considers words as intimately tied to the essence of the beings or things they define, the resemblances of words could not be simply fortuitous but rather convey a relationship of nature, a subtle rapport which the science of the priests will have to define. Names of places, names of divinities, terms designating sacred objects, all ought to be explicable by means of a phonetic etymology--and the door is open to the most extravagant fantasies.

Now we may turn to the various cosmogonic systems.

The Heliopolitan System

While the Heliopolitan system of creation is the first one for which we have extensive literary evidence, we can suspect the existence of a preliminary scheme that featured Horus as the creative god. That the king was the god Horus incarnate ("the Good God, Lord of the Two Lands")[15] seems probable in the writing of the Horus name of the king in a *serekh* (palace facade) having a Horus-falcon above (see Chapter One above), a practice that goes back to the time of the Scorpion king and Narmer just before the beginning of the first dynasty.[16]

The cosmic role of Horus seems to be neatly indicated on a comb of the Horus Wadji found at Abydos (see Fig. II.3). We see, at the top of the figure, Horus in a boat, a boat which rides upon two outstretched wings, and below these wings the figure of Horus appears once more, this time placed above the *serekh*-name of Wadji. It seems certain that the wings represent the sky (and since a boat is riding upon them, the wings become the heavenly waters, an image later applied to the solar boat riding on the heavenly underbelly of the Divine Cow, as was already noted in our quotation from Anthes's account of the various treatments of the sky). The wings could be those of a vulture representing Nekhbet, the goddess of Nekheb across the river from Hieraconpolis, or they could be the wings of the Horus falcon.[17] The heavenly wings seem to be supported by two *wis-* or *dᶜm*-staffs[18] shown on the sides of the *serekh*. A remark in the *Pyramid Texts* (Doc. II.1, Sect. 1156) similarly represents the king after death and ascension to the sky as supporting the sky with a *w's*-staff. The same passage also speaks of his holding up the sky with a life- or ankh$(^c nh)$-sign (and we see in our Fig. II.3 that an ankh-sign is also beneath the wings of the sky and to the right of the *serekh*). Another passage (*ibid.*, Sect. 1456) mentions the imperishable stars "who traverse the Land of Libya, who lean on their $d^c m$-staffs. This Pepi leans with you on a *w's*-staff and on a $d^c m$-staff". The *w's*-staffs on Wadji's comb not only seem to serve as supports for the sky, but they also help to frame the *serekh*-name. Thus it appears that the whole picture offers good evidence that the God Horus, incarnate in the king, travels the sky in the same manner that the deceased king is pictured later as traveling in a solar boat.

. It could be that the boat pits found near tombs of the first dynasty (as for example, that found north of tomb 3357 at Saqqara, which dates from the time of Horus Aha at the beginning of the first dynasty) contained boats that were to be used by the deceased king when he traversed the sky as Horus. Thus it could be that these early boat graves contained Horus-boats rather than solar boats. But surely when the solar cosmology which developed at Heliopolis absorbed that of Horus, these boats became solar boats.

Possible evidence bearing on the identification of the sky-god Horus and the king occurs in the entry for the year X + 8 of the second-dynasty king Ninetjer found in the early royal *Annals* translated above as Document I.1 (see and consult note 60 to that document): "The Year of the First Occurrence [in

Ninetjer's reign] of the Festival of the Worship of Horus of Heaven." It certainly seems probable that the Horus-king would want to celebrate the festival of his heavenly counterpart. Horus is again and again called Horus of the Horizon in the *Pyramid Texts* (e.g., see the many passages presented in the work of T. G. Allen cited in note 15).

Incidentally, it should be remarked that there is plentiful evidence in the *Pyramid Texts* that the king as Horus became at death an imperishable star "which illumines the sky...[for] the sky will not be devoid of this Pepi and this earth will not be devoid of this Pepi forever" (Sects. 1454-55). In another passage where the king propitiates the primeval gods he asks them to tell their father that King "Wenis knows him and knows his name: 'Eternity' is his name, 'The Eternal One, Lord of the Years' is his name. The Armed Fighter Horus, who is over the gods of the sky, is he who vivifies Re every day" (Sect. 448-49). Some other passages referring to Horus as a star are to be found in the following sections of Document II.1: 330, 1301, 1508-9, 1636 (and again see Allen's work referred to in note 15).

It is also thought that the symbol of the Eye, which plays such an important part as the Eye of Re and also as the Eye of Horus in the later mythology arising at Heliopolis, had as its predecessor a falcon's eye which was conceived when Horus was the supreme god. Thus Clark remarks:[19]

> At the beginning of history
> the High God of the Egyptians was a
> falcon which was shown either as
> perching on a building or emerging
> from the Primeval Waters. Its right
> eye was the sun and its left one the

> moon...Certainly, whenever the
> Egyptians pictured the eye of their
> god they depicted a falcon's eye, not
> a human one.

One last point is worth making concerning the possibility that Horus was conceived as the creator god at the time of the union of the two lands. As early as the second dynasty we note that the Horus Sekhemib apparently added to his name Perenmaat, i.e. "the House of Maat", indicating perhaps that Horus established and preserved maat, i.e. the "world order". It must be remembered that, in the later Heliopolitan system, maat was personalized as the daughter of Re and as such was one of the principal creations of the solar deity. Hence it would be surprising if maat had not been considered in the pre-Heliopolitan days to be Horus's creation. Significant evidence that this was so may well be the Horus name of Sneferu, the first king of the fourth dynasty; it was Nebmaat ("Lord of Order"). Also, one of the epithets of the solar god under his name of Reharakhti (Re-Horus of the Horizon) was Nebmaat at the solar temple built in Abu Ghurab by the fifth-dynasty King Niuserre.[20]

The earlier views concerning Horus and the role they may have played in the later Heliopolitan solar scheme is well (but somewhat speculatively) summarized by Anthes:[21]

> In the course of this summary
> of ancient Egyptian mythology the
> reader will have become aware that,
> in Egypt, we have the unique
> opportunity of determining the time
> and the circumstances in which the
> most substantial sector of her

mythology, the myths centering on Horus, originated. The time was the beginning and the middle of the third millennium B.C., starting with the earliest documentation of history, and the circumstances were prompted by the establishment of the kingship in Egypt. The myth of Horus encompassed the concepts of the lineage of Horus [starting from Atum and proceeding through the Ennead to Horus] which then became the Heliopolitan cosmogony of Horus and Seth; of Osiris and Isis, and of the Eye of Horus; it became the prototype of the concept of Re, the sun who was the king of heaven. This myth was rooted in the first known conception of the highest god, the ruler of All, who appeared in the trinity of the Horus falcon, the Horus king of Egypt, and the heavenly Horus. It came into existence through speculations that were conducted in a clearly logical manner, based upon the faith in the universal and eternal character of the king of Egypt, and enriched by cosmogonic ideas that had been transmitted from prehistoric times; and it was made effective by the amalgamation with the rites that were performed in the service for the divine king and, particularly, for his ascension to the throne and his interment.... However...in Egypt, mythology arose out of the creation of a new form of society whose structure was expressed in theological terms. It is true that a few mythological concepts of the sky and the sun, the earth and vegetation had been carried over from the prehistoric period into the myth of Horus and, later, that of Re. Other ideas of the cosmos, however, originated as replicas of ideas of the kingship on earth. One of these more recent cosmic concepts was that of the heavenly king Horus who was incorporated in the sun and a star.

It seems probable that the old Horus of whom we have just spoken merged with the Horus who became the heir of Atum and of the company of nine gods, the Ennead, and who played an essential role in the Heliopolitan system we are about to describe.

There is some evidence of the importance of a solar deity to the united kingship as early as the second dynasty. The reader will recall that one of the kings of that dynasty was named Re-neb ("Re is the Lord") and his stela has been given as Fig. I.14a. Such a title of course tells us little if anything about any cosmogonic role the sun god Re might have been thought to have played at such an early date. But surely it was significant for the king on earth to declare by his Horus name that Re was the lord in heaven, if that is what the title signifies. However, it was later, in the third dynasty, that specific evidence of the importance of

Heliopolis to the kingship undeniably appeared, for the great vizier and architect of Djoser, the famous Imhotep, bore the title of "The Great Seer", the title of the High Priest of the solar city Heliopolis.[22]

Evidence of the interest in Re on the part of the kings was also present in the fourth dynasty, particularly in the names of some of the kings after Cheops: Djedefre ("Re is enduring"), Chephren (i.e. Khafre, "Re rises [or appears in glory]"), Mycerinus (i.e. Menkaure, "Established are the kas of Re"). All three of these names can be regarded as reflecting the Heliopolitan doctrines of Re.

But it was in the fifth dynasty that the greatest influence of Re seems to have been exercised on the monarchy, evident not only in the names of the monarchs: Sahure ("Re is [his or my] protection"), Neferirkare ("Beautiful is the action of the ka of Re"), Niuserre ("Re has power"), and Djedkare ("Enduring is the ka of Re"), but in the fact that several of the kings built solar temples as well as pyramids, the temples apparently being in imitation of the temple at Heliopolis, and they endowed solar shrines and temples throughout Egypt (see my discussion of Doc. I.1 in the preceding section). Furthermore, the use of the designation "Son of Re" for the king, found in the fourth dynasty and more frequently in the fifth and sixth, no doubt has great significance for indicating the spread of the Heliopolitan doctrines.[23] It was also at the end of the fifth dynasty that the *Pyramid Texts* were first inscribed on the walls of the chambers in the pyramid of Wenis, and it is these texts that recount some details of the Heliopolitan doctrines. It now behooves me to describe some of these doctrines.

The creator God Atum (identified in the

Heliopolitan system with Re, Khepri, and the syncretic god Re-Atum) lay inert and formless in the Abyss or Deep of Nun (see Fig. II.4), the primitive waters, which were limitless and dark, and this was before the "first time" when nothing yet existed.

Then in some mysterious manner Atum decided to take form, and the king (identified with him) was born *(msiw)* in the Abyss "before the sky came into being, before the earth came into being, before any established thing came into being" (see Doc. II.1, Sect. 1040). Atum in the name of Khepri or Khoprer created himself *(ibid.,* Sect. 1587). He raised himself on a mound or high hill as a *benben*-stone (shaped like a small pyramid and perhaps thought of as a cluster of solar rays joining the emergent sun and its source) in the Mansion of the Phoenix in On (i.e. Heliopolis) *(ibid.,* Sect. 1652). In the *Coffin Texts* (Doc. II.2, Spell 335) and the *Book of the Dead* (Doc. II.3, Spell 17) the Great Phoenix of Heliopolis identifies himself as the examiner of what exists.

After (or in some accounts before) creating the mound, Atum then created a son Shu and a daughter Tefenet by spitting *(ibid.,* Doc. II.1, Sects. 1652 and 1871) or by masturbation *(ibid.,* Sect. 1248). Both are usually considered as physical acts, though Clark, in a rather extravagant interpretation, believed that "the spitting motif expresses creation through the Divine Word or the entry of the breath of life.... The masturbation motif stresses the reproductive aspect of life, but behind lies the mystery of life itself, the breath of the Divine Soul. Hence the generation of Shu and Tefnut [or Tefenet] has to be described in terms of both the masturbation and spitting myths--they are, in fact, complementary, not alternative."[24] For authority he quotes the *Coffin*

Texts (Doc. II.2, Spell 245).   A later account (Doc. II.8, 26(21) *et seq.*) is couched in more abstract theological terms.   In that account when the creator god came into being "Being' came into being" and indeed all creatures came into being after he came into being.

> Manifold were the beings which came forth from my mouth ere the sky had come into being, ere the earth came into being, ere the ground and reptiles had been created in this place.   I created [some of] them in the Abyss as Inert Ones when I could as yet find no place where I could stand....I alone made every shape ere I had spat out Shu, ere I had expectorated Tefenet, ere there had come into being any other who could act with me.   I planned with my own heart and there came into being a multitude of forms of living creatures, namely the forms of children, and the forms of their children.   I indeed made excitation with my fist, I copulated with my hand, I spat with my own mouth; I spat out Shu, I expectorated Tefenet, and my father Nun brought them up....   After I had come into being as sole god, there were three gods in addition to myself.   I came into being in this land and Shu and Tefenet rejoiced in the Abyss, in which they were.

While Shu and Tefenet were still in the Abyss,

they became lost and Re sent his Eye to find them (see Doc. II.8). Meanwhile Re completed his form with all his members and therefore produced a new Eye. The original Eye, on its successful return with Shu and Tefenet, was angry at his displacement. To pacify him Re put the old Eye on his brow in the form of a rearing cobra, the Uraeus, to serve as Re's protector from inimical activities of the serpent Apep (Apophis). The Uraeus was accordingly adopted by all kings of Egypt to act in the same way as their protector. Thus was explained the role that the Eye of Re played in later ritual. It became thoroughly entangled with the Eye of Horus, whose role in the Osiris legend I shall allude to below.

It is apparent that Shu and Tefenet in the earliest accounts were personifications of elements of the environment, Shu being air or space (and then light) and Tefenet being the female counterpart to allow for the future generation of their children, Geb (the earth) and Nut (the sky). By the time of the *Coffin Texts* (Doc. II.2, Spells 79-80) Shu became the mediating creator between Atum and the subsequent creations in a very elaborate and often confusing doctrine. Tefenet becomes identified with another daughter of Atum, Maat, the world order (*ibid.*, Spell 80; see also Fig. II.5):

> Thus said Atum: Tefenet is my living daughter, and she shall be with her brother Shu, whose name is 'The Living One'. Her name is Maat (Order or Righteousness),... Nu said to Atum: Kiss your daughter Maat, put her at your nose that your heart may live .... Maat is your daughter and your son is Shu.... Eat of your

daughter Maat (i.e. thrive on her); it
is your son Shu who will raise you
up [in the sky].

After the creation of Geb and Nut, their father
Shu separated the two, thus raising Nut as the sky. A
later account of this is found in the *Book of the Divine
Cow*, which I mentioned earlier (and see Doc. II.6 for
the modifications of the cosmos described therein).
There Re rules on earth but is tired of it, particularly
so as the result of the rebellious action of man. Hence
he climbs on the back of Nut and commands that she be
raised to the sky, raising him along with her. Geb and
Nut give birth to Osiris, Isis, Seth, and Nephthys,
completing (along with Atum, Shu, Tefenet, Geb, and
Nut) the Ennead (or Company of Nine Gods). The
relations of Nut to her husband Geb, to her mother
Tefenet, and to her son Osiris are briefly mentioned in
a series of short spells in the *Pyramid Texts* which I
have not included among my extracts in Document II.1.

At this point we should note that the great
Osiris- and Horus-myths (originally separate as shown
by the fact that in the original Horus-myth, Horus was
apparently the brother of Seth, while in the Osiris-myth
he was the nephew of Seth), which were incorporated
into the funerary rites of the kings of Egypt, can be
detected, at least in broad outline, in the *Pyramid
Texts*: the killing of Osiris by his brother Seth, the
dismemberment of Osiris's body, the search for his body
by his sister-wife Isis and his sister Nephthys, the
reassembling of Osiris' body, the birth of Horus and the
protection of him, the struggle of Horus with Seth and
the tearing out of Horus's eye by Seth, the final victory
of Horus (with the recovery of his Eye) and recognition
of him as the king of Egypt, the gift of the Eye to

Osiris, and the establishment of the resurrected Osiris as the king of the underworld, a resurrection mirrored by that of the dead king who is addressed as Osiris "So-and-so" and receives from his son Horus funerary offerings symbolically designated as the "Eye of Horus".

     I have not included all of these passages in Document II.1 below, but I can here mention some sections that may be consulted in Sethe's edition and Faulkner's translation (see the titles for these works in the Introduction to Doc. II.1 below): 1339, 972, 163, 173, 175, 1007, 584, 1630, 318, 746, 828, 830, 632, 1636, 1463, 1242, 609, 639, 643, 317, 957-58. Other later accounts of the Osiris-legend fill in some of the details (e.g. the Great Hymn to Osiris given as Document II.7a below), but one has to go to the work of Plutarch *On Isis and Osiris* to find a truly coherent account.[25] Important as the Osiris-legend was to the concept of life after death, initially for the king and then later for all deceased, it probably did not play a great part in the invention of the Heliopolitan cosmogony.[26]

     One of the most interesting appendages to the Heliopolitan doctrine involves the concept of Atum as a primitive serpent present in Nun before the "First Time". Pepi is identified with such a serpent and is then said to be the scribe of god's book, "who says what will be and what will not be created" (see Doc. II.1, Sect. 1146), as if the ideas go together to present us with a creator-snake.

     This is perhaps a reference to the doctrine of creation by the word. Though this may be the allusion, still all we can assert is that in this passage the king is first identifying himself with a serpent and then separately with the scribe of god's book (i.e. with Atum). We should note incidentally that the phrase "what will be and what will not be created" is no doubt equivalent to the phrase "that which is and that which is not", a favorite one of the Egyptians to describe the totality of things: the nonexistent perhaps being that which was temporally prior to the created cosmos or that which was spatially beyond or limiting the cosmos, and the existent being that which was created (that is, the cosmos), posterior to the nonexistent and spatially limited thereby.

The snake-form of the creator is considered as an earlier form of him, a form he shed and constantly combatted when it was considered to be the primitive chaos. It was the snake Imy-Wehaf in Heliopolis or more widely, in later accounts, the serpent Apep. The earlier snake-form of Atum appears to be identical with the serpent who is named the "Provider of Kas" *(Nḥb-kꜣw)* (see Fig. II.6a), and indeed in the reference to the snake identified with Pepi a variant reading for the word for snake is Nḥb-kꜣw. Presumably, as Clark indicates, this image of the snake-creator was superseded as creation progressed.[27]

It is of interest to our understanding of the cosmological views of the Egyptians that in Document II.3 (Spell 175) it is remarked that at the end of time Atum will revert to the primitive form of a serpent and the world will return to the undifferentiated chaos. Atum speaks to Osiris in order to soothe the unease of Osiris at having to live in the silent necropolis without water, air, and light, and without sexual pleasures. Atum tells him that only he (Osiris) and Atum will remain when at the end of time he destroys creation and returns to his snake forms:

I will destroy all that I have made. This land shall return into the

> Deep, into the flood, as it was
> aforetime. (Only) I shall survive
> together with Osiris, after I have
> assumed my forms of other (snakes)
> which men know not and gods see
> not.

As Clark has observed, this doctrine of the return
to the serpent form at the end of time provided a figure
of speech to the rulers of Asyut when they claimed to
be as important as "that great surviving serpent, when
all mankind has returned to the slime".[28]

To this point I have mentioned mainly the
beginning of creation and especially the creation and
activity of the Ennead, and incidentally the birth of
Horus as the heir of Osiris. I observe that the Horus so
conceived as the beneficiary of the Heliopolitan Ennead
is essentially distinct from the old sky god with whom
the king was first identified, though of course the two
Horuses became thoroughly intertwined. The king
retained many of the characteristics of the sky god as
he was elevated to the sky on his death, which
elevation is described in countless spells of the *Pyramid
Texts.* He was at the same time the devoted son of
Osiris and responsible for his burial so that when he
(Horus) died he would in turn assume the role of Osiris
to assure his afterlife.

Of course, Atum not only created the rest of the
Ennead,[29] the land on which he stood, the light in
which the land was bathed, and the general cosmic
order, but he created man and the animals as well.
Probably, the earliest doctrine concerning man's
creation was that he was produced from the tears of
Atum (see Doc. II.2, Spell 1130), a doctrine appearing in
more than one form. This doctrine seems to have had

its origin in the similarity between the word for human beings *(rmwt)* and that for tears *(rmwt)*, another example of the role of punning in the creative process. In Doc. II.8 (27, 2-3) we find man produced from the tears of the Eye of Re. Still another popular view had man fashioned by Khnum on his potter's wheel (see Doc. II.7e, Text 319, 16 and Fig. II.7).

Not necessarily at variance with these physical descriptions of the genesis of man, which are mythological in character, are the statements we have already quoted from Doc. II.8 that "manifold were the beings which came forth from my mouth" and that the self-begotten creator in his form of Khepri planned in his heart "a multitude of forms of living creatures, namely the forms of children and the forms of their children". Farther along in the same passage (Doc. II.8, 27, 4-5) the Lord of All declares:

> I came forth from the roots, I
> created all reptiles and all that exists
> among them. Shu and Tefenet begot
> Geb and Nut, and Geb and Nut begot
> Osiris, Horus Mekhantenirti, Seth,
> Isis, and Nephthys from the womb,
> one after another, and they begot
> their multitudes in this land.

The references to the manifold beings which came forth from his mouth and to planning the forms in his heart (essentially the mind in Egyptian conceits) seem like veiled references to the concept of the creative word, as does the passage in the *Pyramid Texts* (Doc. II.1, Sect. 1100) in which king Pepi asserts that the "lips of Pepi are the Two Enneads; Pepi is the Great Word" and the passage in the *Book of the Dead* (Doc. II.3, Spell 17, S 2) describing the great god who came into being by himself, created his names, i.e. the names of his members, and consequently created the gods in his Train or Following. But toward the end of the passage from Doc. II.8 quoted above the author speaks of the next generation begetting the succeeding generations "from the womb", which implies ordinary sexual reproduction rather than creation by the word. Incidentally, we should note that in this part of the document Geb and Nut have five children, a form of Horus being added to the usual four (see note 29 above). In placing the creation of reptiles before the generation of the gods, the account seems to reflect the above-mentioned doctrine that the early form of the creator was that of snakes, a form which he shed in creating living reptiles who were hostile to him. Such creation had importance in this document, for its main purpose was the ritualistic destruction of the snake Apep by rites and spells replete with magical jargon and acts, that snake being the great enemy of Re and thus of his son the king. I have not included these rites and spells in the extract which constitutes Document II.8. But I have given a passage in that document (see 26, 2-7) where careful instructions are given as to how to depict and write down the names of the foes of Re, those of their fathers and mothers, what color ink to use, how to write the names on the breasts of wax effigies, and so on.

The further creative activity of Re or Atum is considerably elaborated in the *Book of the Dead*, where we read (Doc. II.3, Spell 15A3):

> Hail to thee, Re at his rising, Atum
> at his setting. Thou risest, thou
> risest, thou shinest, thou shinest,
> having dawned as king of the gods.

Thou art lord of the sky and earth, who made the stars above and mankind below, sole God who came into being at the beginning of time, who made the lands and created common people, who made the deep and created the inundation, who made the water and gave life to what is in it, who fashioned the mountains and brought into being man and beast... (As for) him...who came forth from the deep, Re triumphant, divine youth, heir of eternity who begot himself and bore himself, sole one, great in number of forms, King of the Two Lands, Ruler of Heliopolis, lord of eternity, familiar with everlastingness.... No tongue could understand its fellow except for thee alone [i.e. thou art the creator of language] .... (Spell 85 [not included in my extracts below]:) I am a soul; I am Re who came forth from the deep. The god is my soul. (It was I) who created Authority. (Cf. Doc. II.2, Spell 307).

Unusual is the spell in the *Coffin Texts* (Doc. II.2, Spell 1130) in which the four good creative acts of the Lord of All are specified: (1) he made the four winds so that everybody might breathe, (2) he made the great flood so that the poor as well as the rich might be strong, (3) he made every man equal to his fellows, and "I commanded them not to do wrong, but their hearts disobeyed what I had said", and (4) he made the hearts of men not forget the West (i.e. the deceased) by making offerings to the gods of the nomes (i.e. the local gods). This is unusual since it emphasizes Atum's evenhandedness toward man at the same time that Atum is laying on him the responsibility for his acts, thus proclaiming a nascent doctrine of free will.

Indeed the Heliopolitan scheme became the starting point in the eighteenth and nineteenth dynasties for the detailed accounts that made up the Theban cosmogonies of Amon-Re, expressed in the hymns that were a part of the temple rituals, as we shall see (Doc. II.7b). It was also influential upon the cosmogonic hymns of Akhenaten in Amarna toward the end of the eighteenth dynasty (Doc. II.7c).

We should also note finally that this scheme even invaded the wisdom literature, i.e. the instruction-books, taught in the scribal schools. For example, in the Instruction-book for Merikare we read of the creative activity and power of the god (who is surely Re):[30]

> Well tended is mankind--god's cattle,
> He made sky and earth for their
>   sake,
> He subdued the water monster
>   (the primitive snake?),
> He made breath for their noses
>   to live.
> They are his images, who came
>   from his body,
> He shines in the sky for their sake;
> He made for them plants and cattle,
> Fowl and fish to feed them.
> He slew his foes, reduced his
>   children,

When they thought of making
    rebellion.
He makes daylight for their sake,
He sails by [i.e. across the sky]
    to see them.
He has built his shrine around them.
When they weep he hears.
He made for them rulers in the egg
    (i.e. destined some to be rulers
    from birth),
Leaders to raise the back of
    the weak.
He made for them magic as weapons
To ward off the blows of events,
Guarding them by day and by night.
He has slain the traitors among them,
As a man beats his son for his
    brother's sake,
For god knows every name.

The Cosmogony of Hermopolis

It is not easy, as I have said, to single out from the sprawling Heliopolitan doctrines what we can surely identify as belonging to the priests of Hermopolis. But it is usually agreed (from the constant association of the name Hermopolis with them in the documents) that three key concepts were probably of Hermopolitan origin: a creator in the form of eight primeval gods in the Deep, their production of a mysterious primeval egg, hatched in some accounts from a Nile goose called the Great Cackler, from which egg the sun and ultimately all creatures arose, or alternately the creation by the Eight of a lotus on the initial land from which the sun burst forth to assume its crucial but supplementary creative role.

The eight ancestor-gods, or Ogdoad, as they are ordinarily called, consisted of four pairs of gods, each pair representing an aspect of the primitive waters, and each pair consisting of a male and a female, so that the single, self-created creator Atum in the Heliopolitan system is replaced by a sexually coupled set of Chaos gods. Hence the passive role of the Deep in the Heliopolitan system was discarded in favor of this actively creating company of gods. From this set of eight gods, which we shall describe in more detail shortly, the town of Hermopolis took the name that it had as early as the Old Kingdom and that it still possesses, namely Eighttown (Khmun [i.e. *Ḥmnw*] in ancient Egyptian, Shmoun in Coptic, and el-Ashmunein in Arabic), although it apparently had an older name (identical with that of its nome), Haretown (*Wenu*).[31]

The earliest trace of the Ogdoad in the literature is perhaps a passage in the *Pyramid Texts* (Sects. 446-47), where we find grouped together: Niu and Nenet, Amun and Amaunet, Atum and Ruti (the Twin-Lions, a dual form embracing Shu and Tefenet), and Shu and Tefenet, where only the first four may represent traces of the Hermopolitan doctrine. The next mention of the concepts that go to make up the four male gods dates from the Heracleopolitan period (in the *Coffin Texts*, Doc. II.2, Spell 76). This same spell and indeed Spells 79-80 also speak of the eight chaos-gods who surely are related in some fashion to the Ogdoad even though they are brought in line with the Heliopolitan scheme when they are described (Doc. II.2, Spell 76) as created from the efflux of the flesh of Shu "whose names Atum made when *nw* (Abyss) was created, on the day when Atum spoke in it with Nu in *ḥḥ* (darkness) and in *tnmw* (gloom)".[32] Similarly these chaos-gods seem to be identical with the eight support-gods that are described in Document II.6 as holding up the heaven (see also Fig. II.2, where two of them are shown seated by each leg of the Divine Cow).

After a fluctuation of names in the Middle and New Kingdoms, we find the eight Hermopolitan gods possessing the following names: Nun [or Nu] and Naunet (the formless waters), Hehu and Hehet (indefinitely extended space), Kek and Keket (darkness), Amun and Amaunet [or Amen and Amenet] (invisibility).[33] They are depicted in various fashions [see once more note 33]. In the most interesting representations, the male gods are depicted as having the heads of frogs, the female those of serpents, both animal forms being appropriate to inhabitants of the mud and slime with which chaos is often associated (cf. Fig. II.8).[34]

In addition to the doctrine of the Ogdoad, tradition also associated with Hermopolis a company of Five.[35] In Doc. II.11 (F, 1-5), we read:

Hail to you, you Five Great Gods,
Who came out of the City of Eight,
You who were not yet in heaven,
You who were not yet upon
    the Earth,
You who were not yet illumined
    by the sun.

This company was perhaps comprised of gods representing the four basic concepts of the Ogdoad plus the god Thoth (represented as an ibis [Fig. II.9], an ibis-headed man [Fig. II.9], or a baboon). Thoth was held to be the patron of writing and the inventor of hieroglyphics, the one who planned temples and rituals, the one who was expert in all kinds of knowledge (and especially magic), and, as a moon-god, the reckoner of time. He was the scribe of maat for the Great Ennead and for the Lord of Eternity himself, and indeed the scribe of God's book. He (with his helper Seshat) was the recorder of the king's name on the sacred Ished tree at Heliopolis (Fig. II.10) as well as the recorder at the weighing of the heart of the deceased before the latter was justified (i.e. "acclaimed right"). In addition, he retrieved the Eye of Horus and was the assistant of Isis and Horus in the resurrection of Osiris. Finally he was the patron god of Hermopolis and hence his possible appearance as part of the Five. Or perhaps the Five were related in some fashion to the five gods of the epagomenal days. The High Priest of Hermopolis was known as the "Great One of the Five in the House of Thoth", and indeed this office was held by several royal princes of the fourth dynasty.[36]

Returning to the Ogdoad and their roles in creation, we should observe that the qualities that they personalized represented the negative qualities of the Deep, which in some mysterious way were thought to have become creatively active. In one view they were believed to have come together in the primitive waters and thereby to have produced the primeval egg "in the darkness of my Father Nun".[37] There is perhaps a reference to this primeval egg in the *Coffin Texts* (Doc. II.2, Spell 307): "I am the soul who created the Watery Abyss and made a place in god's land; my nest will not be seen nor my egg broken, for I am the lord of those who are on high, and I have made a nest in the limits of the sky." Hymns to the Sun-god tell us:[38]

> You have lifted yourself up there,
> (leaving) from the mysterious egg as

the infant of the Ogdoad....Your place since the First Time was on the Hill of Hermopolis; you touched the land [that arose] in the Island (*or* Lake) of the Two Knives, and you lifted yourself up from the primitive waters out of a hidden egg.

In the Magical Papyrus of Harris (Doc. II.11, K 5-10) there is what is surely a reference to this egg:

Oh you Egg of the water, Seed of
   the earth
... (Essence?) of the Ogdoad of
   Hermopolis,
Great One in the Heaven and Great
   One in the Netherworld,
Residing in the nest in front of the
   Lake of the Two Knives,
I have emerged with you from
   the water,
I have left with you from your nest.

In another passage of the *Coffin Texts* (Spell 223) the primeval egg is seen as being hatched by a primitive bird, the Great Cackler or Great Honker: "Oh Atum, give to N. (the deceased) this sweet air which is in your nostrils, for I am the egg which is in the Great Cackler." This is elaborated in the *Book of the Dead* (Doc. II.3, Spell 54). The egg of the Great Cackler is referred to Hermopolis in the same work (Spells 56 and 59, of which I have included 56 in Doc. II.3). It was the Great Cackler who disturbed the silence which prevailed before creation:[39]

The Ennead was still joined with your members..., all gods were still joined to your body.... He cackled,

> being the Great Cackler, in the place
> where he was created, he alone. He
> began to speak in the midst of
> silence. He opened all eyes and made
> them see. He commenced to cry
> when the earth was inert. His cry
> spread about when there was no one
> else in existence but him. He
> brought forth all things which exist.
> He caused them to live. He made all
> men understand the way to go and
> their hearts came alive when they
> saw him.

The Great Cackler's honking in the primitive night is also mentioned in Doc. II.11 (M,9).

Apparently, then, from that primitive egg the Ogdoad produced the sun and the sun then assumed its creative role. The shell (*lit.* the half *or* halves) of this primitive egg was said by Petosiris of Hermopolis (ca. 330 B.C.) to have been buried in Hermopolis.[40]

In a second scheme the Eight produced the primitive land in Hermopolis and it was called the "Isle of Fire".[41] It was so named because of the belief that the sun came forth from a lotus flower on it. In the *Book of the Dead* (Doc. II.3, Spell 15B1) we read about the Great God who lived on the Isle of Flame, "the youth (born) of gold who came forth from the lotus" and again (Spell 15A4) about the child "rising from the lotus, goodly youth who has ascended from the horizon and illumines [the Two Lands with] his light" (see Figs. II.8 and II.11, showing the young sun coming forth from the lotus blossom). Earlier in the *Pyramid Texts* (Doc. II.1, Sects. 265-66) the king identified himself with the lotus blossom (Nefertem) from which Re emerged on the Isle of Fire.

The complexity of the sources concerning the Ogdoad is well illustrated by the absorption of the doctrine into the Theban cosmogony where the Ogdoad are subordinated to Amon-Re as another form of his creation (Doc. II.7b[3] [III, 23]; Doc. II.11 [H and K]; Boylan, *Thoth*, p. 113, n. 1).

Though the God Thoth seems not at first to have been connected with the events recounted concerning the creative power of the Ogdoad, there is evidence of late cosmogonic conceptions in which Thoth appears as the creator god and even as the father of the Ogdoad. From them we learn that "at his command (i.e. assertion) heaven and earth were established".[42] And in the *Book of the Dead*, Spell 130, S 6 (not in Doc. II.3) identifies him as Thoth,

> the great one dwelling in his eye,
> sitting or kneeling in the great bark
> of Khepri. Osiris N comes into being;
> and what he (Thoth) says comes into
> being.

Hence the power of the creative word seems also to have been associated with Thoth, as it was on occasion with Re and systematically with Ptah in the *Memphite Theology*. Incidentally, in connection with the *Memphite Theology*, note that Ini-sw, who is probably Thoth, declares that "Hu (authoritative command or creative word) is in my mouth and Sia (understanding) is in my heart",[43] a passage that may imply that the heart and the tongue were as important in Thoth's creative activity as they were in Ptah's. Gardiner, in an early article, suggested the possible origin of the Memphite doctrine of the creative word in the Heliopolitan doctrine of Hu and Sia (see Fig.

II.12).[44]   Boylan, by abundant citation, has made clear that Thoth's epithet "Lord of the Divine Word" implies not merely his invention of hieroglyphics but also his authorship and control of cult-ritual and magical formulae, in short, of creative words.[45]   A series of Thoth's epithets points to his special connection with time and its reckoning: He who made Everlastingness *(Dt)*, Lord of Eternity *(Nḥḥ)*, King of Eternity *(Nḥḥ)*, Ruler of Everlastingness *(Dt)*, He who increases Lifetimes and multiplies Years, the Reckoner of Time, the Reckoner of Time for gods and men, the Reckoner of Years, the One who reckons All Things, He who knows Reckoning, He who gives Length of Life to him who is in his favor, Determiner of Life-time, Lord of Lifetime, Lord of Old Age, the Orderer of Fate, the One who announces the Morning, the One who distinguishes the Seasons, the Months, and the Years, and the One who gives Life to men.[46]

Like the other great gods who became widely worshiped and venerated, Thoth was credited on occasion with being the creator of all. In the temple of Philae, Thoth is described as he who came into being when nothing that was later to come into being had yet been created, and as the one who created everything.[47] There is also a Ptolemaic inscription in the Bab el-Abd at Karnak in which the Ogdoad is subordinated to Thoth:[48] the Eight created

> light in the Height [of Hermopolis]
> and took their place in Hermopolis
> with their father, the Venerable One
> [=Thoth].

The Memphite Cosmogony

Though references to cosmogony in Memphis, and even to Ptah, are virtually nonexistent in the early dynasties and rare even in the Old Kingdom, a bowl from Tarkhan (60 miles south of Cairo), presumably from the first dynasty, bears a representation of Ptah (Fig. II.13). He stands in an open chapel, beardless and with smooth head, and carries a *wʾs*-staff. Later he was ordinarily represented with a beard and standing or sitting in a closed chapel (Figs. II.14-15). When sculpted in the round he wears a close-fitting garment, a skulltight headgear, and a beard, and he grasps his staff with both hands (See BM No. 25261). The early *Annals* refer to a sojourn of King Den in a temple, which may be a temple of Ptah's (Doc. I.1, note 39). References to Ptah increase in the Old and Middle Kingdoms, but they tell us little about him as a creator god.[49]

We do know that in the Old Kingdom there were two officials at Memphis, no doubt high priests of Ptah, who held the title of Chief-controller of the Crafts (see Doc. I.3, n. 4). Such a title appears to have had its origin in the quite early assumption of Ptah himself as a master craftsman. And indeed, as we shall see, he was described as having "crafted" the earth. Furthermore in the tomb of the prince Keti at Asyut in Middle Egypt, dating from the ninth or tenth dynasty, the prince tells us that he has restored a temple of Wepwawet, "which Ptah built with his fingers",[50] again emphasizing the craft activities of the god.

From the time of the New Kingdom on, Ptah was widely mentioned as a creator god. It seems clear that unlike Horus and Re, who were sky-gods, Ptah was an earth-god. His chthonic nature is emphasized by his early association with Tatenen (the deified Land-which-rises, as the name means), who no doubt symbolized the first land which emerged from the formless waters of Nun. The most extensive of the New-Kingdom documents which refer to the creative activity of Ptah is a Berlin Hymn to Ptah, extracts from which we have included as Document II.7d, and it often gives us the compound name Ptah-Tatenen (e.g. see Doc. II.7d, A.1, B.1, C.1). Straightway in that document (A.1-2) he is called the father of the gods and the eldest of the primordial gods. He was the one who produced himself before any other creation had taken place (B.19). He crafted *(ḥm)* the earth according to the plans of his heart *(sḥrw n ib-f)*. This seems to unite the idea of the craftsman-creator with the doctrine of creative will (cf. D.20 and E.8), which we shall see elaborated in the *Memphite Theology*. In brief, Ptah gave birth to everything that exists, having begotten and fashioned all the things that are (B.22). A reference to Ptah as the "father of the fathers of all the gods" (C.4) may reflect the Hermopolitan Ogdoad who were known as the "fathers of the gods" or the "ancestor gods", but on the other hand it may reflect the various forms of Ptah that are outlined in the *Memphite Theology*, as we shall see below. Later in the same passage Ptah is hailed as one who carries Nut [to the sky] and lifts Geb (C.9). He is called Khnum (i.e. the Fashioner, masculine) and the Mother who gave birth to the gods (C.12), and so he is thought of as androgynous, as indeed were most of the creator gods. He it was who begot all men and created their sustenance of life (C.13). Furthermore as Lord of Maat (so-called in a fragment from the time of Amenemhet I of the Middle Kingdom and in several sources of the New Kingdom)[51] he no doubt was considered as the creator of cosmic order. At the end of the twentieth dynasty Amenope introduces his list of created things by saying that he will include "what Ptah has created...". (Doc. I.9, Intro.).

Similarly in Pap. Harris I, Ptah-Tatenen is named the father of the gods, the great god from the primeval time, who fashioned mankind and made the gods.[52] His activity in the primordial time before general creation is outlined in some detail in the Berlin Hymn to Ptah (Doc. II.7d, D.3-13). He is described there as existing before those early gods which he created. His was a body that made its own body before the creation of heaven. He put his own flesh together and counted his members. He was at that first time a being who was alone and who created his own place. He had no father, no mother, but formed himself. The details of such an autogenesis, followed by the creation of all things, are described in a novel fashion in the *Memphite Theology*, which we may now examine (see Doc. II.9).

As I have often said in the preceding paragraphs the so-called *Memphite Theology* is of interest to our cosmogonic investigations primarily because it emphasizes that Ptah created everything by thought in the heart and utterance on the tongue, thus extending the doctrine of the creative word to the whole of the cosmos. We have seen that Gardiner proposed that the Memphite doctrine may have been related to the Heliopolitan view of Sia and Hu as goddesses symbolizing the creative Understanding and Utterance of Re. The *Memphite Theology* was written on a block of stone during the reign of King Shabaka (ca. 700 B.C.) and the introduction claims that it was copied from a worm-eaten original by his majesty (Doc. II.9, lin. 1-2). The document goes on to suggest that the copying produced a work "better than it had been before".

Until recently most scholars believed that the original document from which it was copied was composed in the Old Kingdom or even earlier and that the copy was substantially like the original. But recently it has been argued that the document was composed rather at the time that it was written down on the stone in the twenty-fifth dynasty, or, as another author believes, in the nineteenth dynasty (see the Introduction to Doc. II.9, notes 2 and 3). Even if the document was not composed until the time of Shabaka, it is still likely that it was fashioned out of scattered but firmly held older views concerning the creative power of words, views which we have alluded to in the earlier parts of this chapter and which have been admirably summarized by Zandee.[53] Not only does the doctrine of Hu and Sia appear to have been a possible source of the Memphite scheme but ideas expressed about Ptah himself in the Berlin Hymn (Doc. II.7d, B.19-20) seem to suggest that Ptah had already been looked upon as creator of the earth according to "the plans of his heart" (cf. D.20, where we read "your mouth has engendered and your hands have fashioned"). The latter quotation seems to mix both forms of creation that are associated with Ptah: by will and by handicraft. Earlier, on an amulet of the nineteenth dynasty, we read that Ptah provides for the Living Ka that is Memphis and that there is in his mouth "food-creating utterance".[54]

The cosmogonic section of the *Memphite Theology* begins immediately with a list of the forms of Ptah (Doc. II.9, lin. 48-52): "Ptah-upon-the-Great-Throne

...; Ptah-Nun, the father who made (?) Atum; Ptah-Naunet, the mother who gave birth to Atum; Ptah-the-Great, who is the heart and the tongue of the Ennead [i.e. as creator of the Ennead]; [Ptah]...who bore the gods; [Ptah]...; [Ptah]...; [Ptah]....Nefertem at the nose of Re every day."[55] It is evident that only the first four of these forms of Ptah are clear enough to help us explicate the basic ideas of the Memphite cosmogonic scheme when we join them to what follows. The first form, Ptah-upon-the-Great-Throne, singles him out as the great king, no doubt the creator who was alone before assuming the other forms. By the next two forms he is identified with the primeval Abyss, but here conceived as two different sexual forms, male and female, and so resembling the first two forms of the Hermopolitan Ogdoad. This identification of Ptah with male and female forms of the Abyss allows Ptah to be called the father and mother of Atum, and hence implies that, as Ptah, the Abyss has a more active creative role than it had in the earlier Heliopolitan scheme.[56] I should remark, however, that as early as a gloss in the *Coffin Texts* (Doc. II.2, Spell 335, IV, 188) the Great One, the self-created, is identified as the *nu*, the Watery Abyss, and in the same work (*ibid.*, Spell 714, VI, 343-4) Nu[n] is said to be the

> Sole One who has no equal and who was born on the great occasion of my flood.... I am the one who originated in the Abyss... I brought my body into being with my own might. I am the one who made myself. I fashioned myself at my will according to my desire.

In the later solar scheme Nun was also described

as the father of the gods. This is evident in Doc. II.6, at the beginning: when Re assembles his Eye, the next four members of his Ennead, the ancestor gods and Nun, the last one is called "the father of the eldest ones (gods)" and is addressed by Re as "Oh Eldest God in whom I came into being". Nun replies "My son Re, a god greater than he who made him." Nun's parental role is also evident in the Hymns to Amun, as we shall see when discussing the Theban cosmogonies.

Ptah's fourth form is, of course, the crucial one for the creation doctrine: Ptah-the-Great, who is the heart and the tongue of the Ennead. The significance of this form is evident in the passages that follow the list of forms (Doc. II.9, lines 53 *et seq.*). We first see that the form of Atum took shape in the heart and tongue of Ptah, for, as the account says, "Ptah is the very great one who transmitted [life] to all the gods and to their kas (i.e. souls) by means of the heart in which Horus has taken shape [as an agent or form of Ptah] and by means of the tongue in which Thoth has taken shape as [an agent or form of] Ptah." The document goes on to say (line 54):

> [Thus] it happened that heart and tongue gained mastery over [every] member [of the body] according to the teaching that he (Ptah) is in every body [as heart] and in every mouth [as tongue]: [i.e. in the bodies and mouths] of all gods, all men, all cattle, all creeping things, and of everything which lives. Accordingly [as heart] he thinks out and [as tongue] he commands what he wishes [to exist].

J. A. Wilson interprets this to mean that "the same principles of creation which were valid in the primeval water to bring forth Atum are still valid and operative. Wherever there is thought and command, there Ptah still creates."[57] The next part of the account contrasts (but apparently without abandoning the former) the Heliopolitan creation of Atum's Ennead by masturbation and consequent ejaculation of semen with the verbal creation of Ptah's Ennead, which is before him as teeth and lips. For Ptah's Ennead are the teeth and lips of Ptah's mouth "which pronounced the name of everything, from which Shu and Tefnut came forth, and which gave birth to the Ennead". The faculties of seeing, hearing, and smelling report to the heart, which causes "every understanding (i.e. completed concept) to come forth, and it is the tongue which repeats what the heart has thought out (i.e. devised). Thus all gods were born and his Ennead was completed." Thus the divine order ("every word of the god") was created "by means of what the heart thought out and the tongue commanded". Thereafter the full range of creation is mentioned as being "thought out by the heart" and as coming forth "on the tongue" and so creating "the performance of everything": food, provisions, justice to the good, punishment for the bad, life to the peaceful, death to the criminal, labor, crafts, actions of the hands and feet, and indeed all physiological processes. In short, Ptah has created everything, and hence Ptah, identified with Tatenen, "is the mightiest of the gods". The cosmogonic section of the document is then completed with a poetic passage that celebrates Ptah's creation of gods, towns, and nomes, his putting gods into shrines with offerings to them, and his letting their bodies enter the statues made of various materials. Confusing though this document may be in places, it remains one of the most remarkable compositions from ancient Egypt and justifies Wilson's evaluation of it:[58]

> The creation texts which we have discussed earlier have been more strictly in physical terms: the god separating earth from sky or giving birth to air and moisture. This new text turns as far as the Egyptians could turn toward a creation in philosophical terms: the thought which came into the heart of a god and the commanding utterance which brought that thought into reality. This creation by thought conception and speech delivery has its experiential background in human life: the authority of a ruler to create by command. But only the use of physical terms such as "heart" for thought and "tongue" for command relate the Memphite Theology to the more earthy texts we have been considering. Here, as Professor Breasted has pointed out, we come close to the background of the Logos doctrine of the New Testament: "In the beginning was the Word, and the Word was with God, and the Word was God."

CREATION AND COSMOLOGY

Theban Cosmogonies of Amon-Re

The most prolific and extravagant development of cosmogonic ideas was evident in the hymns and prayers associated with Amon-Re, the most powerful god in Egypt in the New Kingdom when Egypt's military and political influence in the Near East was highest. Amun, whose name means the Hidden One, emerged as a significant god in Thebes at the end of the eleventh dynasty, at least in court circles. Indeed a vizier of the last king of the eleventh dynasty was named Amenemhet ("Amun is at the fore"), and he was elevated to the kingship as the first king of the twelfth dynasty.[59] The god and his wife Amaunet could have been introduced into Thebes from Hermopolis, for we later find their names among the four pairs of gods of the Ogdoad of that city, or he may have been a special form of the early fertility god Min of nearby Coptos.[60]

The cosmogonic ideas which swirl about Amun, particularly in his syncretic form of Amon-Re, are a pastiche of borrowings from the three systems already described: Heliopolitan, Hermopolitan, and Memphite. For example, we find Amun identified with Tatenen, i.e. Ptah-Tatenen, in Doc. II.7b[3] (III,23-25 and IV, 12-15), where he (Amun) is also described as having created the Ogdoad, the primordial gods, and Re himself. But his attributes are not limited to those of the three systems, for we find that he has borrowed from Min (if indeed he was not in fact Min) the latter's ithyphallic form (see Fig. II. 16 and also note 60).

Before considering four great hymns to Amon-Re, it will be useful to list some of the many epithets and brief statements that bear on the cosmogonic aspects of Amon-Re's activities and which are found in tombs from the early part of the eighteenth dynasty:[61]

      The Primordial God of the earth from the beginning, the Illustrious Power who created himself, the Lord of All in each of his places, the One who is complete in form, the Primordial God who created what is and brought forth being, the Lord of millions having no equal, the One who determined the origin of gods and men, the One from whose mouth the earth came forth, He who arose from the primitive waters to the heaven, the Hawk who flies around day and night, the One who gives birth to himself every hour and comes forth from his mother every day and goes to rest in her at his time, the King of unending time or eternity *(nḥḥ)*, the Lord of everlastingness *(ḏt)*, the One who speaks and what should come into being comes into being *(ḏd-f ḫpr ḫprt)*, the Bull (i.e. Progenitor) of the Corporation [of the great Ennead], the One who fashions man and joins together the gods (i.e. produces their forms and joins man's limbs together), the One who illuminates the Two Lands with his right eye, the One who has driven out the ambient darkness when he arose in Nun, the Great Phoenix on his shore when he shines forth as Re (?), the

Great Goose [of creation], the Eldest
of the heaven and earth who created
himself to appear in the primitive
waters, and so on.
The four hymns I have selected to present as
Document II.7b add substance to the various short
epithets I have just given. In Document II.7b[1], we
first see Amun described in column I as the "eldest of
heaven" and the "first-born of earth", the "Lord of what
is, [who is] enduring in all things" (repeated). He is
called "Lord of order (m³ᶜt)". It is he "who made
mankind and created beasts" as well as fruit trees and
herbage, giving life to cattle. He is the "Divine Power
whom Ptah made". Furthermore in column II Amun is
called "the chief one who made the entire earth". He is
celebrated in the two primitive shrines: the Per-wer of
Upper Egypt and the Per-nezer of Lower Egypt (see
above, Doc. I.1, n. 35). It is his fragrance which the
gods love when he descends from Punt. In column III
he is identified as "Min-Amon", and called "Lord of
eternity, who made everlastingness". In IV he is
identified as Re and again said to be Lord of order
(m³ᶜt), "whose shrine is hidden" (thus playing on the
fundamental meaning of Amun as the one who is
hidden), and he is further identified as Khepri "in the
midst of his bark", the one who gave commands and the
gods accordingly came into being (a clear indication of
the presence of the doctrine of the creative word in
cosmogonic accounts long before the *Memphite
Theology* was inscribed on the Shabaka stone). He is
"Atum, who made the people (rhyt), distinguished their
natures, made their life, and separated [their] colors, one
from another". In column V he is said to be "great in
appearances in the Benben-house", i.e. in Heliopolis, the

"lord of the New Moon Feast" and celebrated one of the festival of the Sixth Day and that of the last day of the third Quarter-Month.   As is the case with all creator gods he is called the "sole one" and the one who made everything that is (Column VI).   Mankind came forth from his eyes and the gods from his mouth, both doctrines familiar to us from the Heliopolitan scheme. He creates herbage for cattle, fruit trees for man, nourishment for fish and birds, for that which is in the egg, for serpents, insects, rodents, and so on.   In column VII there is possible reference to his creation of the Ogdoad since he is called there "father of the fathers of all the gods".   He is the "sole one, without his peer" (column VIII).   He lives on maat every day, i.e. he thrives on the cosmos which he has established.

In the next of our hymns to Amon-Re (Doc. II.7b[2]) Amun is addressed as Re, who is described as having a radiance that exceeds that of electrum ($\underline{d}^c m$), and he is a Ptah who fashioned or modeled (nbi) his body.   With use of the verb msi in its meaning to fashion or shape statues he is said to be a "shaper who is not [himself] shaped".   Once more we learn that he is unique.   In one day he races millions and hundreds of thousands of leagues.   Each day is but an instant to Re. He is the creator and vivifier of all.

The third document illustrating the cosmogonic prowess of the great syncretic god of Thebes includes sections or stanzas from Leiden Papyrus I 350 (Doc. II.7b[3]).   In Sect. II,26 of this document Amun is described as crafting (ḫm) himself, reminding us of the form of creation ordinarily associated with Ptah.   No one knows his shapes or forms.   He made his own images as he created himself.   In II,27 we are told that he joined his seed to his body to create his egg within

his secret self. He became a form and image of birth. I
have already mentioned the passage (III, 23) in which it
is stated that the Ogdoad was Amun's first form and
that he made his further transformation as Tatenen in
order to give birth to the Ennead or to the primitive
gods (III,24), suggesting once more the doctrines later
found in the *Memphite Theology*. This was followed in
III,25 by the removal of Amun to heaven and his
establishment there as Re. It is emphasized in III,26
that Amun came into being when there were no other
beings and no land existed outside of him. All gods
came into being after him. When the Ennead was
created it was part of Amun and joined to his body
(IV,1), i.e., all the gods of the Ennead were united in his
body. Then Amun separated himself to produce the
beginning of things and he was Tatenen, shaping
himself as Ptah (IV,2). The fingers or nails of his
members or body were the gods of the Ogdoad, the
account once more reflecting the Hermopolitan scheme.
Note that I have already quoted much of this passage to
throw light on the Hermopolitan doctrine of the Great
Cackler who at creation broke the silence with his
cackle. In IV,9 Amun's solitude at creation is stressed.
Being the first to come into being, Amun's secret image
was unknown:

> No god came into being before him;
> there was no other god with him [to
> whom] he might tell his form. He
> had no mother to produce his name
> and had no father who begot him
> [and thus] could say "This is I" (*or*
> "He is mine").

It was Amun who shaped or modeled his own egg
(IV,11), this "mysterious force of births, who created his

[own] beauty". In the following passage (IV,12-21) many of the cosmogonic ideas already recounted are repeated or elaborated: the mysteriousness of his forms, his shining appearance, the multiplicity of his forms, Re's union with his body, his primacy in Heliopolis, his identification with Tatenen (i.e. Ptah), his coming forth from Nun, his initial form as the Ogdoad, his procreation of the primeval gods who brought Re into being and the completion of himself as Atum, his indefinable mystery, his unapproachable and unknowable power, and his "hidden" name.

In IV,21 we find the remarkable statement that "all gods are three: Amun, Re, and Ptah, and there is none like them" (i.e., they have no equal). Their cities on earth are Thebes, Heliopolis, and Memphis (IV,22), and these will last forever. This is not a trinitarian grouping implying monotheism. Rather it is a statement that reflects the widespread holdings and influence of these three gods and their priesthoods at the end of the fourteenth century B.C. when this passage was written. Finally we should notice the remarks of V,16-17 where Sia (creative understanding or knowledge) is described as Amun's heart and Hu (authoritative command) as his lips, a doctrine probably originating in the Heliopolitan scheme and taken over in the *Memphite Theology*, as I have often noted above.

Our last hymn to Amon-Re (Doc. II.7b[4]) is the most recent since it is probably contemporary with decrees benefitting the High Priest of Amun Pinudjem II (990-969 B.C.) and his wife. It expresses many of the ideas found in the other hymns. It demonstrates Amun's position as the first primeval god from whom all others came into being. Being the Unique One at the beginning, he created what existed in the first time. He was "mysterious of births, numerous of appearances, whose secret image is not known". All forms came from his form. He gave light to the earth at the first time with the solar disk. He sails the sky. He is the Ancient One who early arises as a youth and "who brings forth the limits of eternity". He passes through the Netherworld to give light to it. He is the "Divine God who formed himself, who made heaven and earth in his heart". "Eternity comes under his might, he who reaches the end of everlastingness." He is identified with the Watery Abyss. He makes himself manifest at his time in order to vivify the clay of man that comes off the potter's wheel. This surely is what he has done in the birth scenes of Hatshepsut and Amenhotep III in Deir el-Bahri and Luxor. His eyes are identified as the sun disk and the moon. Man is born from the creator's eyes and the gods from his mouth. He makes food, creates nourishment, and shapes everything that is. He is the everlasting one who wanders through the years without an end to his existence. He traverses eternity, and when old he makes himself young. With his daily reappearance as the circling sun over so many years, he guides the millions by giving light. He created earth by his plans and receives obeisance from the gods and goddesses. "His form is that of every god." He is decisive and unwavering, his word firm, his decree perfect and unfailing. "He grants existence, he doubles the years of him who is in his favor, he is a good protector of him whom he has placed in his heart."

The various doctrines of creation expressed in these hymns are found widely circulated in many other hymns. For example, notice how the doctrine of the creative word is expressed in a Ramesside hymn to Amon-Re-Atum-Harakhti,[62]

> who spoke with his mouth and there
> came into being men, gods, cattle and
> all goats in their totality [and
> further] all that flies and alights.

The hymn goes on to assert that he created all the regions including the Ha-nebu (the Mediterranean Islands), "the fertile meads made pregnant by the Nun (i.e. the Nile) and later giving birth; and good things without limit of their number to be sustenance for the living".

Temple rituals reflected in reliefs and in papyri repeat many of the cosmogonic ideas of the hymns. There is a ritual called the "opening (or uncovering) of the face of Re" which is addressed to Amon-Re. It is accomplished "in the House of Benben" in Heliopolis.[63] The ritual includes a hymn to Amun in which he is described as having constructed (*kd*) himself, and Moret notes a parallel passage to the effect that he (Amun) has "constructed his own members".[64] In another chapter of the ritual book we are discussing,[65] Amon-Re is again addressed in the course of speaking of the divine image

> that came into being in the first time
> (*sp tp*) when no god was [yet]
> created, when the name of nothing
> was known, when you (Amon-Re)
> opened your eyes to see with them
> and everybody became illuminated
> by means of the glances of your
> eyes, when the day had not yet
> come into being. You opened your
> mouth and spoke with it to establish
> the heaven in the West with your
> two arms in your name of Amun, the

image of the ka of all the gods, the
image of Amun is that of Atum and
that of Khepri..., you are the one
who bore all living things, you are
more alive and more powerful than
all the gods, you have seized for
yourself the whole Ennead..., you are
a god who has created with your
fingers and a god who has created
with your nails what has been
created [i.e. you are the one who
created things by touch], [you are]
the Lord of all, Atum, created in the
first time.

We can also mention the hymn appearing in the
Harris Magical papyrus (Doc. II.11, G), which reappeared
in expanded form in the Temple of Amun at the oasis
of el-Kharga in Persian times.[66]   We read in the
magical papyrus:

Adoration of Amon-Re-Harakhti, who
    came into being by himself,
Who founded the land when
    he began
    [to create],
Made by the Ogdoad of Hermopolis
    (or Who made the Ogdoad
    of Hermopolis) in the first
    primordial time...
Amun the primordial god of the Two
    Lands
When he arose from Nun and
    Naunet.
What was said [came into being] on
    the water and on the land.

> Hail to you, the One who
> made himself
> into millions,
> Whose length and breadth are
> without limit,
> Ready Power who bore himself,
> The primordial serpent who is
> powerful of flame,
> The One rich in magic with secret
> forms.

This is a hymn which ties Amun to the Ogdoad of Hermopolis and it may even say that he was made by the Ogdoad, though most often in later inscriptions Amun was said to have created the Ogdoad, usually first creating Ptah (see n. 66). It also seems to say that what he asserted came into being, as in the case of the *Memphite Theology*. It stresses the limitlessness of his creation: one into millions and one who is without limit of length and breadth. It also puts forth the doctrine of the primitive snake-form of the creator god, and it stresses the creator's magical powers and secret forms. In short, this hymn is rich in all kinds of cosmogonic ideas and is a fitting document with which to complete this brief summary of the Theban cosmogonies of Amon-Re.

The Cosmogony of Aten

The hymns to Amon-Re which we have just discussed indicate the elaborate adoration that developed for that syncretic god, reflecting most prominently the Heliopolitan scheme but also revealing strains of the other cosmogonies with which we have been concerned. All of these hymns and eulogies to

Amon-Re (and indeed to the various other gods as well) are addressed to a single god either in simple or syncretic form, but never to such a god considered to be the only god. That is, all the documents we have considered still reflect the polytheistic views of the ancient Egyptians. In our next document, however, the Great Hymn to the god Aten (Doc. II.7c), we find that the hymn is addressed to Aten considered as the only god. It is then a truly monotheistic document. We say this even though it is clear that already, before Akhenaten, the solar disk (i.e. the Aten) had begun to be addressed as an individual personalized god in his own right.[67] It should also be realized that though Aten is considered as the one god, the form and content of the account of his creation are prosaic and everywhere reflect the cosmogonies we have already described, with the obvious exception that he is not credited with creating other gods, he being the only god. We note that in the first part of the hymn it is said that all nature and beings awaken and respond to the Aten on his rise each day, an idea that was conventional by the time this hymn was composed. The hymn (Doc. II.7c,6) treats Aten in largely customary fashion as the one

> Who makes seeds grow in women,
> Who creates people from sperm;
> Who feeds the son in his mother's
> womb....
> To nourish all that he made.

The list of Aten's creations is commonplace: the earth when he was alone and acting on his own desire, people, herds, all that walk upon the earth on legs, all that fly on wings, the various lands and places of the world where men were set, their sustenance, the reckoning of their life-spans, their different languages and colors, the river in the underworld, the rain from the sky, and the mountain rivers, and indeed the millions of forms that spring from him alone.

Cosmogonies at the Temple of Esna

We have already described the cosmogony assigned to Ptah and reflected in the Berlin Hymn to Ptah (Doc. II.7d), and so we may turn immediately to the late cosmogonic material found at the Temple of Khnum at Esna (Doc. II.7e), all of these extracts dating from the time of the Roman Emperor Trajan (98-117 A.D.). I give these extracts as representative of the cosmogonies described on temples built in the Ptolemaic and Roman times. Similar accounts could also be constructed by examining inscriptions in the temples at Philae, Edfu, Kom Ombo, and Dendera.

It is perfectly clear that the god Khnum-Re is credited with the same creative acts as the other creator gods. Indeed he is identified with Ptah-Tatenen as the creator of the primordial gods (Doc. II.7e [Text 394,23]). He is called the "great god who came into being at the very beginning" and the "magnificent ram, at the first time". We hear of his lifting the earth and supporting the sky, and of his shining forth with the form of luminous brightness. "He installed the soul of the spirits in the midst of the waters (?)." "He acted the god when he began to come into being" (Text 394,25). He is "mysterious of aspect" and is called the "modeler of the modelers" (Text 394,26), an obvious reference to his creation of living things on the potter's wheel (a function sometimes also ascribed to Ptah).[68] He is called the "eldest of the primordial gods". He is also the "father of the fathers" and the "mother of the mothers". He made both superior and inferior beings, cities and countries, and the Two Lands (Egypt). He made firm the mountains (Text 394,27). He brought to life those he had modeled on his wheel and he provides continued sustenance for them. "He comes forth at the right time without cease." His most frequent identification is as the lord or god of the potter's wheel (see Texts 319, 378 and 394). Like the other creator gods he is unequaled and he "made that which is and that which is not", i.e. everything (Text 378,9).[69] He is the omnipotent one (Text 319,16):

> You have modeled men on the
>   potter's wheel,
> You have made the gods,
> You have modeled large and small
>   cattle,
> You have formed everything upon
>   your wheel, each day,
> [In] your name of Khnum the Potter.

Also like other creator gods he is described as the "mysterious one whose form no one knows" (Text 378,10). Khnum came forth from the Abyss and appeared with the form of the [solar] flame. Not only does the Nile arise from two caverns under his feet [at Elephantine] but he likewise produces the north breeze "for the nostrils of gods and men". His right eye is the sun and his left the moon. Again we see him identified with Ptah-Tatenen (Text 378,13). He is also described (in Text 378,14) as a Heh god, i.e. a support god (no doubt symbolizing all of the eight Heh gods holding up heaven--gods whom I have mentioned earlier). Finally note that he is also identified with the eldest son of

Atum, i.e. with Shu.

A great many other details concerning Khnum's activities can be milked from these extracts, but I set them aside and pass on to a rather detailed account of creation by the goddess Neith, an account also appearing in our extracts from the Temple of Esna (Doc. II.7e [Text 206]).

Like other Egyptian gods cast in the role of the demiurge, Neith is called "father of the fathers" and "mother of the mothers". Similarly, like other such gods she is described as having come into being from herself at the beginning of time in Nun. This was the time when the land was still in the shadows of the Abyss, i.e. when the land had not yet emerged. In the beginning Neith took more than one form. First she gave herself the appearance of a cow in order to hide her divine form. "Then she changed herself into a lates-fish (ꜥḥ)." Then she went forth and gave illumination with her eyes to what she saw (i.e. to say, when she looked at something she illuminated it), as is said of other creator gods and particularly of solar gods. "Then she said, let this place (where I am) become for me a platform of land in the midst of the Abyss in order that I might stand on it." This is one of the many such commands in this account which show the device of the creative word in action. The first land to be created was Esna, which is equated here in some way with the early home of Neith in Sais.[70] Thereafter Neith created thirty gods, again by using the technique of the creative word, i.e. by pronouncing their names. She ordered her children to stand on the primordial land, which was called "Highland" (ḳ). Then they asked of her what else was to be created. She answered by describing the creative process of conception and verbal command: (1) the enumeration of the four [creative] spirits *(ḥw)*, (2) the giving of form to that which is in the stomach (perhaps the magical forms and concepts in the heart?), (3) the pronouncing *(šd)* of what is on the lips, (4) the recognition or knowing of the resultant beings that will arise that very day. Thereupon they did everything which she described. Then Neith considers what she will produce next. She declares that a god will come into being who will produce light by opening his eyes and darkness by closing them. Men will be produced from the tears of this god and gods will be created from his saliva. Neith will fortify this god by means of her power, making him effective through her own efficacious spirit. She predicts that men will rebel against this god, thus recalling the account of such a rebellion in *The Book of the Divine Cow*, and further that this rebellion will be defeated. The name of this powerful god she will create will be Khepri in the morning and Atum in the evening, and he will be a god who shines forth every day forever in his name of Re. To this the gods reply "we are ignorant" *(ḥm-n)*. From this reply arose their name of Eight *(ḥmnw)*, from which Hermopolis takes its name. So it is clear that here we have Hermopolitan influence.

Further evidence of Hermopolitan influence is seen in the details of the sun-god's birth as described by Neith. He was born from excretions of hers which she had placed in the [primordial] egg, which egg we have already mentioned in connection with Hermopolitan doctrines. Accompanying the birth of the sun came light and the first day of the year (i.e. the solar year came into being). At this point are described the details of the creation of man from the god's tears brought on by his not seeing his mother and the creation of the gods from his saliva produced when he salivated on seeing her again. Finally we notice a passage which states that, from seven commands which Neith pronounced, the Seven Goddesses of Methyer (a cow goddess) were created, one more reference to the Memphite type of creation by spoken command.

Of the various hymns which we have examined in the extracts designated as Document II.7, only one is not primarily cosmogonic. This is the Great Hymn to Osiris (Doc. II.7a), which I have included as an example of a quite extensive account of the Osiris-Horus legend. But in this account we see that even the chief funerary god Osiris has attracted to himself some of the epithets of a creator god. Thus he is described as lord of eternity, king of gods, one whom the sky and stars obey, the ruler of the imperishable stars, the one who sets maat throughout the Two Shores, and, as heir of Geb, the ruler of the land, the water, the wind, the plants, the cattle, all flying creatures, reptiles, desert game, "the leader of all the gods" and the one "effective in the Word of Command".

Cosmology

To this point our concern has been almost entirely with the various views held by the ancient Egyptians concerning the way the world came into being. In the part that remains we shall try to see what kind of world resulted, what sort of visible and invisible beings populated this world, and what was the nature of the forces which were believed to keep the world and its parts functioning harmoniously and of those which were dangerous and threatened the desired harmony of the cosmos. In this brief examination of cosmology I shall deliberately exclude any discussion of Egyptian astronomy, since that topic will be reserved for the next volume.

The world after creation was inhabited by gods (*netjeru*), spirits (*akhu*), man, and all kinds of animals. However present the gods might have been on the visible water and land during the first creation, it is evident that by the time of the first dynasty, when the Two Lands came under pharaonic rule, the gods retreated to the heavens (and soon also to the netherworld beneath the visible world of man). That the gods formed and continued to control the natural world is evident from all of the cosmogonic accounts we have described. But how were they manifest to man? What was their essential nature?

It is sometimes thought that the prehistoric Egyptian saw gods first in fetishes, then in animal forms, then in anthropomorphic forms, and finally in mixed animal and human forms. But surely we have no hard evidence of the course of belief in the early stages of civilized man.[71] True, early Egyptians throughout the Gerzean or Naqada II Period (ca. 3500-3100 B.C.) fashioned palettes in animal forms that may have signified deities. For example see the palette of Fig. II.17, which is in the form of a fish, and remember that one of the forms that Neith took in the account of creation which I discussed at the end of the last section was that of the lates-fish.

Similarly we see numerous vases decorated with ships that have standards which seem to bear emblems symbolic of gods (see Fig. II.18a). Standards of this kind, which probably represented the divine patrons of towns or regions, are later found on a mace-head of the Scorpion king (Fig. I.3). There we see two emblems that may consist of the animal form (a wild dog?) that represents the god Seth, one that is a jackal representing some divinity not surely known to us (compare also Fig. II.18b) and one that is the notched symbol representing the god Min. Before the king a bearer carries a standard with a curious oval-like symbol that sometimes is said to represent the royal placenta and later appears to be called *khons* (but is not to be identified with the god Khons).[72]

On the mace-head of King Narmer and also on his celebrated palette (see Figs. I.8 and I.9) we find the procession of four identical standards: with two emblems consisting of falcons, which no doubt represent the god Horus; one that is a jackal, and one the unidentified oval emblem mentioned above. These fetish and animal forms do not of course tell us how the gods were truly conceived. It is obvious that from the first dynasty (and no doubt sometime before) statues were made to represent gods and celebrations followed in some kind of religious services, as is perfectly plain from the *Annals* we have translated and discussed as Document I.1 (see particularly note 6). The statue was kept in a sanctuary that was the earthly "House of the God". The purpose of the cult-ceremony performed was no doubt to make the statue suitable for its occupation by the god. This was certainly the case later when we have detailed written descriptions of cult ceremonies.[73]

Incidentally, I remind the reader that we have already given a crudely drawn representation of the god Ptah enclosed in an open naos or shrine on a bowl from Tarkhan which can be dated approximately to the first dynasty (see Fig. II.13). Even the depiction of gods by mixed animal and human forms goes back to the first dynasty or before, as is evident from the divinity shown in relief at the top of both sides of the Narmer palette, who has a human face with cow horns and ears and so is probably a figure of the goddess Hathor. See also the figure which has what may be Seth's animal head and a human body, the figure appearing on a sealing that dates from the reign of Peribsen in the second dynasty (Fig. I.19a, middle figure). Examine other anthropomorphic divinities depicted on early-dynastic objects in Fig. II.20, where it is particularly noteworthy that they often carry signs of life and power, the two signs attesting to important attributes of gods throughout Egyptian history. Hence all the main ways of depicting the gods seem to go back at least to the beginning of dynastic history if not before.

I might add to this discussion that the gods depicted in human form often carried on their heads hieroglyphs indicating their names or other symbols by which they could be identified.

Though the gods are shown in forms that are well represented in nature, perhaps exhibiting characteristics that can be related to powerful, dangerous, or clever animals, to men, to plants, to extraordinary natural events like the flooding of the Nile, and even to inanimate objects, most of the cosmogonic accounts we have discussed mention that at least the creator gods have a mysterious divine form or name that nobody knows (or presumably can know). This is illustrated by the well-known tale that centers on Re's secret name and the efforts of Isis to extract that secret name from the mighty god.[74] She succeeds by a stratagem worthy of her magical prowess, causing in him a painful snake bite which she will not cure until the name is revealed to her.

Not being able to know the god's true divine form, Egyptian theologians tended to multiply the god's describable attributes or forms. Thus we notice a work entitled the *Litany of Re* (Doc. II.5), which commences with seventy-five invocations to Re. They allude to manifestations, activities, or properties of Re-Osiris (as "The One Who is Joined Together in the West"), i.e. in connection with his journey in the Netherworld, and his renewal of bodies in the earth, and the consequences thereof for the kings in whose tombs (in the New Kingdom) this litany was inscribed. To these invocations there is added in a rambling way much that tends to identify Re with Osiris. This added material has been omitted in my extracts in Document II.5.

As the attributes and manifestations of the gods proliferate so do the ways of depicting them, that is, iconographic plurality tends to accompany the developing complexity of theological attributes and forms. Hornung comments on this succinctly:[75]

> There is an astonishingly rich variety of possibilities; only to a very limited extent can one speak of a canonically fixed iconography of a god. The goddess Hathor is a good example (Fig. II.21). Her normal iconography...shows a slim woman who wears a wig covering her head and on top of it a pair of cow horns with a sun disk between them. There are, in addition, three more ways of imagining Hathor. In direct contrast to her completely human form, the goddess may have a pure

animal form, as, for example, in the
Hathor shrines of Deir el-Bahri,
where she is depicted as a cow from
whose udder the king drinks or as a
cow stepping forth from the western
mountains of Thebes and taking the
deceased into her protection. In
between there is the unusual form of
the capital of a Hathor column or
pillar [Fig. II.22]...: a cow with human
face, whose ears are animal and
whose eyes, nose, and mouth are
human. Finally the form of a human
body with animal head is not
lacking....

There are other ways in which the Egyptian
theologians attempted to express the manifold
manifestations and complex nature of the gods. Gods
were said to have multiple kas and bas, i.e. vital forces
and souls, which, in their singular forms found in man, I
have already mentioned often in these pages (see
particularly Doc. I.6, notes 16 and 17). Thus Re is
ordinarily said to have fourteen kas and seven bas.[76]
In his analysis of multiple kas, Vandier distinguishes
them from an individual ka possessed by man. He
labels them as *génies*[77]

who personify a certain number of
qualities. These *génies*, when they
are mentioned, are generally seven in
number and have seven companions
who are called *hemsou*. The
fourteen qualities that they personify
are, according to the most current
list: force, power, honor (i.e.

venerableness), prosperity, nourishment, duration of life, radiance, brilliance, glory, magic (=*hike*), creative will (=*hu*), sight, hearing, and understanding (=*sia*). These qualities are properly divine and are those which yield the eternal spiritual force. It is without a doubt that Re possesses them so eminently that he is judged to have fourteen *kas.*

According to Bonnet,[78] these multiple kas are, so to speak, divisions or separate aspects of an individual ka. For our purpose they reveal the characteristics and powers that were thought to be divine by the Egyptians. We notice that the emphasis is placed on power and force, on radiant and brilliant manifestation, on faculties of perception and will (supplemented by hearing and sight) that play a part in the creative word and in magic.) Though they are the most important divine qualities when possessed in the degree in which they are present in Re, they are also obviously the most admired qualities when possessed by man even in a lesser degree.

It is clear that from the very beginning of the pharaonic period Egyptians believed that one of the most precious possessions of the gods was the ability to give the breath of life to man. Recall from Figures I.19c and II.20 that among the earliest depictions of gods in anthropomorphic and mixed animal and human forms, the gods were wont to carry the sign of life, the well-known *ankh*-sign, in one of their hands. This persisted throughout Egyptian history, so that when Akhenaten's artists represented the solar disk, the Aten, his rays ended in hands that held signs of life to the nostrils of Akhenaten and the members of his family (see Fig. II.23). This is essentially what transpired when one of the creator gods whom we have already discussed brought to life the clay model of a person which had been turned out on Khnum's wheel.

Associated with the divine power of vivifying is magical power, which gods possessed in varying degrees, but all certainly in some degree. As Zandee has shown, magical power is essentially the same as the power of the creative word.[79] Magical power was possessed by the king when at death he joined the stars, for "his magic has equipped him" (Doc. II.1, Sect. 250). Indeed when the king has become the Bull of the sky, he lives on the being and entrails of every god, "even of those who come with their bodies full of magic" (*ibid.*, Sect. 397). King Pepi identifies himself as a magician possessed of magic (Sect. 924). In still another spell of the *Pyramid Texts* (Sect. 1324), the deceased king asserts that it is magic and not the king himself that speaks to the gods, the magic being in his belly (Sect. 1318). Presumably the deceased king in these passages, if not a full-fledged god, is at least an *akh* whose ba or ka possesses magical powers in the manner of all gods. Boylan's remarks concerning hike [heka] or magic (and especially the magic of Thoth) are worth quoting:[80]

> Looking at the use of the word *ḥike* generally, we find that it seems to include the whole field of what might be called magical. It is a sort of mysterious power which can produce effects beyond the sphere of man's achievements:...it is something

> before which demons of sickness, and
> of poison--evil demons in general,
> must give way.   Hence the uraeus
> serpents, the deities who guard the
> king, are "great in *hike*...".   Isis and
> Nephthis, as protectors of Osiris, are
> also "Great in *hike*".   Thus *hike* seems
> to include the whole sphere of magic,
> and to extend beyond it .... Thoth
> then, when he is called "Great in
> *hike*" or *Hike*" [himself], appears as a
> god of magic.

Though magical power is in the particular
province of gods, by its equivalence to the creative
powers of words it can be effectively employed by man
(particularly if he calls on the gods for help).   It is
assumed, of course, that the spells that dominate the
documents I have included with this chapter originated
with Thoth or some other god; but if a man speaks
them correctly after he has become deceased (or even
before he is deceased in some cases), then magical
effects are accomplished.   The effectiveness of spells is
declared again and again.   For example Spell 83 of
Document II.2 tells us:

> As for anyone who knows this spell,
> he will not die again, his foes will
> not have power over him, no magic
> will restrain him on earth for ever.

In Spell 146 [not given in our extracts below], we are
told at the end that it is "a spell a million times right", a
testimonial that should have been impressive to the man
who was overseeing the preparation of his coffin.
Similarly in Spell 228 [not given in our extracts] we are
told that the spell is beneficial for any one who knows

it, for he "will complete 110 years of life," this being the desired ripe old age for a man. Spell 335 concludes with the statement that if the deceased goes to the west (i.e. dies) ignorant of this spell, "he shall not [be able to] go in or out [from his tomb], being ignorant". [This conclusion is not included in our extracts below.] There are many similar testimonials and declarations of effectiveness of the spells in the *Book of the Dead*, but we may omit them at this point. I should remark, however, that in the *Coffin Texts* there are a number of spells designed not to let a man's (i.e. a deceased person's) magic be taken from him (e.g., Spells 349, 350, not included in Doc. II.2 below).

As I have suggested, the spell may be effective even if the person is not in the realm of the gods or the dead. For example we may quote a spell against the evil eye:[81]

> Sakhmet's arrow is in you, the magic (*ḥkȝ*) of Thoth is in your body, Isis curses you, Nephthys punishes you, the lance of Horus is in your head. They treat you again and again, you are in the furnace of Horus in Shenwet, the great god who sojourns in the House of Life. He blinds your eyes, oh all you people (*rmt*), all nobles (*pˁ.t*), all common people (*rḥy.t*), all the sun-folk (*ḥnmm.t*) and so on, who will cast an evil eye (*ir.t bin.t*) against Pediamunnebnesuttowi born of Mehtemwesekhet, in any bad or ominous (*dšr*) manner (*ḳd*). You will be slain like Apap, you will die and not live for ever.

ANCIENT EGYPTIAN SCIENCE

Often such spells for the living call upon the gods to perform some action or make some cure. For example,[82] we find a spell for dispelling the *akhu*-demonic spirits from the belly:

Come to me, mother Isis and sister (*sn.t*) Nephthys. See I am suffering inside my body....

Or it may be that the recitation of the god's name and his relatives, coupled with the simplest commands, suffices as in the case of conjurations for any evil swellings in any limb of a man or a woman:[83]

Hail to you Re, in [that] name of his, 'He who has given birth to his children': the children of Re in heaven, the children of Re on the earth, the children of Re in the western desert, the [children] of Re in the eastern desert, the children of Re in the south, the children of Re in the north.... The Great Ennead are children of Re, the Little Ennead are children of Re, (and) Thoth, the great one, sojourning in heaven, the scribe...of Re (and) of the Ennead, the first-born child of Re, who ensures an infinite period for all the gods... He has made the spell applying to you, you evil swelling! He has taken away (the effects of) [your] utterance (*ts*) ! Oh do stand still, do stand still at the throne and the great Ennead, which is next to it. Oh do stand still, fluid of the evil swelling....

To this point I have examined magical power primarily as an attribute of a divinity, though I have briefly mentioned that a person may use a spell to invoke gods on his behalf to cure a disease. A few general remarks on the relationship of heka to religion are in order, since it is obvious that, for the Egyptians, magic was one of the key forces by which the world came into being and continued to run. In a brilliant article[84], Gardiner has made the perfectly valid point that

> So far as Egypt is concerned, there cannot be the slightest doubt that *ḥïke* was part and parcel of the same *Weltanschauung* as created the religion which it deeply interpenetrated.

He adds:

> It would have been strange if the practice of *ḥïke* had been restricted to the narrow circle of the living, when the living shared with the gods and the dead all their other modes of intercourse. In point of fact, it was *ḥïke* more than anything else that welded together the seen and the unseen worlds. The self-protective rites of the living...are full of trafficking with the gods and the dead.... Nothing could better prove the wide range of *ḥïke* than to observe its transference from secular to funerary or divine employments and *vice versa*. In the *Pyramid Texts* and the *Book of the Dead*,

compilations intended to ensure the well-being of the departed, one may often come across spells that must originally have been composed for earthly use--spells against the bites of snakes... or of crocodiles...; for example even erotic charms may be found inscribed on coffins .... It may therefore be taken as proved that *hĭke'* was intimately associated with the presumed existence of the gods and the dead as it was with the real existence of the living. But further than this, a greater or less element of *hĭke'* may have been inherent in all the dealings between men on the one side and the gods and the dead on the other. The two last classes of being were, after all, creatures of a world apart, elusive in their nature and hard to reach by ordinary, matter-of-fact means. The very idea of their existence puts a strain upon the imagination, and for this reason set forms of words, indicative of an effort to break down mystical barriers, had to accompany even such simple deeds of homage as the presentation of food offerings. In other terms, the gods and the dead could hardly be approached save by the medium of what is known as 'ritual', and the attribute which distinguishes ritual from ordinary performance may have been just that attribute which the Egyptians called *ḥike'* .... From the Egyptian point of view we may say that there was no such thing as 'religion'; there was only *ḥike'*, the nearest English equivalent of which is 'magical power.' The universe being populated by three homogeneous groups of beings--the gods, the dead, and human living persons--their actions, whether within a single group or as between one group and another, were either ordinary or uncanny *(ḥike')*. But the gods and the dead were somewhat uncanny themselves, so that all dealings with them or performed by them were more or less *ḥike'*.

I shall make no effort here to examine in any detail the practices of individual magicians as they attempted to defend someone or even themselves, from hostile gods or forces, or as they attempted to practice black magic against some enemy. However, the reader might find interesting the conclusion of Sauneron to the effect that the magical practices of those defending themselves against enemies employed a kind of internal logic beyond the mere sterile repetition of the formulas.[85] First they attempted to mobilize the power of Amun or some other great god through the image of his bas, for it was believed that the gods could project their bas a great distance to serve as a destructive force. So it was the forces of the gods rather than the gods themselves that were being so invoked. The second part of the operation consisted in convincing the adversary that any hostile act toward the magician would be in fact an act against the great god. Then finally the magician had to convince his adversary that the result would be a terrifying response from the great god.

Sauneron also remarked that "each great divinity has the power to act, even at a great distance".[86] This is evident by the supposed fact that the god, who might well reside in heaven, can be persuaded to occupy a statue, at least if that statue has been properly prepared. In the course of the cult activities that prepare that statue, it is purified, washed, fed, and clothed, and hence one sees that the god is in certain respects being treated like an important and respected human being. Needless to say, the priest could not have failed to see that the offerings of food presented to the gods in their temples (or indeed to the Blessed Dead in their tombs) were not in fact consumed. But the fiction was maintained that the god took his fill and the remainder was divided among the attending priests. All of the many cult rituals and their magical overtones have often been described[87] and are not of further importance for our brief cosmological remarks. In connection with the gods' occupation of cult statues it is worth noticing that when the appearance of gods is mentioned it is often in terms that would be applied to a jeweled statue or one composed of precious metals. Thus in the beginning of Doc. II.6 the aging Re is described as having bones like silver, flesh like gold, and hair like real lapis lazuli.

In addition to the sundry manifestations and powers which I have alluded to briefly, we can mention the oft-noted fragrance associated with the gods.

Earlier we spoke of the fragrance of Amon-Re when he descended from Punt, the land of myrrh and incense (see Doc. II.7b[1], II,4). Similarly Ahmose, the mother of Queen Hatshepsut, when Amun came to lie with her in order that the great queen might be sired by the god to assure her right to the throne, first noticed Amun's presence by the fact that the "palace is flooded with divine aroma," which awakened her.[88]   In the early dynastic period an unguent had the name "aroma of Horus".[89]   Of course the fragrance of the gods is tied to the fact that in their temples they are constantly censed. Indeed it may not be unimportant in this regard that the gods were said to have come into being from the exhalations of Atum while men came from his tears.

A god's presence might also be signaled by some great natural uproar or event. It is well known that when the shipwrecked sailor of an early tale was cast upon a desert island, the presence of a great snake-god was made known to him by "a thundering noise".[90]

Other attributes of the gods seem remarkably human. Even the greatest gods were not omniscient: witness the above-noted story of Isis's tricking Re's secret name from him. Furthermore it is clear that Egyptian gods could grow old and even die. It was, of course, the initial death of Osiris that set out the great Egyptian doctrine of resurrection in the other world. Furthermore, other gods were conceived of as dying. Such was the case of the form of Amun and the gods of the Ogdoad who went to Djamet at Medina Habu where they were worshiped as dead gods.[91]   In the story of the shipwrecked sailor, the snake-god recounts a pitiful story of how his family was wiped out by a fire produced by a falling star. He ends the story: "I was not with them in the fire... I could have died for their sake when I found them as one heap of corpses."92 Finally, recall the already mentioned passage in Spell 175 of the *Book of the Dead* (Doc. II.3) which held that all of the gods would die at the end of time and only Atum and Osiris would survive.

Not only were gods thought of as capable of dying but of course they were capable of some kind of sexual reproduction. We have mentioned the various generations between Atum and Horus, and we have also mentioned that Osiris was bored with the Underworld in part because he was deprived there of sexual pleasure.

We have seen that the world (heaven and earth) was full of gods. It also was filled with the Blessed Dead, that is, those who had at one time lived on the earth. When the funerary literature in the First Intermediate Period began to offer deceased human beings the same benefits as those enjoyed by the kings in the Old Kingdom, namely their resurrection or elevation to the heavens, the deceased acquired a kind of divinity as *akhu*. They assumed all the same goals as the kings had earlier, namely to join the sun-god in his solar boat, to have their kas and their bas soar to heaven or back to earth for them. They were given the same kind of spells in the *Coffin Texts* to make their passage to and life in the other world safe and assured.

But there was an intermediary being between the gods, whose powers and manifestations we have briefly described, and human beings, who successfully made the transition from their mortal lives here on earth to their future lives--lives to be lived partly in the Netherworld (where their bodies resided nearby in their tombs in the necropolis) and partly in the heavens (in the forms of their bas and kas). This intermediary being was the king himself. Many scholars have stressed the divinity of the king, for example Moret and Frankfort.[93] Others, like Posener and Hornung, have suggested that he was far from being considered a god himself, though the kingship in some fashion represented divinity.[94] In regard to the latter view, Posener has collected a fair number of statements which reveal that the king was hardly considered a god by those people close to him. Still the king and the priests themselves made much of his relationship to the gods. Indeed, it would seem to me to be significant that when the king's artists fashioned statues and reliefs of the gods they often substituted the face of the king for that of the god, thus underlining the divine nature of the king, though it might better be argued that the objective of this substitution was not to divinize the king but to establish his dominant position by creating an idealized physiognomy of the king that might be applied "not only for the representation of other members of the royal household but also for those of deities as well", as my friend Robert Bianchi writes in an unpublished communication. A spectacular case of this is illustrated by a piece in the Cairo museum where Tutankhamen is shown as the divine son of Amun standing next to Amun (on his left) and the young king's face appears on both statues (see Fig. II.24).

In addition to substituting features of the king's person in representations of the gods (a practice that was no doubt at least as early as the probable use of King Chephren's head on the Great Sphinx in the fourth dynasty and the near replication of the king's face in the statue of the goddess Hathor as she appears in a dyad now in Boston of King Mycerinus of the same dynasty), the king and his priests and artists certainly strove to propagate the idea that the king was of divine birth and that the gods (especially Re) gave to him power, enduring existence, and life like Re's forever by means of his (the god's) magical protection *(s3)*.[95] Everywhere on the reliefs in the temples the king is represented as talking directly to the gods, who grant him his regalia. Even if the king is only a subordinate of the gods as the recipient of their help in protecting and extending the kingdom, he is clearly shown as their intimate. His figure is of the same size as theirs on the monuments, unlike the figures of other mortals. They communicate with him directly in dreams by manifesting themselves and usually in terms that are clearly understandable rather than in the innuendos one finds in the dreams of other mortals. Thus we find on the so-called Sphinx stela, a red granite tablet between the paws of the Sphinx, an account of the appearance of the god of the sphinx (Harmachis) to the future Tuthmosis IV in a dream as he slept near the Sphinx:[96]

> One of those days it came to pass that the king's-son, Tuthmosis, came, coursing at the time of midday, and he rested in the shadow of this great god [Harmachis]. A [vision] of sleep seized him at the hour (when) the sun was in the zenith, and he found the majesty of this revered god speaking with his own mouth, as a father speaks with his son, saying: 'Behold thou me! See thou me! my son Tuthmosis. I am thy father, Harmachis-Khepri-Re-Atum, who will give to thee my kingdom on earth at the head of the living. Thou shalt

wear the white crown and the red crown upon the head of Geb, the hereditary prince. The land shall be thine in its length and breadth, that which the eye of the All-lord shines upon. The food of the Two Lands shall be thine, the great tribute of all countries, the duration of a long period of years. My face is thine, my desire is toward thee. [I do this in order that] thou shalt be to me a protector, (for) my manner is as if I were ailing in all my limbs....The sand of this desert upon which I am has reached me; turn to me, to have that done which I have desired, knowing that thou art my son, my protector...

In short, the god promises Tuthmosis the kingdom if he will keep the sand from engulfing him!

As I suggested above, the gods also communicated with other human beings through dreams, but in a more indirect way. It was well established that the gods were the source of dreams.[97] The meanings of dreams were collected together in dream-books, in which each dream was delineated, its prognostication as good or bad in consequence given, and its significance or meaning revealed. I have included extracts of this kind as Doc. II.10.

Notice first of all that similarity of the sounds of key words in the dream with those of key words in the meaning given to the dreams plays an important part in the dreams recorded in Doc. II.10. For example (2,23) the dream of being "up a growing tree *(nht)*...means his loss *(nhy)* of...[something]" and (3,4) a dream of "white

ANCIENT EGYPTIAN SCIENCE

(ḥḏ) bread being given to him...means [that] something
[will happen] at which his face will brighten up *(ḥḏ)*
and (9,10) a dream of "uncovering his own backside
(pḥwy)... [means that] he will be an orphan later *(ḥr
pḥwy)*. The reader will discover that many of the
dreams and their interpreted meanings concern prosaic
matters.   Thus one dream means his good fortune,
another his elation at something, a third his finding
something he has lost, and a fourth his sitting among
his [distant] townsfolk. Others may be interpreted with
more serious omens: the killing of his enemies, the
absolution of all his ills, the pardoning of him by his
god, the passing of a judgment against him, and so on.
Notice that the list of dreams and their interpretations
is followed by an incantation to Isis to protect the
dreamer after he awakens.
     There is another class of dreams in which the
dreams are brought about by sleeping in a holy place
with the hope that the god of that place will come to
the sleeper in a dream and give him the answer to some
question or help him in some fashion.[98]   There are also
many examples of the statues of gods being addressed
for oracles as they passed in procession, and there is
one well-known case recounted in a speech of
Tuthmosis III, inscribed in the Karnak temple of Amun
in one of the king's additions. In this case the god
Amun sought out Tuthmosis III, when he was a young
man serving in the temple and thus long before his
elevation to the throne. When the young Tuthmosis
was found, Amun, i.e. his statue, made him stand in the
"Station of the King," i.e. the place usually occupied by
the king.[99] The purpose of this story was obviously to
demonstrate the selection of the king by divine oracle.
     I have already mentioned that ordinary people

sought divine help by magical means when sick. Needless to say, they also called upon the gods by magical means for other purposes. Late examples of this occur in the Leiden and London magical papyrus, and I quote only one to illustrate the use of a lamp and a small boy as a medium:[100]

> An inquiry of the lamp. You go to a clean dark cell without light and you dig a new hole in an east wall and you take a white lamp in which no minium or gum water has been put, its wick being clean, and you fill it with genuine Oasis oil, and you recite the spells of praising Ra [Re] at dawn in his rising and you bring the lamp when lighted opposite the sun and recite to it the spells as below four times, and you take it into the cell, you being pure, and the boy also, and you pronounce the spells to the boy, he not looking at the lamp, his eyes being closed, seven times. You put pure frankincense on the brazier. You put your finger on the boy's head, his eyes being closed. When you have finished you make him open his eyes towards the lamp; then he sees the shadow of the god about the lamp, and he inquires for you concerning that which you desire. You must do it at midday in a place without light .... The spells which you recite <to the lamp> to the wick previously

before you recite to the boy [are the following]... 'Art thou the unique great wick of the linen of Thoth? Art thou the byssus robe of Osiris, the divine Drowned [one], woven by the hand of Isis, spun by the hand of Nephthys? Art thou the original band[age] that was made for Osiris Khentamente? Art thou the great bandage with which Anubis [the embalmer] put forth his hand to the body of Osiris the mighty god? ....The spells of the great Sorcerer are those which I recite to thee. Do thou bring me the god in whose hand is the command today and let him give me answer as to everything about which I enquire here today truly without falsehood.'

To this point I have emphasized the magical power of the gods and its consequences for relations between the gods and the Blessed Dead on the one hand and human beings on the other, and I have discussed various attributes of the gods, focusing on those mentioned among the fourteen kas of Re. But we have not said much about the first two attributes of Re in their general expressions as force and power. Černý has some interesting general remarks about the attribute of power:[101]

The most conspicuous attribute of a god was his power; thus gods are sometimes referred to as *sekhem* "powers" and are then represented materialized in a sceptre of special form also called *sekhem* (lit. *powerful one*). Osiris is a *sekhem* or *sekhem o*, *power* or *great power*, and at the same time also a *sekhem-sceptre*, or *great sekhem-sceptre*, since despite his entirely human nature he was given the material form of a sceptre in his temple at Abydos. A large *sekhem*-sceptre was kept there in a shrine and carried through the town in religious processions. A golden cap with a human face was placed over the top of the sceptre to recall the original human form of the god.

But surely to the ancient Egyptian the god's power was known primarily by its effectiveness, just as a human ruler's power was judged. Cosmologically speaking, the god's power was most importantly tested in his ability to ensure the continuation of the cosmic order, that is its maat. And presumably maat was present as long as the flooding of the Nile was the right height for an effective yield of crops and as long as social conditions were tranquil. Again and again we hear, in times of crisis such as in the first or second intermediate periods or when the Nile was too low and there was drought, that the gods had deserted Egypt.[102] The rituals to be followed by the king and his priests to preserve the life of the king and hence the maintenance of the cosmos were constantly studied and practiced both at the Houses of Life and the various temples.[103] A corollary of a great god's cosmic power was his power to assist the king in his political and military ventures. The power of such assistance is expressed in the famous poetical stela of Tuthmosis III, whose prologue I now partially quote:[104]

> Speech of Amon-Re, Lord of the
>   Thrones-of-the-Two Lands;
> You come to me in joy at seeing my
>   beauty,
> My son, my champion, Menkheperre,
>   everlasting!
> I shine for love of you, my heart
>   exults
> At your good coming to my temple.
> My hands have endowed your body
>   with safety and life,
> How pleasant to my breast is
>   your grace!
> I placed you in my temple and
>   did signs for you,
> I gave you valor and victory over
>   all lands.
> I set your might, your fear (i.e. fear
>   of you) in every country,
> The dread of you as far as heaven's
>   four supports.
> I magnified your awe (i.e. awe of
>   you) in every body,
> I make your person's fame traverse
>   the Nine Bows.
> The princes of all lands are gathered
>   in your grasp,
> I stretched my own hands out
>   and bound them for you.
> I fettered Nubia's Bowmen by
>   ten thousand thousands,
> The northerners a hundred thousand

captives.

I made your enemies succumb
        beneath your soles,

So that you crushed the rebels and
        the traitors.

For I bestow on you the earth, its
        length and breadth,

Westerners and easterners are under
        your command.

We may conclude our treatment of the gods and their relations to the other classes of beings by reiterating that Egyptians, at least by the time that religious literature was composed in the Old Kingdom, were compelled to treat the gods, no matter how exalted, in human terms (for they had no others). Again we can quote the observations of Černý:[105]

> In the Old Kingdom a god is said to "abide" or to "appear (like the sun)". Gods "live" (or "belong to life", are "lords of life"), they are "great", "powerful" and "strong", "good" ("beautiful"), "merciful", "noble", "high" and "just". Like men they have a *ka* or several *kas* and these are also powerful, good, pure, great noble and abiding. The *bais* (external manifestations) "appear (like the sun)" and are "great" and "good". They "make" or "bring" a child, "love it", "bring it up", "protect" it while they stand "behind" it, "keep it alive" or "nourish" it, "clothe" it, and "make it happy", "favour" it, "come" to it, "lift it up", in short "its life is in the hand

of the god, for man is his "*servant*"
and "*adores*" the god.... The Middle
Kingdom names have little to add to
this picture. The gods are also
"*sweet*" and "*pleasant*", people are
their "*sons*" and "*daughters*" and the
gods "*make them good*". For the first
time we hear that gods are "*in
festival*" and though they are said to
be in the "*columned hall*" or in the
"*courtyard*" of the temple, they also
appear in public "*on the lake*" or
"*navigating*" on the Nile.... The
prayers--or "hymns", as they are
u s u a l l y   c a l l e d   b y
Egyptologists--down to the end of
the Middle Kingdom are singularly
void of any reference to the relation
between the worshipper and his
god.... It is only in the New Kingdom
that we meet with prayers referring
to the personal feelings of
individuals towards divinities.

In the previous discussion we have learned a
certain amount about the role of human beings in
Egyptian cosmic schemes: their divine origin in the tears
of a creator god or in the plans of his heart, their
consequential designation as "god's cattle" or the "cattle
of Re", the formation of their overall form and shape on
the potter's wheel, their animation by the god's gift of
the breath of life, their possession of spiritual elements
or separate personalities called kas and bas (no doubt
reflecting godlike attributes), their death upon the earth
followed by their reappearance as Blessed Dead in the

Beyond if they received the judgment "acclaimed right" (m*ᶜ-ḫrw*). Indeed a few notable human beings achieved a status approaching that of a divinity. The wise-man Kagemeni was worshiped at the end of the Old Kingdom (though never unequivocally called a god).[106] On the other hand, the great architect Imhotep achieved the status of a god, a god of healing like the Greek Asclepius, by the time of the Saite dynasty.[107]

A word must now be said concerning the geography and character of the regions occupied by the three kinds of beings we have described, the gods, the Blessed Dead, and live human beings. We have seen that the gods had their chief habitations in the stars (witness our remarks earlier concerning Horus), though they of course inhabited properly prepared statues in their temples in the real world. In this connection it is evident that they often had their special regions in this world: Re in Heliopolis, Ptah in Memphis, Thoth in Hermopolis, and so on. Now it also is obvious upon reading the *Pyramid Texts* that the gods had special regions in the sky. In one spell (Doc. II.1, Sect. 480) the god Geb says to the king: "The mounds of my mound (i.e. realm) are the Mounds of Horus and the Mounds of Seth...."

The deceased king is described again and again in the *Pyramid Texts* as becoming a star. In Sect. 263 the king is called a "star brilliant and far-traveling, who brings distant products to Re daily". In Sects. 934-36 the king says that he goes up "on this eastern side of the sky where the gods were born...Sothis (i.e. Sirius) is the sister of Pepi, and the Morning Star is Pepi's child." The king is also often said to join the solar bark. For example, in Sects. 710-11, the king declares: "Teti will assume his pure seat which is at the bow of the Bark of

Re." The sailors who row the bark will "convey Teti round about the horizon." In Sects. 906-07, the king says that he takes his oar and he "occupies his seat, this Pepi sits in the bow of the ship of the Two Enneads. Pepi rows Re to the West." During this journey "The doors of *Bȝ-kȝ*, which is in the firmament, are opened to this Pepi, the doors of iron which are in the starry sky are thrown open for this Pepi, and he goes through them." So evidently the king is considered to be a star and traveling companion of Re.

In the course of the king's celestial travels he visits many ill-defined regions, such as the High Mounds, the Mounds of Seth, and above all the Field of Rushes and the Field of Offerings. In Sect. 936, he says "This Pepi will come with you and wander with you in the Field of Rushes; he will serve as herdsman with you in the Field of Turquoise." In Sects. 1086-1087 the Field of Rushes is distinguished from the Field of Offerings:

> He (Pepi) takes for himself his throne which is in the Field of Rushes and he descends to the southern region of the Field of Offerings.

In another spell (Sect. 918) the king reports that "This Pepi has bathed in the Field of Rushes, this Pepi is clothed in the Field of Khoprer, and Pepi finds Re there." At times the king reaches the mysterious Field of Rushes by means of a ferry (Sect. 1188 [not given below in Doc. II.1]: "O you who ferry over the righteous boatless as the ferryman of the Field of Rushes."); the same is true for the Field of Offerings (Sect. 1193), which may be identical or at least connected in some way with the Field of Rushes, perhaps the prototype of the Greek Elysian Fields.[108] In Sect. 1196 the king identifies himself as "the potter (*or* plumb-line) of the Two Enneads by means of which the Field of Offerings was founded". A further detail of celestial geography is given in Sects. 1199-1200, when the king asks Osiris to commend him "to the supervisors of the Causeway of Happiness north of the Field of Offerings.... Let Pepi eat of the fields and drink of the pools within the Field of Offerings."

Though these fields may on occasion have been shifted to the Netherworld by the time of the composition of the *Book of the Dead*, that work retains and expands on the theme of their agricultural plenty. In Doc. II.3, Spell 99, we read:

> If one recites this spell, he goes forth (by) day from the Field (of Rushes). Given him are a cake, a jar, a *pz(n)*-loaf, a chunk of meat, and (fields of) barley and ⌈Upper Egyptian⌉ wheat 7 cubits (high). It is the Followers of Horus who reap them for him.

In Spell 110, the two fields are linked together in its title:

> Beginning of the spells for the Field of Offerings..., attaining the Field of Rushes, existing in the Field of Offerings, the great settlement..., gaining control there, becoming a blessed one there, plowing there, reaping (there), eating there, drinking there, copulating there, doing everything that is done upon earth.

Hence it is obvious that by the time of the *Book of the Dead*, when the funerary practices and benefits for the dead were extended widely to other than the royal family and their select courtiers, the ideal life of the Beyond was that which they left behind but without trials and tribulations. This latter conclusion is emphasized by the invention in the Middle Kingdom of the so-called shawabti, washabti, or shabti figures, figurines of wood or wax or stone, to be buried with the deceased in order to be available to perform hard labor in the afterlife when called upon by the deceased.[109] The manner in which the life in the Fields of Offerings and Rushes was to be passed by the deceased is illustrated by vignettes that are included with Spell 110 in various copies of the *Book of the Dead* (see Figs. II.25-26) or by paintings on the tomb walls (see Fig. II.27).

Another topographical feature of the celestial regions which was mentioned often in the *Pyramid Texts* was the so-called Winding Waterway. This was conceived as meandering through or around the sky in some fashion and giving access to the Field of Rushes. Thus in Sect. 340 we read: "The Fields of Rushes are filled [with water], and Wenis ferries across on the Winding Waterway." For other mention of the Winding Waterway, see the following Sections of the *Pyramid Texts* which I have not given in the extracts of Doc. II.1 below: 594-97, 599-600, and 1084. Incidentally, in one further reference to the Winding Waterway in Doc. II.1, Sects. 2172-73, the king is said to board the bark "like Re on the banks of the Winding Waterway" and the king "shall be rowed by the Unwearying Stars and shall give commands to the Imperishable Stars". This is fine confirmation of the view that the gods in the stars acted as oarsmen in the Bark of Re, with the Imperishable Stars being the circumpolar stars that do not set and the Unwearying Stars being the planets and the decans of stars (as we shall see in Chapter Three in the next volume). In the hymns of the New Kingdom the day-journey of the solar bark is said to be accomplished by the Imperishable Stars and the night-journey by the Unwearying Stars.[110]

Still another place frequently mentioned in the *Pyramid Texts* is the Jackal-Lake in which the king is purified. It is mentioned once in Sects. 1164-65 together with the Lake of the Dat when the king's son says: "...wash yourself in the Jackal-Lake, be cleansed in the Lake of the Dat, be purified on top of your lotus-flower in the Field of Rushes. Cross the sky, make your abode in the Field of Offerings among the gods who have gone to their kas." This last phrase is often used as a euphemism for dying, and if that is what it means here, we have one more instance of gods being said to die. As we move from the Old Kingdom and its references to the places located in the other world, we find an increasing specification of the locales and inhabitants of the Netherworld. There was a rather vaguely expressed belief in the Old Kingdom that the Dat or Duat (the land where the deceased lived in company with the gods) had an upper part in the skies and a lower counter-sky in the Netherworld, though surely the term Dat originally must have been principally used in connection with the celestial regions, since it was written with a star enclosed by a circle. Be that as it may, the doctrine of the daily coursing of the solar bark through the sky in the daytime and an inferior world at night was clearly present. Indeed the passing of the sun into the western horizon to begin its night course and its subsequent passage until rising again in the morning not only was thought of as counting the hours and delineating the days and nights but was probably looked upon as evidence of rebirth in nature and thus of human resurrection.[111]   At any rate, the doctrine of the death and birth of the sun each day exerted enormous influence on funerary practice in the Middle and New Kingdoms.   Indeed it was the nighttime journey which stimulated the imagination of the priestly authors of the New Kingdom, who recounted that journey in word and picture in the tombs of the kings in the Valley of the Kings at Thebes.   Among these accounts are those entitled the *Book of Amduat* (so called, but perhaps better *Amdat* or *Amdet*), the *Book of Gates*, and the *Book of Caverns*; the first of these works will serve as a model for this type of work.

In fact these works of the New Kingdom were to some extent anticipated by a composition found among the *Coffin Texts* which is usually called the *Book of Two Ways*.[112]   This work consists of an obscure journey of the solar bark.   The goals of the deceased in undertaking this journey, aside from the purpose of his resurrection, are by no means clear, but an ultimate sojourn with Osiris appears to be involved.[113]   The deceased seems to embark on the boat at Heliopolis (Doc. II.2, Spell 1030):

> See, its starry sky (or collection of stellar deities?) is in On (i.e. Heliopolis), the sun-folk are in Kheraha.... I will go with them aboard the lotus-bark at the dockyard of the gods.... I will ascend in her to the sky.   I will sail in her in the company of Re.... I will act as pilot

in her to the polar region of the sky,
to the stairway of the bark of
Mercury.

The journey is beset with dangers and the hostility of demons. Thus in Spell no. 1034, the deceased recites an incantation against hostile snakes, and he declares that Re's protection is his protection. In the very next spell the traveler says that he has passed along the ways of Rostau, i.e. the paths from the gate of the other world (perhaps originally thought to be at Saqqara). We are told that these are the paths or ways of Osiris and they form the border of the sky. The rubric of Spell 1131 indicates that it is a guide to the double doors of the horizon and it emphasizes the importance of the written expression of their keepers' (collective) name. Similarly knowledge of the names of doorkeepers and their gates and doors was important for the deceased when he entered the judgment hall in Spell 125 of the *Book of the Dead* (Doc. II.3). There is a reference to Hu, the personalization of the creative word, in Spell 1136 of the *Coffin Texts*, a reference that may refer to the original creation in darkness: "Hu who speaks in darkness belongs to me". That is, by Creative Utterance, or magical words, the way can be opened for the traveler. Spell 1146 speaks of an image of a mansion, presumably one of the goals of the voyage. It is the "place of a spirit, the place of excellent magic". A rubric for Spell 1162 relates the Field of Offerings to Osiris and Thoth: "Spell for being in the Field of Offerings among the Following of Osiris and among the Following of Thoth every day."

The most interesting feature of the *Book of Two Ways* is the map of the two paths around which the spells are grouped. It varies from coffin to coffin (see

Fig. II.28). I shall make no effort to treat this bizarre map of the two ways but will confine myself to a brief comment from Lesko's work:[114]

> The map is divided horizontally into two compartments each having a zigzag path .... The blue path or way in the upper compartment meets or almost meets the black lower way at the far end of the two compartments .... The upper way of the map has Osiris, who is in the sky, as its central figure.

Continuing our geographical survey of the nightly other world in which resided gods, spirits of various forms, and the dead, we can now turn to the three works of the New Kingdom which we mentioned above. The first of these works chronologically was the *Book of Amduat*, i.e. the *Book of What Is in the Netherworld*. I shall give a short summary of this work, referring to the extracts of Doc. II.4, which are accompanied by Figs. II.29-II.40.

The contents of the *Book of Amduat* are epitomized in the introductory text, where we are told that the work will inform us of the locations of the various beings of the Netherworld (souls, gods, shades, and spirits), their power, their activities, their rituals for Re, their mysterious powers, their conversations with Re as he travels through their regions, the movement of the hours and their gods (i.e. the gods who guide the Great God through their hours), who are the powerful ones and who are the annihilated. We can note that the names of the gates of entrance for the hours are usually given but they are not emphasized and are not depicted in the accompanying illustrations as they are in the *Book of Gates*.

The bark of Re often changes form in the course of the journey and its crew of gods varies somewhat as to number and names, though it is of some interest that Sia and Hu are usually present, as seems appropriate for the main purpose of the voyage, the rebirth of Re. Some of the same activities occur in each successive cavern. The sun-god communicates with the resident gods, he illuminates them, and in a sense he brings them alive each night, even though he leaves them behind. He also often commends to them various fields, as he does to the gods of his own Following. Sometimes he greets the resident gods simply as corpses and other times as disembodied souls. The sun-god when shown in his bark throughout the journey, until its end, is represented as ram-headed and he is called Flesh, i.e., he too is a kind of corpse, though the use of the ram-form seems to imply that it is the ba (or soul) of Re that completes the night journey since the ram is one of the signs for ba as soul. There are, however, constant indications in the various hours that he will be reborn at the eastern horizon: the beetle is introduced into the text as a portent of the sun-god's rebirth in the beetle form of Khepri (e.g., the third register of the illustration of the very first hour contains a beetle in a bark with two gods adoring him).

The journey starts at the western gateway, and he makes his transformations [to his ram-headed form] after passing that gate. The distance through the gateway to the next cavern is 120 *iteru* (each *iteru* being about 10.5 km.). Re's bark is towed by Two Truths (represented as goddesses). He dispenses fields to the gods in his Following. The name of this field of the first cavern is Water of Re.

The second cavern is called Wernes and is 309 *iteru* in length and 120 *iteru* in breadth. In this cavern Re makes further grants of fields to the gods and talks to the inhabitants. In one of the boats that precedes the sun bark a beetle replaces one of the customary symbols at the prow, again indicating the ultimate purpose of the voyage. The resident gods call out to the sun-god and live through his voice when he replies. Indeed they are said to breathe by means of his voice, when he grants them their duties *(irw)*. They are accordingly able to supply plants, i.e. vegetables, to the gods in Re's Retinue. And so we see here and elsewhere that agricultural activities are as important in the Netherworld as they were in the Field of Rushes when it was located in the sky. In the third register depicting this hour we see gods carrying signs for the year *(rnpt)* and branches that represent the ages, and the text tells us: "These gods...present this Great God with the year-signs... [and] with ages-branches which they hold in their hands."

The cavern in the third hour is called the Field of the Offering-dwellers in the realm of Osiris. It too is 309 *iteru* in length. Above the gods depicted in this cavern, that is, in its first register, we read: "They (i.e. the gods) are like this in the Netherworld in the flesh of their own bodies. Their souls (i.e. bas) speak for them and their shades (or shadows) rest in them." In view of this description it is not surprising that they are shown standing on water. We are further told that these gods must overthrow the enemies of Re by causing them to be drowned in the flood of water from the Abyss and blown about by winds drawn from the earth. Re stops at the city where Osiris resides and gives orders to him and his followers.

A mysterious cavern of the West called Cavern of the Life of Forms is reached in the fourth hour. Its name is not surprising since we find there the creator-snake mentioned earlier in this chapter, the Provider of Forms (Neheb-kau). As I suggested, he perhaps represents an early stage of creation in the Abyss. We must also remember that among the crew of the bark the gods of the creative word, Sia and Hu, are likewise present. Both this cavern and the next are a part of the abode of the dead Sokaris, the ancient god of the dead at Memphis. In the fifth cavern we see this great mound which constitutes his burial ground. But he is depicted sticking his head out of the top of the mound to see Re pass. The third register accompanying this part of the journey shows the inside of the great mound of Sokaris. The diagram of the whole cavern is referred to as the plan of access to Sokaris. It is said to be executed "according to the plan which is drawn in the hidden region of the Netherworld". We note the zigzag descending tunnel that appears on the illustrations of both the fourth and fifth caverns, and we are reminded of the similar zigzag route in the earlier *Book of Two Ways*, though there the zigzag path no doubt represented a route in a horizontal plane and here we seem to have a vertical tunnel being depicted.

In the sixth hour Re arrives at a field close to the body of Osiris. Thus in the third hour we had the living Osiris as the ruler of the Netherworld and here we have his body. Here it is emphasized that Re talks to the resident gods (who are of course also dead) and illuminates their darkness. They can hear his voice and they can accordingly breathe. The creative activity of snakes is emphasized in the second register of the accompanying depiction where a five-headed snake with tail in mouth encloses a god with a beetle on his head, another portent of the sun's rebirth. In the seventh hour the bark is drawn through the Cavern of Osiris, along which it is towed by the magical utterances of Isis and by the magical utterances of the Elder One, the magic being directed against Re's archenemy, the snake Apep. In the middle register of this cavern's depiction the snake is given the name Neha-her, i.e. Evil Face, and is said to be on a sandbank named Sadjau, which is 440 cubits long and 440 cubits wide and which is filled by the snake's coils. It is an interesting feature of these fanciful accounts that often great precision as to size and form is given, though as usual with scribes and artists in all ages there is considerable variety in the reporting of these precise numbers from one copy to the next. Knives are taken to Apep by four goddesses. Horus is cast here as a protector of Re when he orders the help of gods and goddesses who bear stars on their heads.

In the eighth hour the sun-god comes to other banks or mounds of dead gods, and the name of the city here is "Sarcophagi of her Gods". Here Re "calls to their souls [i.e. those of the deceased gods] after he has entered this city of the gods who reside on their sand". Further, "it is his voice that the gods hear after he has called them while the forms of their bodies remain on their corpses which are under the sand". "When this Great God calls them, what is in them comes alive." Here is further evidence of the general belief that gods die and may be reborn like Osiris or indeed like Re on this very trip. The dead gods hide after Re passes. Darkness returns.

In the ninth hour the Great God and his crew

rest from rowing. The bark is shown as preceded by a file of twelve gods with paddles. In both the first and the third registers gods are shown seated on stools that are the hieroglyphs for "clothing", which means they are "in their own flesh". In the tenth hour Khepri the beetle appears in the presence of Re, a sign of what is to come at the end of the journey. We read: "They are like this in the Netherworld in the forms and births of Khepri when he carries his egg toward this city in order to come forth afterwards in the Eastern Horizon of Heaven." In this hour, in the third register, we see depicted Horus addressing the "drowned ones" who are shown stretched out on their backs in the water. They are said to be in the Abyss, i.e. the primordial water that enters the Netherworld. It is clear, from this and preceding references in this book, that always near at hand in the regions of the underworld the Abyss threatens. I have already mentioned early in the chapter that the cosmology of the Egyptians assumes the tension and balance that are maintained between the created, existent cosmos and the threatening nonexistence of Chaos.

The eleventh hour takes the sun-god through another mysterious cavern. Here we see anticipations of the climactic rebirth to take place at the end of the next hour. In this penultimate hour the rebels, who constantly threaten during the journey, are disposed of by The Starry One, the Mistress of the Bark. Portentous is the statement that "Everlastingness swallows up her images before the Seeing One, who is in this city, and she gives them back [again] upon the birth of Khepri on earth." The figure of swallowing images to regurgitate them is also used with respect to a goddess who is mounted on the back of a serpent

above the constellation of Shedu. The text tell us that
"what she has to do, is to live by the voice of Re every
day. She swallows her images in this city [of the
eleventh hour]."

Now the travelers are in their last nocturnal
hour, the twelfth, when the glorious rebirth is to take
place. The sandy borders at the top and the bottom of
the depiction of each hour are shown to meet in the
middle of the semicircular arc at the end of the picture.
Where they meet we see the rising Khepri and the sun's
disk. Clearly the rebirth is accomplished. The action of
this hour is epitomized in its introductory text:

> Born will be this Great God in his
> forms of Khepri at this cavern. Nun
> and Nunet, Heh and Hehet (i.e. four
> of the primordial Ogdoad of
> Hermopolis) arise in this cavern at
> the birth of this Great God that he
> may come forth from the
> Netherworld, let himself down in the
> Daybark, and arise from the thighs of
> Nut.

The importance of the creator-snake in the final
process of rebirth is evident in the middle register of
the depiction of the hour where the towers of the bark
are shown leading it to the tail of the serpent and we
read:

> This god travels...along the backbone
> of this secret image of the serpent
> Life of the Gods, when his gods tow
> him. He enters into its tail and
> comes out of its mouth, being born
> in his forms of Khepri...

The completion of the renaissance of the sun-god

is emphasized in the illustration which shows the discarded mummified form of the night traveler cast aside at the bottom of the arc that provides the eastern boundary of the underworld.

Needless to say, I have only skimmed the surface of this curious and difficult text. Further help with its contents may be had by consulting the studies of Piankoff and Hornung mentioned in the introduction to Document II.4 below.

The nightly journey to the Netherworld by the solar bark which we have just described by examining the contents of the *Book of Amduat* brings us to Egyptian concepts of time and eternity. The calendaric achievements that resulted from their attempts to measure time will be discussed in the next volume. Here we wish only to note that at a very early period the Egyptians conceived of time as measurable in terms of repetitive natural events: the day by the continually repeated rising and setting of the sun, the month by the waxing and waning of the moon, and the year by the repeated inundations of the Nile (and only later in pharaonic times related by them to the heliacal rising of the star Sirius). They also felt time to continue in a linear way indefinitely into the future.[115] This is clear from their very early conception of the continuous and successive rule of the gods and men on the earth since the time of creation. This conception is embodied in the lists of kings and in early annals like Document I.1 given in the first chapter. The remarkable point in this view of time was that it tied time to the cosmos and specified that time began with the activity of creation. As we have seen again and again the cosmogonies reported creation as taking place in the "first time". It certainly seems likely that the Abyss, inert as it was,

ANCIENT EGYPTIAN SCIENCE

was timeless before the creator first established his form within it. And no doubt when a creator god was designated as the Lord of Time, it was his invention of time as an aspect of creation that was implied. The connection between existence (which is indeed the cosmos) and time is asserted in a gloss given in Spell 335 of the *Coffin Texts* (see Doc. II.2 below):

> The Examiner of what exists. *Who is he? He is Osiris. As for what exists, it is eternity (nḥḥ) and everlastingness (ḏt). As for eternity, it is day. As for everlastingness, it is night.*

Thus if we consider eternity and everlastingness as time in its full sweep, i.e. all the days and all the nights, then this gloss certainly identifies it with existence (i.e. "that which is"). These components of time were personified and in one figure shown as props of the sky and thus as a major aspect of the cosmos (see Fig. II.52). The logical corollary of considering time as a function, or perhaps better as a limit, of the cosmos that pertains to it, is that if the creator did decide to destroy everything that he had made and return to the Abyss, as Spell 175 of the *Book of the Dead* declares, then time would also be destroyed.[116] But such a possibility must have seemed unlikely to Egyptians who were so convinced or at least so hoped that the deceased king (and perhaps later any dead person who had been justified at Osiris's hall of judgment) would "live like Re forever (or forever and ever: *nḥḥ ḏt*)", as the conventional phrase had it. And indeed the "eternity" *(nḥḥ)* so desired throughout the whole history of pharaonic Egypt is occasionally used in the same context as the word "million" *(ḥḥ)*, which is often written with the palm-branch sign for "year" as a determinative or mounted on the head of the goddess who represents the word and accordingly means a million, or in fact an almost countless number, of years.[117]   Even the most fastidiously logical Egyptian priest would be glad to settle for this as a definition of eternal life.   Indeed we read in the *Book of the Dead* (Doc. II.3, Spell 42) of the deceased expressing his confidence in or perhaps his hope for lasting a million years or even millions of years:

> I am one who has ascended sound,
> whose name [is not known]. I am
> yesterday; my [name] is He Who
> Sees a Million Years, who has gone
> ...along the roads of the Chief
> Examiners.   [I am lord of
> everlastingness].... I am your
> protector for millions ⌜(of years)⌝.... I
> shall not die again.

A similar hope was implicit in naming Re's bark "The Bark of Millions of Years" and in the designation given to the mortuary temples of Seti I, Ramesses II and others in western Thebes and elsewhere: "The Mansion of Millions of Years". But in identifying time with existence, the glossator of the *Coffin Texts* surely did not mean to exclude the other aspects of existence which express its great variety.   We have already described the rich complex of divine, quasi-divine, and human beings that constituted the heart of the cosmos. But of course the Egyptian cosmos included far more: the animate and inanimate beings of the visible world, or as Amenope put it in his Onomasticon (Doc. I.9, Introduct.):

> all things that exist: what Ptah

> created, what Thoth copied down,
> heaven with its designs, earth and
> what is in it, what the mountains
> belch forth, what is watered by the
> flood, all things upon which Re has
> shone, all that is grown on the back
> of earth....

Indeed we may conclude this summary of Egyptian cosmology by urging the reader to study the wide range of entities listed by Amenope in the document just quoted and from which I have given extensive extracts in the previous chapter. He will find there none of the mythological cosmology that I have mentioned often in this chapter: the sky as a cow's belly or the wings of a vulture or a falcon, the sky's support as the legs of the cow, the morning sun as the beetle, and so on. Instead he will find a sober listing of all the categories of existence which the author thought his scribal readers should know. No doubt if he had wished to describe the entities in addition to listing them, he would have resorted to mythological description, as his remarks concerning Ptah and Thoth suggest.

Notes to Chapter Two

1. This conclusion is evident enough when one studies the documents that appear at the end of the chapter. P. Derchain, *Le Papyrus Salt 825 (BM 10051), rituel pour la conservation de la vie en Égypte* (Brussels, 1965), Chap. 1: "Physique et théologie", p. 4, rather turns my conclusion around when he declares that religion in Egypt "n'était pas une mystique, mais une physique". But as one studies that physics it is evident that it is unlike any physics for which we now customarily use the term, since it regularly included contradictory symbols to represent natural entities and events, expressed contending forces by conflicting gods, made wholesale use of divine agencies to describe creative acts, and everywhere employed magical terms and pronouncements to bring things into existence and to effect communication between human and divine beings. It is of some interest that Champollion, at the very beginning of modern studies of religious documents in Egypt, made some remarks concerning the inscriptions and figures in the royal tombs which have some pertinence for the whole of Egyptian religious literature: *Lettres écrites d'Égypte et de Nubie en 1828 et 1829* (Paris, nouv. ed., 1868), p. 201, describing the burial chamber of the tomb of Ramesses V: "Les parois de cette vaste salle sont couvertes, du soubassement au plafond, de tableaux sculptés et peints comme dans le reste du tombeau, et chargées de milliers d'hiéroglyphes formant les légendes explicatives; le soleil est encore le sujet de ces bas-reliefs, dont un grand nombre contiennent aussi, sous des formes emblématiques, tout le système cosmogonique et les principes de la physique

générale des Égyptiens."

    2. It should be observed, however, that the so-called Heliopolitan cosmogony, reflected so dominantly in Documents II.1-II.3 and indeed in most of the other documents, tended to absorb and alter the doctrines devised at the other religious centers. This was particularly true in the case of the Hermopolitan system, whose paramount beliefs have to be sifted from essentially Heliopolitan accounts. See the remarks of S. Sauneron and J. Yoyotte, "La naissance du monde selon l'Égypte ancienne," *Sources orientales:* Vol. 1, *La naissance du monde* (Paris, 1959), p. 52 (whole article, pp. 19-91).

    3. H. Frankfort, *Kingship and the Gods* (Chicago, 1948), pp. 151-54, and particularly p. 152: "In fact, each and every temple was supposed to stand on it [i.e. the Primeval Hill]....The identity of the temples with the Primeval Hill amounts to a sharing of essential quality.... Each temple rose from its entrance through its successive courts and halls to the Holy of Holies [i.e. the sanctuary], which was thus situated at a point noticeably higher than the entrance. There the statue, barge, or fetish of the god was kept, resting upon the Primeval Hill." Primeval Hills are mentioned by Frankfort for Heliopolis ("The High Sand"), Hermopolis ("The Isle of Flames"), and Karnak ("The Venerable Hill of the First Time"). Note in Leiden Papyrus I 350 the description of Thebes as the place of creation: "Waset [i.e Thebes] is the pattern for every city. Both the flood and the earth were in her in the First Time [i.e. the beginning of time], the sands came to delimit her fields, to create *(shpr)* her ground upon the mound when earth came into being *(hpr)*. Mankind came into being *(hpr)* within her....." (See C. F. Nims, *Thebes of*

the Pharaohs, Pattern for Every City [London, 1965],
text on the page opposite the title page and translation
[slightly modified] on p. 69; cf. J. Wilson's translation
of it found in J. B. Pritchard, ed., *Ancient Near Eastern
Texts Relating to the Old Testament* [Princeton, 1950],
p. 8). For the full text, see Zandee, in the work cited
below in the introduction to Doc. II.7b[3] (Pl. II, lines
10-11). Incidentally, in his dedicatory inscription to the
forecourt, pylon, and obelisks at the temple of Amun in
Luxor, Ramesses II says: "Now His Majesty did research
in the office of archives, and he opened the writings of
the House-of-Life. He thus knew the secrets of heaven
and all the mysteries of earth. He found Thebes, the
very Eye of Re, as being the original plot of earth
which arose in the beginning." (See K. A. Kitchen,
Pharaoh Triumphant [Warminster, 1982], p. 48.) The
concept of the primeval land or hill in creation was
examined at length in the remarkable study of A. de
Buck, *De Egyptische Voorstellingen betreffende den
Oerheuvel* (Leiden, 1922). Cf. the brief summary by H.
R. Hall in a review in *The Journal of Egyptian
Archaeology*, Vol. 10 (1924), pp. 185-87. Also, see R.
David, *A Guide to Religious Ritual at Abydos*
(Warminster, 1981), p. 2: "Thus, the first shrine
symbolised creation. Each 'new' temple which was built
throughout Egyptian history was regarded as being a
representative of the island where life was thought to
have started, and each religious locality in Egypt later
claimed to be the actual island of creation. The
sanctuary of each temple was envisaged as the
primaeval mound where the falcon [or whatever form
the demiurge was supposed to have had] alighted, a
centre of great sanctity and power....[Therefore
Egyptians came] to regard every temple as the 'House

of the God'. The form which the deity took varied in the different localities, but the temple was the sacred place where the statue of the god could rest, where the deity could be attended to, and where the gods, otherwise formless and inaccessible, could be approached by the king or mediator [i.e. priest]."

4. Sauneron and Yoyotte, "La naissance du monde," p. 27. Notice that I have included *hpr* (or its causative form *shpr*) in parentheses everywhere it occurred in the preceding footnote in the passage concerning Thebes as the place of creation.

5. E. Hornung, *Conceptions of God in Ancient Egypt: The One and the Many* (Ithaca, N. Y., 1971).

6. *Ibid.*, p. 91, quoting H. Bonnet, *Reallexikon der ägyptischen Religionsgeschichte* (Berlin, 1952), p. 239.

7. A. Erman, *A Handbook of Egyptian Religion* (London, 1907), p. 3.

8. H. Frankfort, *Ancient Egyptian Religion: An Interpretation* (New York, 1948), pp. 3-4.

9. See R. Anthes, "Mythology in Ancient Egypt," in S. N. Kramer, ed., *Mythologies of the Ancient World* (New York, 1961), pp. 1-92. Cf. Anthes, "Egyptian Theology in the Third Millennium B.C.," *Journal of Near Eastern Studies,* Vol. 18 (1959), pp. 169-212.

10. Anthes, "Mythology," p. 21.

11. *Ibid.*, pp. 21-22.

12. Hornung, *Conceptions of God*, pp. 236-39, 242. Cf. E. Drioton, "La religion égyptienne," in M. Brillant and R. Aigrain, eds., *Histoire des religions* (Paris, 1955), pp. 37-38, commenting on what he believed to be the apparent contradiction of the simultaneous presence of monotheistic and polytheistic views in the Egyptian instruction-books: "L'attachement aux affirmations traditionnelles--C'est que l'Égyptien jugeait moins une

doctrine sur son fond tiré au clair que sur les circonstances d'ancienneté, de tradition, de présentation qui l'entouraient. La tradition surtout était, pour une société qui plaçait tout son idéal dans le passé, à l'âge d'or des dieux, la touche décisive de l'autorité d'une assertion. Que si deux traditions contradictoires se présentaient avec des titres équivalents, force était bien de les admettre toutes deux comme valables. Cela faisait simplement pour les Égyptiens un mystère de plus, dont le sentiment non seulement ne leur causait aucune inquiétude, mais leur donnait l'impression de toucher aux arcanes de la science cachée aux mortels par la divinité. Et puisque, croyaient-ils, les deux assertions se conciliaient dans l'inconnaissable, la sagesse la plus haute--nous dirions de nos jours la science la plus avertie--permettait de parler de l'une en empruntant des expressions à l'autre. Voilà ce qu'il y a au fond de ce 'conciliatisme' foncier, qui est une des marques de la pensée égyptienne et qu'on lui a trop souvent reproché comme un manque de fermeté dans le jugement, une phobie de rien abandonner, voire un scepticisme inconscient. C'était en soi une position rationnelle, mais viciée par une fausse information. Ainsi s'explique que dans une série d'écrits monothéistes il se trouve partout des infiltrations polythéistes. Le fait prouve que les anciens Égyptiens qui ont composé ces livres de sagesse tenaient les deux croyances contradictoires pour également vraies, parce que toutes deux bénéficiaient d'une longue tradition dans le pays." Hornung and others would deny that the wisdom literature is fundamentally monotheistic but would hardly deny Drioton's basic view that the role of tradition is fundamental in what Drioton calls the doctrine of "conciliationism".

13. Hornung, *Conceptions of God*, p. 239.

14. S. Sauneron, *Les prêtres de l'ancienne Égypte* (Paris, 1957), pp. 123-25.

15. This "expression" was common for the king throughout the whole period of Egyptian history, at least in written accounts from the sixth dynasty on. The identification of the king with the god Horus appears in countless references in our earliest sustained religious literature, i.e. the *Pyramid Texts*. Such references were collected in the useful dissertation of T. G. Allen, *Horus in the Pyramid Texts* (Chicago, 1916). Hornung, *Conceptions of God*, pp. 141-42, throws doubt on the simple identification of Horus as king with Horus as god. In general Hornung reflects the views of G. Posener, *De la divinité du pharaon* (Paris, 1960), who marshals the evidence distinguishing the pharaoh from a divinity. Hornung's summary (*Conceptions*, p. 192) is of interest: "Proponents of this view [of the declining power of the king after the early dynasties] have always assumed that in the early dynastic period the king had been, as 'Horus,' entirely a god, so that in the Fourth and Fifth Dynasties he subordinated himself as the 'son' of the Highest god. But I have shown... that it is quite uncertain that as 'Horus' the king was identical with or an 'incarnation' of Horus. All we can safely say is that from the beginning of Egyptian history the king was termed Horus, just as from the Fifth Dynasty on the deceased king was termed Osiris; for the early dynastic period and Old Kingdom we do not know precisely in what form the relationship between Horus and the king was envisaged. The extensive textual evidence of the Middle and New kingdoms suggests that at his accession Pharaoh took on the role of Horus, and at his death he took on the role of Osiris, adopting the

attributes of these gods without being identical with them. This form of divinity does not relate to him as an individual but to his office."

16. See the various early examples of the use of a *serekh* surmounted by the Horus falcon collected by S.A.B. Mercer, *Horus, Royal God of Egypt* (London, 1942), pp. 9-12, 18-24. Perhaps the earliest *serekh* with a falcon is one on pottery that may be of Amratian date (*ibid.*, pp. 8-9).

17. A. H. Gardiner, "Horus the Beḥdetite," *JEA*, Vol. 30 (1944), pp. 46-52, discusses the winged figure on this comb in relationship to the winged solar disk that was to become identified with Horus the Beḥdetite in Edfu. Full article pp. 23-60.

18. A. H. Gardiner, *Egyptian Grammar*, 3rd ed. (London, 1957), p. 509, sign S 40, notes that the same sign stood for both the *w*ʾ*s*-staff and the *ḏ*ᶜ*m*-staff. Both phonetic readings are explicitly given in the passages from the *Pyramid Texts* quoted below in the text. A. Moret, *Du caractère religieux de la royauté pharaonique (Annales du Musée Guimet: Bibliothèque d'études*, Vol. 15) (Paris, 1902), p. 293, had long since remarked that in temple reliefs the *w*ʾ*s*-staffs were shown as supporting the heavens.

19. R. T. R. Clark, *Myth and Symbol in Ancient Egypt* (London, 1959; paperback ed. 1978), p. 219.

20. H. Kees, *Der Götterglaube in alten Ägypten* (Berlin, 1956), p. 234, n. 1. Cf. F. W. von Bissing, ed., *Das Re-Heiligtum des Königs Ne-Woser-Re*, Vol. 3: H. Kees, *Die grosse Festdarstellung* (Leipzig, 1928), p. 41 and plate 21, Nr. 346.

21. Anthes, "Mythology in Ancient Egypt," pp. 85-86.

22. The pedestal of a statue of King Djoser

includes the name and titles of Imhotep: "The chancellor of the King of Lower Egypt, the first after the King of Upper Egypt, administrator of the great palace, hereditary lord, Great Seer (the High Priest of Heliopolis), Imhotep the builder, the sculptor, the maker of stone vases...." (see J.-P. Lauer, *Saqqara: The Royal Cemetery of Memphis. Excavations and Discoveries since 1850* [London, 1976], p. 92 and plate 89).

23. For the epithet and (later) title "Son of Re", see H. Müller, *Die formale Entwicklung der Titulatur der ägyptischen Könige* (Glückstadt/Hamburg/New York, 1938), pp. 63-73.

24. Clark, *Myth and Symbol*, p. 44.

25. For a penetrating consideration of the original Osiris and Horus myths as reflected in the *Pyramid Texts,* see J. G. Griffiths, *The Origins of Osiris and his Cult* (Leiden, 1980), Chap. 1, where a good many passages from the *Pyramid Texts* are translated and analyzed. See also Plutarch, *De Iside et Osiride*, edited, translated, and commented on by J. G. Griffiths (Cardiff, 1970). A brief account of these myths with some attention to the Middle Kingdom and later sources was given by Anthes, "Mythology in Ancient Egypt," pp. 68-85. See also Clark, *Myth and Symbol*, pp. 97-180. Though it is often said that from the earliest days Osiris was a god of vegetation, the first evidence of an unambiguous nature indicating any connection of Osiris with vegetation or fertility appears in the *Coffin Texts* (Spell 80, II,90; not included in our extracts below) where the deceased identifies himself with Osiris and says that he is one "whom Atum made into Neper (the Grain-god)...when I became Osiris". Similarly in Spell 300 (also omitted from our extracts) entitled "Becoming Neper" the deceased says (IV, 167-69): "I am Osiris....I

have grown fat through you, I flourish through you....I live and grow as Neper....I live and die, for I am emmer and I will not perish." Griffiths, *The Origins of Osiris*, pp. 165-66, throws some doubt on the usefulness of this passage for identifying Osiris and Neper, suggesting that the deceased is identifying himself with a series of gods of which Osiris and Neper are two. But there is no doubt from this passage that the deceased, who is most commonly identified with Osiris from the fifth dynasty, is at the same time identified with the grain itself. This idea of connecting rebirth with vegetation may be very old, but the identification of Osiris with vegetation may have followed the practice of also identifying the reborn deceased with Osiris. For Seth's role in the legends, see the thorough study of H. Te Velde, *Seth, God of Confusion* (Leiden, 1977).

26. This is borne out by the fact that there is no mention of Osiris in the *Annals* for the first four dynasties and part of the fifth which we have presented as Document I.1. The earliest known pictorial representation of Osiris is on a block of the fifth-dynasty king Djedkare (see the photograph opposite the title page in Griffiths, *The Origins of Osiris*). Furthermore Griffiths in the same work summarizes on page 41 what we know about the cult of Osiris in the early period: "The earliest evidence for the cult of Osiris is still confined to the closing phases of the Fifth Dynasty. His name occurs in the Pyramid Texts of Wenis in Saqqara, and Wenis is the last king of the Fifth Dynasty. His name also occurs in private mastabas of this dynasty, especially in the offering formulae.

"While there is every likelihood that the Osirian material in the Pyramid Texts derives in part from a much earlier date, so far it has not proved possible to track down the god or his symbols tangibly to the First or Second Dynasty. An interesting find was made by Zaki Y. Saad in a tomb of the First Dynasty at Helwan--two ivory pieces which, in his opinion, form the most ancient example of the *djed*-pillar, which in turn he describes as 'the symbol of the god Osiris'. The *djed*-pillar, however, is not consistently an Osirian symbol, at least not in its early forms. Only in the New Kingdom does it become unambiguously Osirian. Even so, do these pieces represent *djed*-pillars? They seem to imitate papyrus-columns, with four papyrus flowers superimposed one over the other. It may equally be doubted whether the ivory toilet spoon [another of Saad's pieces] is at this time a symbol of the goddess Isis, or again the knot represented on the adjacent box lid [a knot later associated with Isis]." In a footnote to this passage Griffiths acknowledges that some scholars, such as Drioton, Vandier, Westendorf, Emery, and Clark, accept Saad's claims concerning these pieces, though Helck does not.

27. Clark, *Myth and Symbol*, pp. 51-52. Hornung, in his *Conceptions of God*, p. 178, stresses the connection of snake-forms with the Abyss: "These limitless depths also house the enemies of the gods, in particular Apopis, who daily stretches out his snake's head to attack the sun god, and must forever be driven into nonexistence. For the Egyptians the form of a snake... has a particular affinity with nonexistence. The primeval god who outlives the existent world changes into a snake at the end of time, and after the Amarna period the Egyptians devised the image of the snake coiled back on itself, called 'tail-in-mouth'; in the Roman period this image was called Ouroboros, 'the

tail-swallower' [see Fig. II.6b]. The complete circle of the snake's body illustrates--so far as it is possible to depict it--the nonexistent which encompasses the world continually on all sides.... There is a similar image in the New Kingdom underworld books; a snake, out of which one hour is mysteriously 'born,' and then 'swallowed' again when the hour is passed--which thus embodies the limitless, vertiginous aspect of time." See pp. 172-85 for Hornung's brilliant excursus on the nonexistent identified temporally and spatially with chaos as opposed to the existent identified with the cosmos. See also his "Chaotische Bereiche in der geordneten Welt," *ZÄS*, Vol. 81 (1956), pp. 28-32. Incidentally the snake with his tail in his mouth is also depicted in the *Book of Amduat* (see Fig. II.34) and at the beginning of the *Book of Gates* (Fig. II.41). For the Kematef-snake in Medina Habu and the Earth-Creator snake, see the end of note 66 below. See also K. Sethe, *Amun und die acht Urgötter von Hermopolis: Eine Untersuchung über Ursprung und Wesen des ägyptischen Götterkönigs* (Berlin, 1929), pp. 88-89.

28. Clark, *Myth and Symbol*, p. 52.

29. I may have given the impression above that the four generations of gods embraced by the Ennead were neatly and canonically described in the *Pyramid Texts*, including just the nine gods we have mentioned: Atum, Shu, Tefenet, Geb, Nut, Osiris, Seth, Isis, and Nephthys. This is far from the truth. I have already mentioned that at times Horus appears as the brother of Seth rather than as his nephew, thus increasing the number of gods of the basic four generations to ten instead of nine. Furthermore, this augmentation persists in the tradition that the children of Nut, whose births were celebrated on the epagomenal days, included Horus

the Elder along with Osiris, Seth, Isis, and Nephthys (see Doc. I.1, n. 112). I have also indicated above that Maat was often described as another daughter of Re, though she was at times identified with Tefenet. For other divergencies from the constitution of the Ennead described in the text, see Anthes, "Egyptian Theology," pp. 194-202. As he notes (p. 196): "The deities who belong to the pedigree [of Horus], with the exception of Horus, are called 'the great Ennead' as early as the Pyramid Texts (Pyr. 1655 [see Doc. II.1, Sect. 1655]). For the later periods, H. Brugsch, *Thesaurus inscriptionum aegyptiacarum* (Leipzig, 1883-84 [reprint, Graz, 1968]), pp. 724-30, quotes thirty-nine enumerations of the members of the Ennead. One of them, No. 11, is the duplicate of Pyr. 1655..., but none of the other thirty-eight lists contains the same nine gods completely and exclusively." Whatever diversity there might have been in the composition of the Ennead, in the Heliopolitan system it was surely considered as having issued from Atum as the creator god either directly or indirectly and the gods making it up were considered as a single corporation or company. G. Jéquier, *Considérations sur les religions égyptiennes* (Neuchâtel, 1946), pp. 114-16, stresses that the nine signs for god *(ntr)* used for "Ennead" were arranged in three columns of three signs and thus constituted a kind of super plural (three signs being an accepted form of the plural in hieroglyphic writing). As such, "Ennead" merely stands for a company of gods without specification of the number of gods in the company. This suggestion had been made in a preliminary form long since by C. R. Lepsius, *Über die Götter der vier Elemente bei den Ägyptern* (Berlin, 1856), p. 227. Hornung's remarks on the Ennead (*Conceptions of God*, pp. 221-23) also stress its variable number and composition. Cf. Kees, *Götterglaube*, pp. 150-51, and K. Sethe, *Dramatische Texte*, p. 49 (see full title in Introduction to Doc. II.9 below). As E. Otto notes in his *Egyptian Art and the Cults of Osiris and Amon* (London, 1968), pp. 46-47, the Great Ennead of Abydos in the time of Tuthmosis I consisted of Khnum of Herewer, Khnum of Kebehu, Thoth of Heseret, Horus of Letopolis, Horus the defender of his father, Wepwawet of Upper and Lower Egypt (the dualized person of the Upper Egyptian royal god).

30. M. Lichtheim, *Ancient Egyptian Literature*, Vol. 1 (Berkeley/Los Angeles/London, 1975), p. 106. For a discussion of this work of Merikare's, editions of the text, other translations, and studies, see Miss Lichtheim's introduction to this document, pp. 97-98. The references to "shines in the sky" and to "sails by [across the sky]" confirm that the god understood here is Re. Cf. Drioton, "La religion égyptienne," pp. 36-37.

31. For a discussion of the Egyptian names for Hermopolis and the doctrines of the Ogdoad, see above all Sethe, *Amun und die acht Urgötter von Hermopolis*, pp. 36-38. Also consult G. Roeder, "Die Kosmogonie von Hermopolis," *Egyptian Religion*, Vol. 1 (1933), pp. 1-37 (passim); Roeder, "Zwei hieroglyphische Inschriften aus Hermopolis (Ober-Ägypten)," *Annales du Service des Antiquités de l'Égypte*, Vol. 52 (1954), pp. 315-74, and particularly pp. 371-72. For evidence of the town name Khmun in the Old Kingdom, see L. Borchardt, *Das Grabdenkmal des Königs Saḥu-Reᶜ*, Vol. 2 (Leipzig, 1913), pp. 99 and 101 and Pl. 21, and C. R. Lepsius, *Denkmäler aus Ägypten und Äthiopen*, Abt. II (reprint, Geneva, 1972), 112d (column on extreme left). Cf. Jéquier, *Considérations sur les religions égyptiennes*, p.

162, fig. 58.

32. Cf. Sauneron and Yoyotte, "La naissance du monde," pp. 52-54. J. Assmann, *Zeit und Ewigkeit im alten Ägypten* (Heidelberg, 1975), p. 21, interprets the negative characteristics of pre-existence as "lightlessness" *(kkw)*, "placelessness" *(tnmw)*, and "endlessness" *(ḥḥw)*.

33. Sauneron and Yoyotte, "La naissance du monde," p. 53. But see the classic treatment of the Ogdoad in Sethe's *Amun und die acht Urgötter*, where the variation in the names of these primitive gods over the whole period of pharaonic history is given in Tafel I appended to the volume. An interesting collection of illustrations of the Ogdoad was added by Lepsius, *Über die Götter der vier Elemente*, Taf. I-V. It shows the Ogdoad represented in a number of different forms of eight gods: (1) all sitting--four frog-headed male human forms and four serpent-headed female human figures, (2) all standing--four short-skirted male figures and four long-skirted female figures, (3) all sitting--four bearded males and four beardless females, (4) eight baboons, no distinction between male and female, (5) all standing--grouped as pairs, each pair consisting of a frog-headed male and a serpent-headed female, the first couple followed by Ptah, the second by Thoth, and the last two by no other god; (6) all sitting--four serpent-headed male gods and four lioness-headed female gods; and a number of other representations that are variations on the five listed above. As an example, see my Fig. II.8a.

34. See Sauneron and Yoyotte, "La naissance du monde," p. 53; Kees, *Götterglaube*, p. 307; and Clark, *Myth and Symbol*, p. 55.

35. Sethe, *Amun und die acht Urgötter*, pp. 39-40,

doubts Maspero's theory that the Five consists of four gods personalizing the basic concepts of the Ogdoad plus Thoth. For an extended treatment of Thoth, see P. Boylan, *Thoth: the Hermes of Egypt* (Oxford, 1922). Still another view of the company of Five is given by Jéquier in *Considérations sur les religions égyptiennes*, pp. 53-59. There we find an interesting account of the development of the Ogdoad. He begins with the study of four cynocephalic baboons, which he sees as the earliest representatives of the four qualities of the Primordial Abyss. Then next, he believes, followed the creation of the Five by the addition of a female goddess, namely, the nome and city goddess, The Hare. From this then developed a more satisfactory arrangement where instead of one goddess each of the principal male gods was matched with a female counterpart, and so the Ogdoad was born. He believes this to have taken place at the end of the prehistoric period but he has no evidence earlier than the evidence I have already mentioned that shows the name of Hermopolis as The Eighttown appearing in the Old Kingdom. Of course, he may be correct in assuming that the name goes back to a time just prior to the first dynasty but there is no way to test the assumption.

36. See H. Kees, "Die Feuerinsel in Sargtexten und im Totenbuch," *ZÄS*, Vol. 78 (1942), p. 43 (full article pp. 41-53).

37. So Clark, *Myth and Symbol*, p. 55, interprets this spell. But Faulkner, *Coffin Texts*, Vol. 3, 167 (Spell 1129) [full bibliographical reference in Doc. II.2 below] translates it very ambiguously: "This portal has closed on me as on the body of the egg from which I emerged. It is the darkness of my father Nu which does it, being far from this portal." Faulkner in note 7 says: "This

passage is unintelligible to me." But even if Clark is wrong in so interpreting this spell, the passage above the next note clearly conveys the basic ideas expressed by Clark here, especially as regards the Ogdoad's parentage of the Primeval Egg. For this parentage also see Sethe, *Amun und die acht Urgötter*, pp. 62 and 66 n. 2.

38. Sauneron and Yoyotte, "La naissance du monde," p. 61.

39. See Doc. II.7b[3] (IV,1-IV,8). For its association with the Hermopolitan doctrine of the Great Cackler, see Sauneron and Yoyotte, "La naissance du monde," p. 61.

40. Sauneron and Yoyotte, "La Naissance du monde," p. 61; Roeder, "Die Kosmogonie," p. 10, and G. Lefebvre, *Le tombeau de Petosiris* (Cairo, 1923-24), I, p. 140 and II, pp. 56-57. See also Lefebvre, "L'oeuf divin d'Hermopolis," *Annales du Service des Antiquités de l'Égypte*, Vol. 23 (1923), pp. 65-67.

41. Kees, "Die Feuerinsel," pp. 41-53, and his *Götterglaube*, p. 309.

42. Roeder, "Kosmogonie," p. 11. In the hymns to the gods found in Haremhab's tomb at Saqqara we see that Thoth, who is entitled "Lord of Hermopolis", has some characteristics of a creator god, for he is said to be "a self-created one who was not born". But in the same verse he is mentioned as "he who gives prescriptions to the Westerners who are in the Following of the sun god", which seems like a purely scriptorial function. See J. Assmann, *Ägyptische Hymnen und Gebete* (Zurich and Munich, 1975), p. 168.

43. Boylan, *Thoth*, p. 73; H. Brugsch, *Religion und Mythologie der alten Ägypter* (Leipzig, 1891), p. 49, gives a passage in which Thoth was designated not only

as the "Heart of Re" (as he was often called in other Ptolemaic sources) but also as the "Tongue of Atum". Cf. A. H. Gardiner, "Some Personifications. II. *ḤU, 'Authoritative Utterance.' 'SIA' ', 'Understanding,'" PSBA*, Vol. 38 (1916), pp. 50-51 (full article pp. 43-54, 83-94), where he gives examples in which courtiers assert to the king (whose powers on earth match those of his solar father) that he has Hu in his mouth and Sia in his heart.

44. Gardiner, *ibid.*, p. 52: "Wherever, in fact, Ḥu and Sia' appear as attributes of kingship, it is by virtue of the old legend which tells how Re^c, on emerging from the Nun, invented 'Utterance' and 'Understanding' to aid him in his creation and governance of the world. The myth...whereby Re^c fashioned Ḥike', 'Magic,' for the identical purpose, now appears as a variant version of the same idea, Ḥike' [or Heka] implying both the power of knowledge and the power of speech, but adding to these conceptions the notion of mysterious efficacy." P. 53: "It is not unjustifiable, therefore, to suppose that the legend of Sia' and Ḥu provided the model for that curious analysis [in the *Memphite Theology*] of Ptah into 'heart'..., the seat of the intelligence, and into 'tongue'..., the organ of speech, the interaction of which two sources of purposeful will is said to have resulted in the creation of all things." See also Gardiner's postscript in Vol. 39 (1917), p. 139: "I have tried to prove that the so-called philosophical text from Memphis (*Brit. Mus.* No. 135), in explaining the creation of the universe as due to Ptah, who took shape in Thoth as 'heart' or 'intellect' and in Horus as 'tongue,' has merely adapted to its special purpose the Heliopolitan legend according to which Atum divided into Ḥu 'Creative Utterance' and 'Sia' 'Intelligence' (see

pp. 53-54 of my first article)." Note that here Gardiner (following a common misinterpretation of the relevant passage of the *Memphite Theology*) reverses the roles of Thoth and Horus. The proper roles are Horus as heart and Thoth as tongue. For a recent summary of the creative role of Hu and Sia, see the article "Hu" by H. Altenmüller in W. Helck and W. Westendorf, eds., *Lexikon der Ägyptologie*, Vol. 3 (Wiesbaden, 1980), cc. 65-68. We should also note the scene at Dendera where Hu and Sia appear in the following of Thoth and Maat and are accompanied by Seeing and Hearing. They are preceded by the Ogdoad (see Fig. II.8f). Hu and Sia often appear in the solar bark as personalized gods (see Fig. II.12b). On more than one occasion Hu is replaced by Heka, the god of Magic or Magical Word (cf. Jéquier, *Considérations sur les religions égyptiennes*, p. 80). Jéquier correctly associates Sia and Hu with the rebirth of the sun every morning after its night voyage through the Underworld (see also Doc. II.4, n. 2).

45. Boylan, *Thoth*, pp. 92-97.

46. *Ibid.*, pp. 180-200. I have sometimes translated epithets differently from Boylan, but without omitting any important ones.

47. H. Grapow, "Die Welt vor der Schöpfung," *ZÄS*, Vol. 67 (1931), p. 37 (full article pp. 34-38).

48. Boylan, *Thoth*, p. 109, n. 1.

49. In the *Pyramid Texts* there are only two direct mentions of Ptah (Sects. 560 and 1482). M. Sandman Holmberg, *The God Ptah* (Lund and Copenhagen, 1946), pp. 24-25, says that these citations are interesting not because of their content but because they are the only ones in this large collection. After all, Ptah was the principal god in the capital city and hence one might expect more references to him. There

are perhaps two explanations. By the time the *Pyramid Texts* were put upon the walls of the pyramids, Re had become the most important god and references to him far outnumber or tend to mute references to other gods. Furthermore, since Ptah's center was in Memphis, the residence of the king who was the Living Horus, it is not surprising in the early period to find Ptah taking a position inferior to Horus.

50. Sandman Holmberg, *The God Ptah*, p. 27. His craft activities were still being emphasized at Edfu (E. Chassinat, *Le Temple d'Edfou*, Vol. 2, [Cairo, 1918], p. 37): "Words to be said by Ptah 'south of his wall', the Lord of the Life of the Two Lands (=Memphis or a district of it), the great god at Edfu, the father of men and women, the splendid god who came into being alone at the beginning. He has no equal, he who has molded himself in the beginning without having father or mother. He made his body completely alone, he who created the gods, he who created without being created, the one who lifts the heavens by the work of his hands...."

51. Sandman Holmberg, *The God Ptah*, pp. 30, 33-34.

52. *Ibid.*, p. 33.

53. J. Zandee, "Das Schöpferwort im alten Ägypten," *Verbum: Essays on Some Aspects of the Religious Function of Words dedicated to Dr. H. W. Obbink* (Rheno-Traiectina, Vol. 6, 1964), pp. 33-66.

54. Sandman Holmberg, *The God Ptah*, pp. 41, 14* (51).

55. Of all the treatments of the cosmogonic section of the *Memphite Theology*, the most useful is that found in Sethe's *Dramatische Texte*, pp. 46-70 (for full title see bibliography in the introduction to Doc.

II.9 below).

56. Note that in the Hymn to Ptah (Doc. II.7d, K.23) Re is referred to as "his (i.e. Ptah's) son".

57. H. and H. A. Frankfort, J. A. Wilson, T. Jacobsen, and W. A. Irwin, *The Intellectual Adventure of Ancient Man* (Chicago and London, 1946; Phoenix ed., 1977), p. 58.

58. *Ibid.*, p. 56.

59. According to Nims, *Thebes of the Pharaohs*, p. 18: "The name borne by the new king was known as early as the reign of Intef III [eleventh dynasty] and the sheets in which were wrapped the bodies of sixty soldiers who had fallen in the siege of some fortress in a campaign of Montuhotep II [the uniter of the kingdom] have in ten instances names compounded with Amon. One already shows Amon's claims to power, Sankh-Amensekhemtawy, meaning, 'Amon, the (most) powerful (god) of the Two Lands, sustains life'. But while names compounded with Amon were popular in court circles, none occurs in the list of more than eighty persons in the letters of Hekanakht [eleventh dynasty] and another contemporary archive. However, in the latter a blessing is pronounced in the name of Amon-re, the earliest evidence of Amon's identification with the ancient sun god." For the reference in the reign of Intef III, see Sethe, *Amun und die acht Urgötter von Hermopolis*, p. 32. See also pp. 11-12 for references to Amun in the eleventh and twelfth dynasties.

60. Sethe, *Amun und die acht Urgötter von Hermopolis*, p. 79, develops the thesis that Amun was imported into Thebes from Hermopolis. This is vigorously combatted by G. A. Wainwright, "The Origin of Amun," *The Journal of Egyptian Archaeology*, Vol.

49 (1963), pp. 21-23, and earlier in his review of Sethe's book in that journal, Vol. 17 (1931), pp. 151-52. Wainwright argues that Amun was essentially a form of Min. H. Kees, *Götterglaube im alten Ägypten*, p. 345, accepts Sethe's view. No one disputes that Amun took over the ithyphallic form and accompanying fertility aspects of Min (see Sethe, *Amun*, pp. 19-21).

61. Epithets and eulogies are found in German translation in Assmann, *Ägyptische Hymnen und Gebete*, Nos. 72-86, pp. 188-99. The textual sources and studies of them are conveniently given in Assmann's commentaries to Nos. 72-86. Needless to say, I have made no effort to include all the epithets, but I have given the most common and the most distinctive ones referring to Amon-Re's cosmogonic activities. See also H. M. Stewart, "Traditional Egyptian Sun Hymns of the New Kingdom," *Bulletin of the Institute of Archaeology*, University of London, Vol. 6 (1967), pp. 29-74.

62. A. H. Gardiner, *Hieratic Papyri in the British Museum: Third Series, Chester Beatty Gift*, Vol. 1 (London, 1935), p. 32, slightly altered.

63. A. Moret, *Le rituel du cult divin journalier en Égypte* (Paris, 1902), p. 108.

64. *Ibid.*, p. 123, and p. 123 n. 1.

65. *Ibid.*, pp. 129-30. Cf. Assmann, *Ägyptische Hymnen und Gebete*, No. 122, pp. 264-66.

66. Assmann, *Ägyptische Hymnen*, No. 129, pp. 293-99, and N. de Garis Davies, *The Temple of Hibis in El-Khargeh Oasis*, Part III, *The Decoration* (New York, 1953), plate 32. Incidentally, we should note the investigation of the relationship between Amun and the Ogdoad made by Sethe in his *Amun*, where (p. 56) he quotes an inscription to the effect that Amun "created Ptah in order to produce the Ogdoad" and another one

that asserts that he "created Ptah the goldsmith for building the Ogdoad". Still we also find (*ibid.*, p. 49) that Amun is called the "heir of the Ogdoad". As a matter of fact, Sethe concludes (p. 60) that a very complicated relationship between Amun and the Ogdoad developed as the result of the splitting of the primordial form of Amun into four different gods: (1) Amon-Re, the father of the father of the Ogdoad, the one who was the primordial snake Kematef in Medina Habu; (2) Amenapet I, the father of the Ogdoad, equivalent to Ptah-Tenen of Memphis, who every ten days appeared in the Temple of Amun at Luxor, the one who was the Earth-Creator snake; (3) Amun, who was one of the Ogdoad of Hermopolis, and like them was the father of the solar god Re, and who was worshiped as a deceased god in Medina Habu, being the primordial form of the gods; and (4) Amenapet II, the heir of the Ogdoad, the great living god, the chief of the gods, equivalent to Horus the Son of Isis and Osiris. This situation shows how complicated the later developments became.

67. On the history of the personifying of the Aten before Akhenaten, see the brief remarks of A. Piankoff, *The Shrines of Tut-Ankh-Amon* (New York, 1955), pp. 5-6.

68. Sandman Holmberg, *The God Ptah*, p. 48, quotes a statement from the Temple of Horus at Edfu that the king "had created Edfu on a potter's wheel, like 'Him who is south of his wall' (Ptah)".

69. S. Sauneron, *Esna*, Vol. 5: *Les fêtes religieuses d'Esna* (Cairo, 1962), p. 213, translates this phrase as "que fit ce qui est et ce qui n'est pas (encore)". This gives the negative half ("that which is not [yet]") the sense of a potential existence rather than the sense of nonexistence defined as that which is in the realm of

chaos (cf. Hornung's interpretation referred to in note 27 above).

70. Sauneron, *Esna*, Vol. 5, pp. 249-50, 255.

71. For example, Jéquier, *Considérations sur les religions égyptiennes*, pp. 14-25, describes the history of Egyptian religion as passing through three stages: fetishism (=veneration of gods in the form of inanimate objects), zoolatry (=the veneration of gods in animal forms), and anthropomorphism. Hornung mentions this theory in the course of analyzing the hieroglyphs used for "god" in his *Conceptions of God*, pp. 33-42. The three glyphs for "god" discussed by Hornung are shown in Fig. II.19. The wrapped pole on the left may indicate some early veneration of a god by means of an inanimate object, the falcon on a perch veneration by means of an animal form, and the seated figure with the beard veneration by means of a human form. The first two go back at least to the beginning of writing, while the third appears as early as the beginning of the Old Kingdom. But, as Hornung points out, the use of the wrapped pole for *ntr* (=god) may show us a fetish, but it tells us nothing more about the early Egyptian conception of god (and indeed we might well add that neither do the other two signs). A fourth sign for god, a star, is said by Hornung to be attested only from the beginning of the Ptolemaic period. We can point out, however, that the appearance of a star in the name of a fortified place whose name may be translated "The Might of Horus the God" (F. Petrie, *Royal Tombs*, Vol. 2, pl. 23, 200) and which dates from the second dynasty would (if the translation is correct) indicate the use of the star as a glyph for "god" at a much earlier time. From this we could infer that in this early period the gods were thought of as at least residing in

the stars, as they were somewhat later in the *Pyramid Texts.* Another translation less favorable to my interpretation would be "The Might of Horus the Star", which, however, would still confirm the view that at least Horus was conceived as a star in the sky. We have again and again in this chapter referred to the personification of abstract concepts as gods or goddesses: Maat (Order or Justice) represented as the daughter of Re, Sia (Understanding), Hu (Utterance), Heka (Magic), and so on. Černý has some succinct observations on the phenomenon of personification, *Ancient Egyptian Religion*, pp. 58-59: "Both the deities dwelling or manifested in objects and animals, and the gods who are personifications of natural phenomena and are manifested in the phenomena themselves, underwent at a relatively early date a personification in human form; but besides these two classes there are a number of divinities who are personifications in human form of certain abstract conceptions or activities. Analogy on the original fetishes and animal and nature gods played its part here and underlying human characters were added to the abstract nouns of the language which made it possible to treat them on the same footing as other deities in pictorial art or in myths. In representations they were usually provided with certain marks which made them at once recognizable to an Egyptian. We have already met personifications of Shoy *'Fate'* as a man and of Renenet *'Nursing'* as a woman, and may add here personifications of certain materials, like Napri *'Corn'* as a god, Nub *'Gold'* as a goddess (because for some reason or other *'Gold'* became early an epithet or attribute of the Goddess Hathor), Kebhowet *'Cold Water Libation'* as a goddess, and activities such as *'Weaving'* (the goddess Tayet) and 'Winepressing' (the god Shesmu). Certain conceptions of time are found personified in the goddess Ronpet 'Year', Akhet 'Flood-season' and Proyet 'Spring' and the god Shomu 'Summer', the sex of the deity being decided by the gender of the Egyptian words. There are also geographical conceptions such as the goddess Sokhet 'Cultivable Plain', the god Ha 'Desert' and the goddess Amentet 'West', who bear on their heads hieroglyphic signs for 'field', 'desert' and 'west' respectively. The most important among all the personifications, however, is Ma^cet, personifying both 'Right' and 'Justice'....[her] name appears as early as the IInd Dynasty; very early too she is represented bearing on her head an ostrich feather which for some unknown reason had become her symbol. She is 'daughter of Re', for Re, the sun-god, rules the universe according to the principles of 'right' and 'justice' (both ma^cet) which he has laid down, and Ma^cet is, therefore, regularly seen standing on the prow of the sun-barque accompanying the sun-god on his course across the sky."

72. See Kees, *Der Götterglaube im alten Ägypten*, pp. 101-02; Jéquier, *Considérations*, pp. 175-76, and Černý, *Ancient Egyptian Religion*, p. 18.

73. Moret, *Le rituel du culte divin journalier en Égypte*, passim.

74. For translations of this story of Re and Isis, see that of Wilson in J. B. Pritchard, *Ancient Near Eastern Texts Relating to the Old Testament* (Princeton, 1950), pp. 12-14, and that of A. Piankoff, *The Litany of Re* (New York, 1964), pp. 56-59. The story is in the form of a spell, whose opening lines encapsulate Re's activities as a creator god: "The spell of the divine god, who came into being by himself, who made heaven, earth, water, the breath of life, fire, gods, men, small

and large cattle, creeping things, birds, and fishes, the king of men and gods at one time *(for whom) the limits (go) beyond years*, abounding in names, unknown to that (god) and unknown to this (god)" (Wilson). At one point in the story Isis asks Re his name, "(for) a man lives who is called by his name". This shows once more the creative power of naming.

75. Hornung, *Conceptions of God*, p. 110.

76. Moret, *Du caractère religieux de la royauté pharaonique*, p. 57, n. 2: "Il est bien caractéristique du caractère religieux de la royauté que le Pharaon ait officiellement quatorze 'doubles' [i.e. 'kas'] comme son père Râ. De même, au *décret de Phtah-Totunen* [i.e. Ptah-Tatenen] (1.13) on apporte au roi les '14 doubles de Râ'. Le soleil possède en effet sept âmes (*biou* [i.e. *b*'*w* or bas]) et quatorze doubles (*kaou* [i.e. *k*'*w* or kas]), ainsi que l'atteste un texte du temple de Philae (Mariette, *Denderah*, texte, p. 219, n. 3). Ces quatorze doubles figurent souvent sur les murs des temples ptolémaïques; ils portent tous un nom d'une faculté ou d'un sens (ouïe, vue, entendement, puissance, etc.) et sont 'comme les émanations de la divinité par lesquelles la divinité vit et qu'elle transmet a l'homme.' (Mariette)." See also J. Dümichen, *Altägyptische Tempelinschriften in den Jahren 1863-1865*, Vol. 1 (Leipzig, 1867), pl. 29, where it is noted that prayers are offered to each ba and ka. In an inscription on a stela at Abu Simbel dating from Year 35 of Ramesses II's reign the fourteen kas of Re are said to have been given to him by Thoth (Lepsius, *Denkmäler*, Abt. III, Bl. 194, line 13; J. F. Champollion, *Monuments de l'Égypte et de la Nubie*, Vol. 1 [Paris, 1835], Pl. 38, line 13). See also Budge's *An Egyptian Hieroglyphic Dictionary*, Vol. 2 (London, 1920) under *k*'*w*. Gardiner, "Some Personifications...," (1916), pp.

84-85, 94-95, discusses eight lists of the kas of Re, seven of which include the same names. For the full title of Gardiner's article, see note 43 above.

77. J. Vandier, *La religion égyptienne* (Paris, 1949), p. 132.

78. H. Bonnet, *Reallexikon der ägyptischen Religionsgeschichte* (Berlin, 1952), p. 359. For information on the ten bas of Amun, see J.-C. Goyon's treatment in R. A. Parker, J. Leclant, and J.-C. Goyon, *The Edifice of Taharqa by the Sacred Lake of Karnak* (Providence, Rhode Island, and London, 1979), pp. 73-79, where reference is given to the discovery by C. Traunecker of the ten bas of Amun painted in fresco on the walls of the north crypt of the temple of Opet. The identical scene of the procession of the ten bas was apparently present on the south and north walls of room F of the edifice of Taharqa.

79. Zandee, "Das Schöpferwort im alten Ägypten," p. 60: "Das Schöpferwort und das magische Wort sind identisch. Auch eine Beschwörung ist ein Schöpferwort. Es beraubt Dämonen ihrer Kraft. Es errichtet Ordnung statt Chaos. Es beseitigt Gefahren und lässt einen erwünschten Zustand eintreten. Es vertreibt den Tod und bringt das Leben."

80. Boylan, *Thoth: the Hermes of Egypt*, pp. 126-27. Boylan also says (p. 126) that *hike [heka]* "seems...to resemble, somehow, other qualities, or endowments needed for the full perfection of the glorified Dead--something, that is, on the same plane as the so-called Kas of Re. It deifies to some extent. Again it is clear from a number of passages that *hike* implies powers over things demonic and evil.... The power thus employed against evil is often described as if it were something carried in the mouth, and put into

action by utterance."

81. J. F. Borghouts, *Ancient Magical Texts* (Leiden, 1978), p. 2.

82. *Ibid.*, p. 22.

83. *Ibid.*, pp. 33-34.

84. A. H. Gardiner, "Magic (Egyptian)," J. Hastings, *Encyclopedia of Religion and Ethics*, Vol. 8 (Edinburgh, 1915), pp. 262-63 (whole article, pp. 262-69).

85. S. Sauneron, *Le papyrus magique illustré de Brooklyn* (New York, 1970), pp. 16-17.

86. *Ibid.*, p. 13.

87. See the work of Moret cited in note 63, which, despite its relative age, is still the most penetrating examination of Egyptian rituals. For a short, lucid account of temple rituals, see the work of Sauneron mentioned in note 14.

88. Hornung, *Conceptions of God*, p. 133.

89. P. Kaplony, *Die Inschriften der ägyptischen Frühzeit*, Vol. 1 (Wiesbaden, 1963), p. 291.

90. Lichtheim, *Ancient Egyptian Literature*, Vol. 1, p. 212.

91. Sethe, *Amun und die acht Urgötter*, pp. 53-61.

92. Lichtheim, *op. cit.* in n. 90, p. 213.

93. See the work of Moret cited in note 18 and that of Frankfort in note 3. See also G. Steindorff and K. C. Seele, *When Egypt Ruled the East* (revised ed., Chicago and London, 1957), pp. 82-83, who say that from the earliest time the king was considered as an embodiment of the falcon-god or as the son of the sun-god. They mention the depiction of the divine birth of Amenhotep III in the temple of Amun at Luxor. They quote a flowery courtier's speech in which we read (p. 83): "If you sayest to the waters, 'Come upon the mountain,' a flood floweth directly at thy word, for

thou art Re...and Khepri.... Authority is in thy mouth and perception is in thy heart; the activity of thy tongue is the temple of Maat... and God sitteth upon thy lips." These authors concede that not often in the time of Tuthmosis III or his immediate predecessors was the king the object of worship in the temples devoted to him. But they point "to the temple of Soleb in Nubia where Amenhotep III was worshipped 'as the living image of Re on earth,'...".

94. See the references to Posener and Hornung in note 15.

95. Moret, *Du caractère religieux*, pp. 43-48, displays from Lepsius, *Denkmäler*, Abt. III, plate 121a, the figure from the tomb of Haremhab of the solar disk with the signs for power, duration, and life hanging from the bottom of the disk. He translates the inscription somewhat close to the figure as follows: "Re makes magical protection *(sʲ)* of your body." He suggests that this magical protection is that involved in the phrase: *sʲ ᶜnḫ ḏd* ("the magical protection of life-power-duration"), which he then interprets as a kind of fluid that the god imparts to the king. I would prefer to translate the inscription *(wnn Rᶜ m sʲw ḫᶜw-k)* "Re will be as magical protection to your body." This would modify the idea that Re transfers some kind of fluid to the king. Still, the basic idea that Re will somehow provide the king with magical protection is certainly intended.

96. J. H. Breasted, *Ancient Records of Egypt*, Vol. 2 (New York, 1906; repr. 1962), pp. 323-24. I have altered the spelling of the king's name to Tuthmosis to conform to my practice in this volume. Furthermore I have changed Breasted's reading of the name of the earth-god from Keb to Geb to follow the now generally

accepted reading. I have added the phrases in brackets.

97. Bonnet, *Reallexikon der ägyptischen Religionsgeschichte*, p. 835.

98. *Ibid.*, p. 837.

99. Breasted, *Ancient Records*, Vol. 2, pp. 60-61.

100. F. Ll. Griffith and H. Thompson, *The Demotic Magical Papyrus of London and Leiden* (London, 1904), pp. 50-53. This papyrus dates from the third century A.D. and shows considerable Greek influence, including passages in the Greek language, though the gods named are mostly Egyptian.

101. Černý, *Ancient Egyptian Religion*, p. 59.

102. For example, see the Prophecies of Neferti, in W. K. Simpson, *The Literature of Ancient Egypt* (rev. ed., New Haven and London, 1973), p. 238, which appears to describe in the literary form of a prophecy the bad conditions preceding the Middle Kingdom: "The land is diminishing, though its controllers are many; he who was rich in servants is despoiled and corn is trifling, even though the corn-measure is great and is measured to over-flowing (i.e. the dispensers of corn are hoarding it). Re separates himself from men; he shines that the hour [of dawn] may be told [lit., exist], but no one knows when noon occurs, for no one can discern his shadow [the sun being too weak]....". This is a poetic way of saying that Re has all but quit caring about the earth and its inhabitants. Similarly in the Admonitions of an Egyptian Sage (*ibid.*, p. 212) we read that "Khnum fashions (men) no more because of the condition of the land", and later after recounting more miseries the sage says "Indeed, the hot-tempered man says: 'If I knew where God is, then I would serve him.'" (*Ibid.*, p. 216). Furthermore, the sage says concerning Ptah (p. 217) "Why do you give to him? There is no reaching him."

103. Derchain in the work cited in footnote 1 of this chapter has a great deal to say about the role of the House of Life and its rituals in the preservation of maat and in the protection of the life of the king. The two are intimately tied together. Posener has expressed this succinctly: "Tout changement sur le trône prend une signification cosmique. Si, à la mort d'un roi, le chaos menace l'ordre de l'univers, l'avènement de Pharaon renouvelle la création originelle, rétablit l'équilibre de la nature. 'Rejouis-toi, pays entier! Les temps heureux sont arrivés. Un Maître s'est levé dans toutes les terres,..... l'inondation monte haut, les jours sont longs, la nuit a ses heures exactes, la lune revient avec regularité.' L'harmonie du monde dépend de la condition du roi, il doit garder tous ses moyens pour la bonne marche du cosmos." See G. Posener, et al., *Dictionnaire de la civilisation égyptienne*, 2nd ed. (Paris, 1970), p. 219.

104. Lichtheim, *Ancient Egyptian Literature*, Vol. 2, pp. 35-36.

105. Černý, *Ancient Egyptian Religion*, pp. 54-56.

106. *Ibid.*, p. 49. Cf. Bonnet, *Reallexikon*, p. 858.

107. Bonnet, *Reallexikon*, pp. 323, 858-59.

108. See H. Kees, *Totenglauben und Jenseitsvorstellungen der alten Ägypter* (Leipzig, 1956; 4th printing, 1980), pp. 73-74; Jéquier, *Considérations sur les religions Égyptiennes*, p. 67; Vandier, *La religion égyptienne*. pp. 76-81 (and particularly p. 78); R. Weill, *Le champ des roseaux et le champ des offrandes dans la religion funéraire et la religion générale* (Paris, 1936), and A. Bayoumi, *Autour du champ des souchets et du champ des offrandes* (Cairo, 1941).

109. A. J. Spencer, *Death in Ancient Egypt* (Harmondsworth, England, 1982), pp. 68-70. The

well-known spell from the *Book of the Dead* for putting the shawabti to work (no. 6) runs as follows: "Spell to cause the shawabti to perform work for a man in the Netherworld: O shawabti, if So and So (i.e. the deceased) is called upon or if I am listed to perform any work that is performed in the Netherworld, as a man to carry out his duties, to cultivate the fields, to water the banks [of the river], to transport the sand of the East to the West, 'Present' (i.e. 'I am here'), so shalt thou say." Černý, *Ancient Egyptian Religion*, p. 93.

110. Stewart, "Traditional Egyptian Sun Hymns," p. 38. As Stewart also remarks, "The day journey was thought to begin through the doors of heaven beyond the mythical eastern mountain of Baku, and end at the western mountain of Manu, where he [i.e. the sun-god] was received by the welcoming arms of his mother Nut. According to an early belief, already recorded in the Pyramid Texts (2173), the solar barque was rowed by the stars, who represented the spirits of the dead, and in the hymns of the New Kingdom the day journey is said to be accomplished by the circumpolar stars, 'those which can never set', and the night journey by 'those which can never weary'...."

111. Jéquier, *Considérations sur les religions égyptiennes*, pp. 54-59.

112. L. H. Lesko, *The Ancient Egyptian Book of Two Ways* (Berkeley / Los Angeles / London, 1972), includes an English translation and extensive notes and comments. However, I have for the most part followed Faulkner's later translation (see the introduction to Doc. II.2 below).

113. *Ibid.*, pp. 4, 6-7, Lesko characterizes the *Book of Two Ways* as follows: "Usually the *Book of Two Ways* was copied on the inside bottoms of the nobles'

coffins, probably so that the deceased would have this guide at their feet when walking in the underworld....The *Book of Two Ways* includes a number of different gods and goals....In addition to Re and Osiris...[it] also involves Thoth the god of the moon who is accompanied in the sky at night by the deceased as stars. To some extent he is as important as the other gods providing as he does a goal for the deceased, but since all the coffins having these texts are from his city [Hermopolis] this is not surprising....The last major deity in these texts is Horus....the eldest son of Re, who with wings outstretched represents the whole sky with his eyes as the sun and the moon... Seth...can also turn up unexpectedly as one of the guides on the bark of Re at the end of the book.... For goals of the deceased in the *Book of Two Ways* there is not only the famous 'Field of Offerings'... but also the mansion or palace of Osiris, the mansion of the moon, and the solar bark. Of the demons who guard the flaming red gates many are the same as those known from the two chapters (144 and 147) of the *Book of the Dead* devoted to the subject of gatekeepers."

114. *Ibid.*, pp. 40-41.

115. S. Morenz, *Egyptian Religion* (Ithaca, New York, 1973), pp. 75-80. If we take the end of the cosmos seriously, as does Hornung, *Conceptions of God*, p. 183, then of course we cannot say that time extends indefinitely.

116. Cf. Hornung, *Conceptions of God*, pp. 178-79, who mentions the view that "the primeval god who outlives the existent world changes into a snake at the end of time".

117. Eternity itself is sometimes given as *ḥḥ* (Erman and Grapow, *Wb*, Vol. 2, p. 299; *Belegstellen*,

Vol. 2, p. 435). We find the two expressions joined together as "millions of eternities" (*ibid.*).